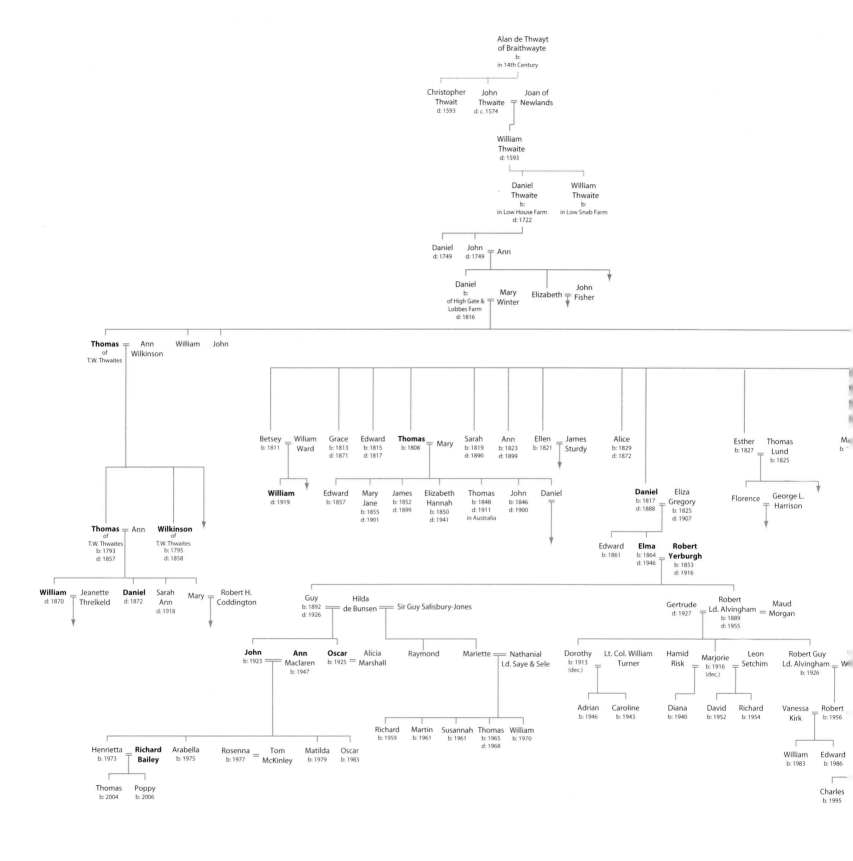

THWAITES and YERBURGH FAMILY

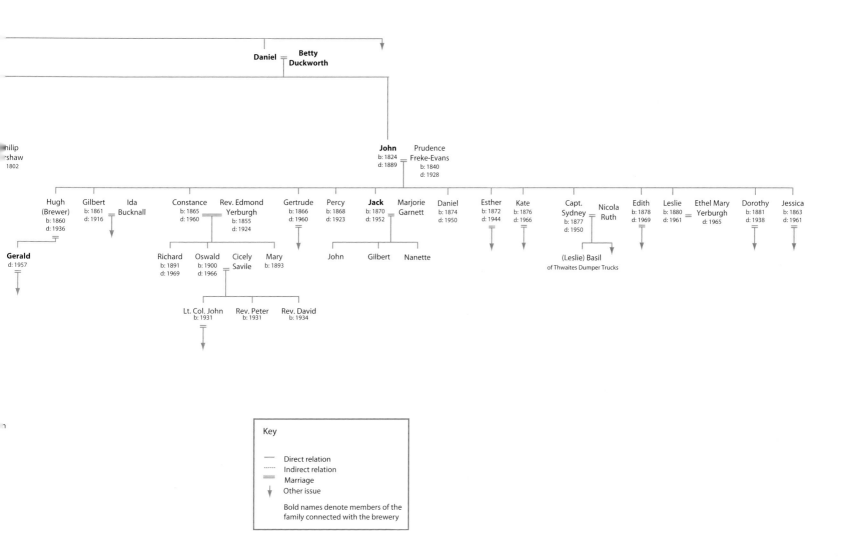

Daniel = **Betty Duckworth**

?hilip
?shaw
1802

John
b: 1824
d: 1889
= Prudence
Freke-Evans
b: 1840
d: 1928

Hugh
(Brewer)
b: 1860
d: 1936

Gilbert
b: 1861
d: 1916
= Ida
Bucknall

Constance
b: 1865
d: 1960
= Rev. Edmond
Yerburgh
b: 1855
d: 1924

Gertrude
b: 1866
d: 1960

Percy
b: 1868
d: 1923

Jack
b: 1870
d: 1952
= Marjorie
Garnett

Daniel
b: 1874
d: 1950

Esther
b: 1872
d: 1944

Kate
b: 1876
d: 1966

Capt.
Sydney
b: 1877
d: 1950
= Nicola
Ruth

Edith
b: 1878
d: 1969

Leslie
b: 1880
d: 1961
= Ethel Mary
Yerburgh
d: 1965

Dorothy
b: 1881
d: 1938

Jessica
b: 1863
d: 1961

Gerald
d: 1957

Richard
b: 1891
d: 1969

Oswald
b: 1900
d: 1966
= Cicely
Savile

Mary
b: 1893

John

Gilbert

Nanette

(Leslie) Basil
of Thwaites Dumper Trucks

Lt. Col. John
b: 1931

Rev. Peter
b: 1931

Rev. David
b: 1934

Key

—— Direct relation

---- Indirect relation

= Marriage

↓ Other issue

Bold names denote members of the
family connected with the brewery

THWAITES

THWAITES

The Life and Times of
Daniel Thwaites Brewery
1807–2007

Jehanne Wake

First published in 2007 on behalf of Thwaites Brewery plc
by Scotforth Books, Carnegie House, Chatsworth Road, Lancaster LA1 4SL.

© Jehanne Wake 2007

ISBN 10: 1-904244-46-7
ISBN 13: 978-1-904244-46-2

Printed by Cambridge Printing, Cambridge

The Black Bull, Livesey, is the oldest surviving Thwaites public-house; it has been in the firm's ownership for nearly 200 years.

Contents

Elma Yerburgh, Chairman and proprietor of Daniel Thwaites Brewery, 1888-1946

Dedication

THIS BOOK is dedicated to my grandmother Elma Yerburgh. She guided the Brewery through years of difficulty and two world wars as well as ones of steady expansion and post-war reconstruction. She was a brilliant businesswoman and it is through her skill and foresight that Daniel Thwaites still exists as a family company. As she recognised, the strength of any firm lies in its people. The calibre of the employees today will ensure that the high standards she set for quality and innovation at Thwaites will continue for another 200 years.

John Yerburgh

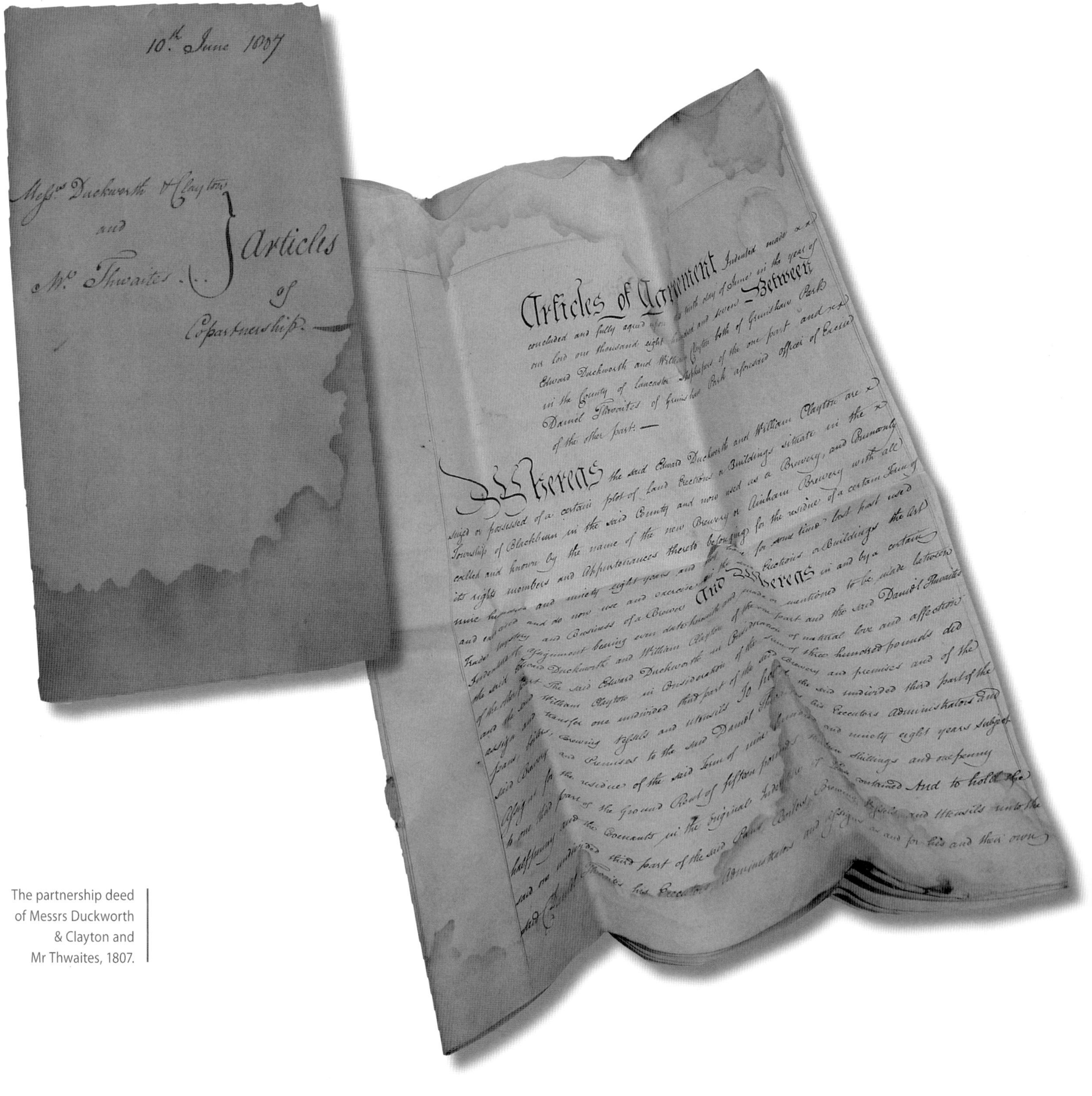

The partnership deed
of Messrs Duckworth
& Clayton and
Mr Thwaites, 1807.

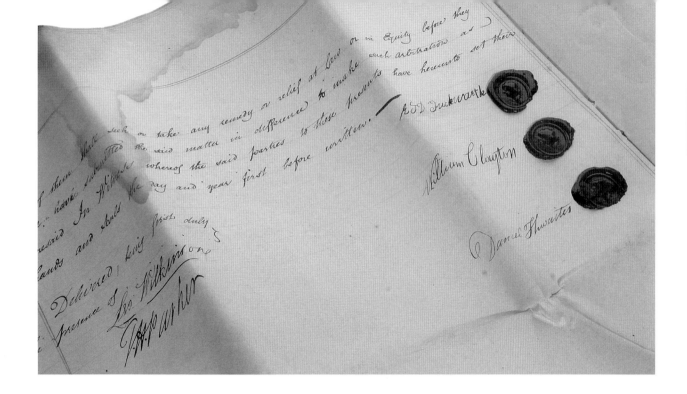

The deed bearing the
signatures of Edward
Duckworth, William
Clayton and Daniel
Thwaites on 10 June
1807.

CHAPTER ONE

Daniel Thwaites 1777–1843

Men are every day starting up from obscurity to wealth
Daniel Defoe

O N 10 JUNE 1807 two mercantile gentlemen
Edward Duckworth and William Clayton called on
their attorney Leonard Wilkinson at Penny Street in
Blackburn in the county of Lancaster. They were taking on
another partner, Daniel Thwaites, to manage their brewery
business and, in the presence of Wilkinson and his clerk, the
three men proceeded to sign the agreement for the new
partnership of Duckworth, Clayton and Thwaites. This was an
auspicious moment in Daniel's career. He was taking a considerable step of advancement up the ladder of fortune and
independence, moving from an employee to a proprietorial
position, one replete with the prospect of profit, status and
preferment.[1]

It was not, however, a step taken without attendant risks
for any of the new partners. The spectre of failure
oppressed many a partnership in those days of unlimited
liability. That very autumn, for instance, Lt-Colonel John
Watson, founder of the Loyal Preston Volunteers, chief
supporter of Lord Derby's Whig interest and senior partner
of the second largest cotton firm in nearby Preston, would
see his well-established family business fail 'in insolvent
circumstances beyond redemption.' The sudden discharge
from the three Watson mills of up to five hundred
aggrieved men, many of them drilled as volunteers in the
Loyal Preston, at a time when the country faced the
external threat of Napoleon and the internal one of

economic distress, was seen to threaten domestic order. A Deputy-Lieutenant of Lancashire warned the Home Secretary, Lord Hawkesbury, 'as the Winter is fast approaching and the Trade here in a most depressed state, some Danger may be apprehended from the discontent of these Men among whom there are many Irish of the lowest Class.' In such testing conditions it was all the more important for Duckworth and Clayton to safeguard their business by placing the direction of 'the Art, Trade, Mystery and Benefits of a Brewery', as the partnership deed described it, in the hands of a man with sound proven experience. Yet they had chosen Daniel Thwaites to be their working partner, a man who had never previously managed any firm before and for whom the art of managing a brewery might, indeed, prove to be a 'Mystery'.[2]

This was all the more surprising because neither Edward Duckworth nor William Clayton were themselves experienced brewers. They were grocers. This did not mean,

Lang's map of Blackburn in 1759, one of the earliest in existence. The original is in Lambeth Palace. It remained largely unchanged until after Daniel's arrival, after which 10,000 of its population of 15,000 were said to be dependent upon the cotton trade for their livelihood.

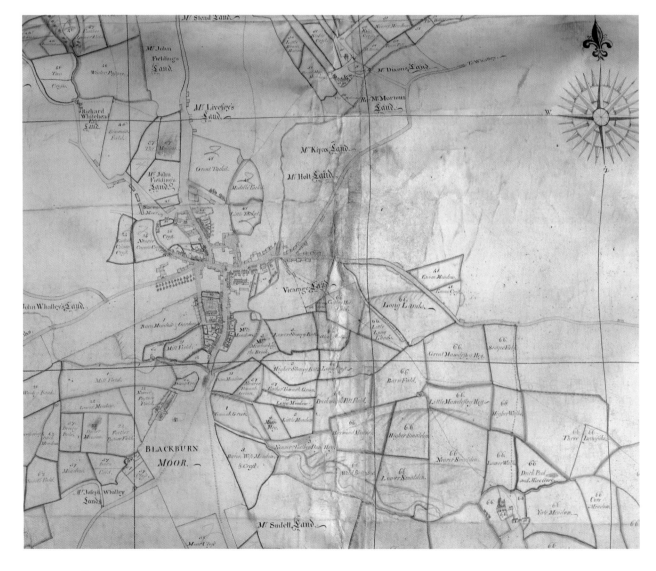

however, that they stood behind a counter in a shop and confined themselves to selling foodstuffs to customers. Grocers in the 18th and early 19th centuries not only sold a wide range of goods but acted also as opportunistic wholesale dealers in commodities and raw materials. Richard Prescott, a Preston grocer, imported 'a Quantity of choice Rum' from the West Indies to be sold in amounts exceeding two gallons at a price of 7/6d per gallon in mid-century. And in that ebullient commercial climate, the more fortunate could end up with a portfolio of occupations. Thus Abraham Dent, a successful 18th-century Westmorland shopkeeper and grocer, also made money as a brewer, bill-broker, small landowner and then wholesale hosier with the reputation of slipping into a Government contractor's order the tasty *douceur* of a Westmorland ham.[3]

Edward Duckworth, born in 1756, appears to have been an equally enterprising businessman. In addition to supplying goods, such as candles, soap, salt, meal, dyes, cheese, paper and twine in his shop, he owned a bakehouse, which he rented out, as well as thirteen other properties with land lying in the then rural area of Grimshaw Park, south of the town of Blackburn. He was also a wholesale flour merchant which in Lancashire could refer only to oats. 'If any ask why this grain, growing commonly all over England, is here entered as an eminent commodity of Lancashire,' commented the historian Fuller, 'Let him know that here is the most and best of the kind;' and he warned strangers to the county: 'say not that oats are horse grain, and fitter for a stable than a table'. For the oats that were ground into oatmeal for porridge and oatcakes and jannock formed the staple diet of Lancastrians and, according to the Lancashire historian Whittle, the middling ranks of society generally liked to take their oats genteely as porridge with milk, treacle or beer.[4]

Duckworth also made money from the cotton trade, as did most of Blackburn's inhabitants in the opening years of the 19th century. Of a population that would grow from about 12,000 in 1801 to some 15,000 in 1811, over 10,000 residents of the Blackburn area were said to depend solely upon the cotton trade for their livelihood. By this time, the first cotton spinning manufacturers, such as Peel and Yates,

had moved elsewhere and it was in cotton weaving rather than spinning that Blackburn's reputation then rested; the trade acted as a magnet to draw people into its employ and swell the population; the majority weaving cotton pieces on handlooms in their own cottages. Edward Duckworth also acted as a calico manufacturer or "putter-out"; he provided the weavers with the raw material, the cotton yarn, and then stored the finished woven calico pieces in his basement room or cellar until he sold them in the market. Thomas Livesey, for instance, a more extensive calico printer, used the basement floor of his elegant 18th-century house in King Street as a warehouse to store the calico pieces in which he traded. Duckworth's cotton trade, however profitable, could not compare with that of the principal merchants whose long established families dominated Blackburn society. Amongst such as the Hindles, the Liveseys, the Feildens and the Claytons, Henry Sudell Esq. of Woodfold Park was the wealthiest and most influential; such was his authority that his word could determine prices and command the market.[5]

Whether or not William Clayton, also a grocer and living at Grimshaw Park, was a partner in some of these other Duckworth ventures has not been recorded. Nor is much else known about Clayton except that he and his father William Clayton senior had, since 1780, owned land and several properties (including one which later became the Bridge Inn, a public-house long held by Thwaites in Clayton Street by Joiners Row) in Grimshaw Park. There is, however, evidence to suggest that Edward Duckworth and William Clayton had invested in another brewery at the end of the 18th century and that they had disagreed with a previous working partner.[6]

Their erstwhile partner was Thomas Dutton descended from an arms bearing family of gentlemen farmers in Clitheroe, though born in 1750 in St Helens. At some stage, and for reasons unknown, in the 1790s he decided to bring his family to Blackburn. Indeed, a haze now descends upon events concerning Dutton which effectively obscures his exact connection with Duckworth and Clayton and the nature of their brewery business during these years. Dutton's daughter Martha married Thomas Clayton landlord of a respectable public-house, the Holy Lamb Inn at Northgate, Blackburn and this event has been seen as the means of bringing Dutton into Duckworth and Claytons' brewery. It is, however, by no means certain that Thomas Clayton was related to William Clayton, Clayton being a common name in Lancashire and it is just as possible that the three partners already knew each other through family connections, they were all members of established local families after all, or that Dutton moved to Blackburn specifically to join Duckworth and Claytons' brewery venture.[7]

Moreover this brewery was probably not the one that Daniel Thwaites was brought in to manage in 1807. In his description of Blackburn in 1795, Dr John Aikin writes, 'A little to the South is a capital brewery, close by which the new canal from Leeds to Liverpool takes its course.' It has always been assumed that Aikin was referring to the commercial brewery erected by a John Nicholls at Park Place in 1793. From the outset, Nicholls saw it as a "spec", an investment to make money, and, together with four other businessmen, he formed a partnership which, according to the *Blackburn Mail*, traded as Nicholls and Co. and did not then include Duckworth, Clayton or Dutton. Nicholls employed 'the most judicious brewers and workmen that could be acquired' and it is possible that amongst these judicious brewers was Thomas Dutton.

The Brewery opened on 5 February 1794 and in March the local paper praised 'its salutary effects' on producing good beer as 'in the houses of the humble industrious handicraftmen, as well as the cellars of the more opulent, a sound wholesome and exhilarating beverage is now to be met with, congenial not only to the palate but also to the pocket of the consumer.' Whether this puff, and a similar report the following month mentioning 'the fame and excellence of the ale lately manufactured at the new brewery, at Park Place', served to produce such a 'wholesome and exhilerating' return on capital that Nicholls decided to realise his investment, two months later, in July, he dissolved the partnership, leaving his four partners to carry on the business. Whilst several changes in the partnership are recorded in the press over the ensuing

years, none mentioned either Duckworth, Clayton or Dutton as being involved, though no details are extant for 1798–1803. Yet Thomas Dutton and his son are recorded elsewhere as being in partnership in a brewery, which 'was known as Park Place, near the Canal bridge at Windham Street', and was terminated in 1807. Furthermore, the local respected historian George Miller describes Messrs Duckworth and Clayton as 'the Park Place brewers', and Thomas Dutton and his son William as '[H]aving been discharged from' their employment there in 1807.

Thus, all that can be said with any confidence of the few facts known about Duckworth and Claytons' brewery business and their relations with the Duttons is that they are riddled at the least with ambiguity and at the most with misinformation. The 18th century was neither so accurate nor so concerned about dates and nomenclature as the 21st century – it was by no means uncommon for even educated people to be ignorant of their own birth dates and exact ages and to use variety in their spelling.

The puzzlement about the brewery business was compounded by three notices placed in the *Blackburn Mail* published in April and May 1807. One was placed by the Park Place partnership to the effect that two quarter shares in the Brewery were to be sold but gives no details of whose shares. The other notices had a more direct bearing on Daniel Thwaites's future and were placed by Duckworth and Clayton themselves. The second notice, which also appeared in the *London Gazette*, stated boldly 'Partnerships Dissolved: Duckworth, Clayton and Dutton, Blackburn, Lancashire, brewers.' The first notice, dated 27 April 1807, declared that 'Edward Duckworth and William Clayton, Brewers of Blackburn having this day discharged from their Employ, Thomas Dutton and William Dutton, who had the Management of their Brewery at Blackburn aforesaid, commonly called The New Brewery', would not pay any debts contracted thereafter by either of the Duttons.

Although, from this latter notice, it would appear that there was a second brewery, the New Brewery, situated at Blackburn separate from both the Park Place Brewery and the one described in the Duckworth, Clayton and Thwaites partnership deed as the 'Aynham Brewery', it is more likely

that they were two names for the same brewery. A sale notice on 23 October 1805 for two dwelling houses describes them as 'adjoining a new street called Larkhill street, being very near to the intended new Brewery, and to the line of the Leeds and Liverpool Canal. They are bounded on the north side by glebe land which has lately been laid out for building upon.' The 'intended new Brewery' must be the 'Aynham' or Eanam Brewery, which was built on glebe land bounded on one side by Larkhill street and at another side by Eanam where the new canal was planned. Thus, the original Thwaites Brewery was being built in October 1805.

There appears to have been a chilly falling out between Duckworth and Clayton and the Duttons; it is most unusual for a notice of partnership dissolution to stipulate any reason for the termination, let alone one of discharge which, in that era, could imply transgression of some kind. The reason behind the discharge of the Duttons remains unverifiable. It does seem likely, however, that Daniel Thwaites was involved in the rupture, despite his lack of management experience as a common brewer (as a commercial brewer was then called). It is possible, for instance, that Thomas Dutton wanted to bring his son William aged 27 years into the partnership, whereas Edward Duckworth and William Clayton preferred to bring in Daniel aged 30 years; similarly, a case can be made for Daniel playing on his advantageous situation to usurp Dutton's position and take a place in the partnership for himself and his family. [8]

The one advantage that Daniel possessed over both Thomas and William Dutton was that, unlike them, he was Duckworth's new son-in-law. Four months previously, on 9 December 1806, Daniel had married Betty Duckworth at the Parish church of Blackburn. Betty had three sisters: Mary, who was married to Robert Yates a yeoman farmer of Duckworth Hall in Oswaldtwistle, and Grace and Ellen, who were then unmarried. Betty, however, had no surviving brothers. And, like her father, William Clayton also lacked sons to bring into the business. Thus any slight inconvenience to the Duttons was set against the infinitely greater convenience to the Duckworths of having a younger

trustworthy member of the family to protect their interests at the Brewery. It also had the merit of ensuring that Daniel and Betty continued to reside in Blackburn. Unlike the Duckworths and the Claytons, Daniel was not a native Lancastrian. In deciding to settle in Blackburn and to seize this opportunity to improve his prospects he was forsaking the hearth and heritage of Cumberland which had sustained the Thwaites family for over five centuries.

Daniel's ancestors were Dalesmen of Viking stock, arriving with the Norse invasion that began in 925 and continued into the twelfth century. Unlike the preceding Danish invasion, exemplary for a ferocity which included the sacking of Carlisle with such brutality that it remained derelict over the ensuing two hundred years, the Norsemen evinced nothing but peaceful intentions. They came not directly from Norway but from Ireland and the Isle of Man where they had lived and farmed for many years before crossing the Irish Sea and arriving at West Cumberland. While many settled on this flat coastal belt, others braved the inhospitable Cumbrian mountains to the East to penetrate the hinterland and settle in the lower ground of the northern Lake Country. Here they cleared the valley floors to provide pasturage for their animals and crop-

The inhospitable if beautiful Newlands Valley near Keswick where Daniel Thwaites was born and raised.

bearing land which they enclosed with stone walls thereby producing the landscapes familiar in the present day. Gradually venturing further up the dales, clearing the woods and keeping their horses and cattle on the fells, these farming colonists integrated with the local Britons and passed on to their descendents, the Dales people, the distinctive names given to the landscapes of Cumberland. Thus fells, tarns, becks, dales and gills are all Norse words. One Norse word is particularly relevant to Daniel's family history and the area in which his ancestors settled, namely 'tveit' meaning a clearing. Over time 'tveit' evolved into 'thwayt' and 'thwaite', the original names of Daniel's ancestors. It was also the name given by these Norse settlers to innumerable places including, for example Braithwaite, Thornthwaite and Dowthwaitehead, all situated in the northern country around Keswick, the area colonised by Daniel's ancestors.[9]

The Thwaites emerged from the shadows of the medieval world in the fourteenth century. Before then the rugged landscape insulated Cumberland from conquering forces. There was no mention of most of the county in the Domesday Book of 1086, for instance, as northern Cumberland had been ceded to Scotland and did not return to English rule until 1092 when William II seized Carlisle. During King Edward III's reign, however, the Crown granted him a subsidy to be raised according to the value of people's estates. The accounts for Cumberland show that William de Thwaytes from Kirkstanton, near Millom, paid £4–10–0. This sum reflected the considerable estate held by the family of the Thwaites of the manors and lordships of Thwaites near Millom, and of Unerigg, near Maryport; both on the West Cumbrian coast where the first Norsemen had settled. This arms bearing branch of the family would prosper until the 17th century when Joseph Thwayts of Unerigg, described in Sanford's *Cursory Relation* as 'one of the wittiest, brave monsirs for all gentile gallentry, hounds, hawkes, horse courses, boules, bowes & arrows, and all games whatsoever; play his £100 at cards, dice and shovelboard … and had not above £200 p. an', became so indebted in 1609 that his son John Thwayts 'in computation for the payment of his debts and for raising portions for his younger children' sold the manor of Thwayts to Sir John Lowther while Unerigg passed to the Christian family. However, one of Daniel's descendents wrote anonymously, 'I do not think [we] make any claim to be descended from the ancient family of Thwaites of Thwaites'; a statement corroborated by parish records.[10]

Daniel's branch of the family was, nonetheless, sufficiently established to provide the only other Thwaite prosperous enough to be listed in the 14th-century accounts: Alan de Thwayt, who paid the much smaller sum of £0–16–0d for land held at Braythwayt [now Braithwaite], a few miles west of Keswick. By this time the valleys surrounding Keswick were benefitting from the benevolent patronage of the two large monasteries of Furness Abbey and Fountains Abbey. Medieval Cumbrians, such as Alan de Thwayt, could enjoy a steadier existence as the 'abbeys gave great alms to poor men', helped the sick and aged and generally improved social conditions in the harsh environment of the lake country fells. More importantly for the Thwaites and other yeomen farmers, the abbeys also

The church close to where the Thwaites family had settled at Low House Farm in the 15th century.

helped hill farmers to make a better living from the unproductive land by introducing methods of sheep farming and of draining land to increase the pasturage of the 'thwaites'.[11]

By the 15th century the Thwaites had decided to move southwards from Braithwaite to take advantage of some of this newly drained land down in the lower dale known as The New Lands – the name adopted and still used to designate the whole valley. Travelling along the western bank of Newlands beck, passing by the hamlet of Little Town and crossing Keskadale beck they reached the heart of the Newlands Valley where they found a tiny church of Norman origin. Despite rebuilding, Newlands Church, with its plain whitewashed walls, bell turret and porch, remains the simple dales church which inspired Wordsworth to write a stanza 'To May' and Beatrix Potter to write the Vicar's daughter Lucy Carr into her story of *Mrs Tiggy-Winkle,* and which would not be unrecognisable to the various Thwaites, buried in the small churchyard, whose tithes doubtless had sustained the priest and contributed to the new lecturn and pulpit in 1610.[12]

They settled close to the church at Low House Farm and also nearby at High and Low Snab and Gillibrow Farms. Here successive generations of Thwaites lived and farmed in one of the most beautiful, secluded areas of the Lake Country, adjacent to the southern end of Derwent Water and Borrowdale and encircled by a panorama of ridges and peaks of the high fells that form a natural backdrop to the valley. Thomas Gray wrote to his friend Dr Wharton in 1769 of 'the most delicious view, that my eyes ever beheld: behind you are the magnificent heights of *Walla-crag*; opposite lie the thick hanging woods of Ld Egremont, and *Newland*-Valley with green and smiling fields embosom'd in the dark cliffs; to the left the jaws of *Borodale*, with that turbulent chaos of mountain behind mountain roll'd in confusion; beneath you, & stretching far away to the right, the shining purity of the *Lake* [Derwent Water], just ruffled by the breeze enough to show it is alive, reflecting rocks, woods, fields, & inverted tops of mountains, with the white buildings of *Keswick, Crosthwait*-church, & *Skiddaw* for a back-ground at distance, Oh Doctor!'[13]

It was, however, less from the pastoral 'smiling fields'

and more from the 'turbulent' mountains that, in Tudor times, Christopher and John Thwaite looked to augment their fluctuating farming income. The encroaching fells glowering down upon the isolated farmsteads in Newlands valley contained mineral wealth sufficient to warrant the attention of an acquisitive majesty. In 1564 Queen Elizabeth entered into a contract with two gentlemen to found the Company of Mines Royal. Thomas Thurland was a clergyman, the Master of the Savoy, and possessed some knowledge of mining in Bavaria and his partner was Daniel Hőchstetter, representative of a large trading and mining concern, Haug, Langnauer & Co., of Augsburg in Bavaria; at this time, England lacked the technical capability to mine that Bavaria had already mastered. The partnership agreement empowered the gentlemen, but in reality Daniel Höchstetter, to 'search, dig, try, roast and melt all manner of mines and ures of gold, silver, copper and quick-silver'. Regal liberality naturally warranted consideration; the Crown in return was to receive one-tenth of the gold and silver and 'the preferment in bying of all Precious stones or pearl to be found in the working of these mines', with shares to be given to Sir William Cecil (Lord Burghley in 1571) and her Lords Leicester and Pembroke.[14]

The inducement for such a noble interest was Germanic rather than ecclesiastic: not only were the Germans ahead

Low House Farm, Newlands, where generations of the Thwaites family lived and which is still inhabited today.

of the English in mining – a German had managed the Alston lead mines in 1350 – but Hang Langnauer & Co. was also one of the great Continental trading houses, their branches stretching across Europe and dealing with bill discounting, banking, silks and cloths, East Indies spices and, in particular, Austro-Hungarian copper mines. It was, according to the firm's account books, from their branch near Innsbruck, a celebrated mining centre, that in 1565 it sent some forty or fifty 'Almaynes' miners to the new Company's main centre of English mining activity, which was in the Keswick area. The first group of mines was in the Newlands valley where, in August 1566, Thurland informed Cecil that a coppermine 'the richest in England' had been discovered; known by the Germans as "Gottesgab", meaning God's Gift, the name evolved in English into Goldscope.[15]

Whereas formerly only border raids or some unique national event, such as the Pilgrimage of Grace, had ever pierced the remoteness of the area, by 1567 the mining industry required six furnaces and a stamp house in Keswick and timber and peat from the surrounding forests and bogs to process the ore from mines in Newlands and the Caldbeck Fells, not to mention the swarms of Bavarians and dalesfolk required to operate them and produce the raw materials, with all the attendant noise and bustle of economic prosperity. Hardly a dale was unrepresented in the lists of people employed by the Company and, according to George Bowes and Francis Needham who inspected the mines in 1600, 'about 500 persons dwelling near about the works are enriched by this means to the great benefit of the country'.

Among them was John Thwaite, who in 1569 was one of the large number of people engaged in transporting the considerable quantities of peat used for fuel to the furnaces. He was joined in 1573 by his son William Thwaite who is listed in the 1574 accounts as 'son of Joan Thwaites of Newlands'. John's brother Christopher Thwaite was employed in building works on Vicar's Island in Derwent Water where a windmill, brewery, pigsties, pigeon-house, and garden were made for the use of the Bavarian management. He used his boat in 1571 to bring 'manure from Miladi's stables to put on the garden on the Island'

and was paid 26/- on account but for taking 300 apple and pear trees there he earned £4. Severe weather was clearly not allowed to interrupt business for he dragged manure on sledges across the frozen lake to the Island, earning £1–0–8, and managed to dig a ditch round the gardens as well. The first known link between the Thwaites and beer appears in 1577 when Christopher supplied the Island Brewery with 180 lbs hops at 7d.[17]

In a region inclined in the 16th century towards poverty rather than wealth, dearth rather than abundance, the success of the Company's operations was paramount. Where John, who died c. 1574, and Christopher, in 1593, had prospered, their descendents were less fortunate. Although James I had renewed the Company's charter, overall output steadily decreased as management changed – Höchstetter had died – and demand for Cumbrian copper faltered in the early 17th century. On top of the series of devastating harvests of the 1640s came the disruption caused by the Civil War, during which Parliamentary troops attacked and destroyed the Keswick mines; and then the royal monopoly was abolished by the Commonwealth after 1649. The sound of pick and copper-smith's hammer no longer rang through the Newlands valley and surrounding fells.

People everywhere knew extreme poverty and hardship during the 17th century but the few travellers to penetrate the now lonely, economically isolated Cumbrian countryside were shocked by conditions there nonetheless. Hammond wrote in 1635 of 'poore cottages … I think the Sun never shone on them … sicke they were as are never saw before, nor ever shall see againe.' The intrepid Lady Celia Fiennes who rode through 'villages of sad little hutts' on her notable journey at the end of the century, in 1697, 'tooke them at first sight for a sort of houses, or barns to fodder cattle in, not thinking them to be dwelling houses' and found the going heavy on the stony hills: Cumbrian 'miles are tedious to go both for illness of way and length of the miles' that she had to get her horses shoed every 2–3 days. By the turn of the 18th century the decline in even once thriving Keswick had, noted a German visitor, 'occasion'd the Town to become much poorer than formerly, less inhabited and frequented, and to contain only one street.'[18]

This generation of Newlands Thwaites, Daniel at Low House and William at Low Snab farm, great-great-grandsons of Christopher and John, managed to survive by eking out a living as sheep hill farmers. It certainly required hardness and skill to do so. That renown 18th-century commentator Daniel Defoe described the landscape as 'eminent only for being the wildest, most barren and frightful of any that I have passed over in England'; while William Benson, the son of another Lake Country hill farmer, recalled 'the dangers and hardships' that his father underwent in tending sheep 'in the mountain districts about Stangend, more particularly in winter, and when the precipes were concealed by drifting snow.' Unlike the Bensons who removed to the nearest towns, Hawkshead and then Kendal, in search of prosperity, Daniel clung on at Newlands where he died in 1722, leaving an inventory of his estate valued at £158 including debts owed to him. From his will, however, it would appear that more adventurous younger members of the family looked beyond the confines of the secluded valley and desolate surrounding fells. He left £30 to his younger son Daniel 'if it shall please God that he returns and arrive safe and alive at Whitehaven from his Virginia voyage'; this the young man would do, though the nature of his American sojourn was not revealed. Daniel of Newlands left his 'great' Bible to John Thwaite, who as the elder son was automatically heir to Low House farm under the ancient rights of northern tenure.[19]

The Thwaites were statesmen (estatesmen), as families of ancient yeoman farming lineage were known in Cumberland, holding their farms as customary tenants, akin to freeholders and retaining certain immemorial privileges. The Crown at the time of James I, believing statesmen only held land by Border tenure, that is on condition they repelled Scottish invasion, tried to claim back the land but the English courts ruled that the tenants' estates were 'estates of inheritance at the will of the lord, descendible from ancestor to heir according to the several customs of the several manors whereof they are hidden', quite apart from Border service. Thus, after his father's death, John Thwaite had to appear at the manor Court of Lord Egremont, the lord of the manor, to pay a fee of £30 by

which his admittance as tenant was entered on the court roll, and to pay a customary annual rent. When a neighbouring Newlands statesman, Reuben Grave, took over the tenancy of Skelgill farm in 1771 he paid Lord Egremont a rent of 13s 10d yearly 'at the feasts of St Michael the Archangel and the Annunciation of the Blessed Virgin Mary … '. John Thwaite expanded his farming, taking on the High Howes farm and High Saab. He had five surviving children, his eldest daughter Elizabeth marrying her cousin John Fisher; an event that heralded generations of intermarriage between Thwaites and Fishers until a Fisher Thwaite Fisher inherited Low House Farm in 1832. John Thwaite died in 1749 leaving his 'beloved wife' Ann sole executrix and all his furniture, sheep and wool at the loft at High Hawes farm to his eldest son another Daniel with instructions to settle £40 and £100 lent out on mortgage upon his three younger children once they reached their majority.[20]

It was this Daniel who took the decision to move away from the Newlands valley, leaving his younger brother to take over the tenancy of Low House farm, which would thereafter be occupied by John's branch of the family until the end of the 19th century. Daniel preferred the opportunities presented by enfranchisement and enclosure, developments which diminished the number of statesmen from the mid-18th century onwards. Although many statesmen were enfranchised by agreement, it proved costly so that some were unable to bear the financial strain of paying a sale price of say £545 and a further £83 for timber and woods to Lord Egremont as Reuben Grove did for Skelgill. Daniel Thwaite, however, purchased Lobbes and High Gate farms from a different lord of the manor, Henry Howard of Greystoke, by Penrith.

To get there, Daniel would have crossed Derwent Water to Keswick, then taken the packhorse route eastwards across to Threlkeld, a village tucked under the mountain of Blencathra – always known locally as Saddleworth – with Skiddaw and the region's finest fells spread around it; and from there over unenclosed Threlkeld Common to the old High Gate and Lobbes farmhouses by Mosedale Beck near Matterdale Common. He would thus have seen the farms when he rode past them with his father en route to Penrith market by the old Roman road, which still passes by High Gate in the present day; he and his father might well have tarried a while at the neighbouring Wallthwaite farmhouse, the date 1720 still legible above its door lintel, where Thwaites kinsmen lived.

Daniel of High Gate remained predominantly a sheep farmer and he took over a basic flock of sheep at both High Gate and Lobbes for, following Cumbrian custom, a flock always remained with its farm, as did the grazing rights on the fell. He, in turn, had handed over the flock at Newlands to his brother, free though he was to take away or sell any additional sheep he had bred or bought in his own right. All these sheep bore sant and ear marks; a page from Hodgson's *Shepherds' Guide* shows Daniel Thwaite's sheep: 'Cropped near ear, upper halved far' with a T-stroke 'over the fillets'.[21]

Besides providing excellent pasturage for sheep, the Threlkeld and Matterdale area proved more attractive than ever when, in 1760, Daniel decided to marry Mary Winter,

Derwent Water as seen from Castle Head.

daughter of John Winter of Threlkeld. They were married in the 13th-century church of St Mary where the marriage register dating from 1573 warned 'Formal contracts of marriage are herein recorded; and sureties entered for the payment of five shillings to the poor by the party that draws back.' Accordingly, it became customary, as a preventative measure, to tie the two churchyard gates securely together during a wedding service. Daniel and Mary began their married life at Lobbes farm, south of High Gate and by the recesses of the fells looking towards Helvellyn on one side and Saddleworth and Skidlaw on the other. It was a bleak area and, in keeping with most of Cumberland, still backward and comparatively little known in 1760. There was no turnpike, little passing traffic and few travellers to bring the news of the day and country gossip. This situation was well illustrated by an old spinning woman, who lived near Brampton. Coleridge and the Wordsworths liked to respeat the authentic story of how, talking to the gentlefolk outside church one Good Friday, she said of the Crucifixion "I hope they haven't killed the poor gentleman – Well it is so long ago and so far away, that I hope it is not true – O well – we live up under the Hill here – we do never hear a bit of news!"[22]

It was at the remote Lobbes farmhouse that, at the beginning of June 1777, the youngest of their eight children Daniel, the founder brewer, was born. The Cumberland in which Daniel grew up had been transformed from the county that his parents and forebears knew. People who could read, unlike the spinning woman, could keep abreast of events and prices through newspapers and periodicals. Daniel was born during the American War of Independence which British people could follow in the expanding press. News of Colonel (later General Lord) Howe's success in taking Philadelphia in May, of American privateers terrorising British ships in the channel near Whitehaven together with accounts of George III's birthday, celebrated throughout Britain with naval salutes and processions, appeared in the weekly paper *The Cumberland Chronicle or Whitehaven Public Advertiser* on 7 June, the day after Daniel's baptism at Threlkeld church. News both printed and oral was disseminated more easily in the North by the establishment

of a turnpike road system that connected London with Carlisle and eventually Edinburgh. A turnpike road had been extended from Kendal to Keswick and via Braithwaite to Cockermouth in 1761 and, later, one ran from Keswick to Penrith. These roads altered the way of life of Cumbrians. Daniel grew up seeing post-chaises and carriers' wagons and, most impressive of all, that "flying-machine": the London stagecoach which, for a fare of six guineas, took passengers on a 36-hour journey from London to Carlisle; the fare being commensurately higher for the fourteen day journey to Edinburgh.[23]

And with the roads in the north-west country came people; not just the working packmen, quarrymen, miners and peddlars, but more often the leisurely visitors, in search of the sublime scenery to be found everywhere in what these tourists dubbed the Lake Country (and the dalesmen had always known as the waters). Devotees of Romanticism and the cult of the Picturesque, influenced by Rousseau and Edmund Burke's *Philosophical Inquiry into the Origin of our Ideas on the Sublime and Beautiful* (1756), gazed ecstatically at the mountains, lakes, clouds, cataracts and ruined castles which invoked exquisite sensations of foreboding. As John Brown wrote to Lord Lyttelton in a famous published letter of 1767, 'the full beauty of Keswick consists of three circumstances, *beauty*, *horror* and *immensity* united … ' Painters, poets and nobility arrived on sketching and journal-keeping tours with the effect of making such visits to the Lake Country *le dernier cri* for the late 18th-century fashionable world. Keswick was especially popular and *The Cumberland Chronicle* reported that, during the summer of Daniel's birth, 'such numbers of genteel company were never seen in it before – The Nobility and Gentry from all parts have honoured it with their presence. They greatly admire its romantic beauties and universally allow it to be the most agreeable place in the Kingdom.' Anyone of sensibility was soon seen carrying a copy of William Gilpin's *Observations* (1786) which defined 'picturesque rules' such as '*roughness* forms the most essential point of difference between the *beautiful*, and the *picturesque*'; though it must have puzzled the reader when Nature did not quite

conform. Gilpin, however, had no compunction about correcting Nature's 'errors' in his landscape sketches: 'I am so attached to my picturesque rules, that if nature goes wrong, I cannot help putting her right'.

Forthright, practical, independent dalesmen had little time for such notions. They would doubtless have enjoyed hearing James Clark, author of *A Survey of the Lakes* … (1789), condemn 'that cant style of painting which Gilpin and some others have introduced into their writing' whereby 'a poor harmless cow can hardly go to drink, but they find fault with a want of grace in her attitude … ' but they, nevertheless, welcomed the financial benefits brought by the influx of tourists to their region. Matthew Brockbank of the Royal Oak Inn at Keswick was quick to advise visitors in May 1777 that 'he has for their better Accomodation of pleasuring upon the LAKE, provided an elegant and safe PLEASURE BOAT, entirely new, which will at all times be ready, for their Reception, with Skilful Rowers, as also an intelligent Person to describe the different Islands, Views & c' on Derwent Water. Others provided their services as

guides on the fells, held in exaggerated awe by tourists. Where one visitor, Joseph Budworth, was so terrified he bandaged his eyes so that he could not see the dizzy heights and perilous paths of an ascent, and had to be helped down by a guide holding his hand and placing his feet, young Daniel, as a dalesman's son who helped on the Lobbes farm, respected the fells but worked in them, gathering sheep upon the highest ground. He and his three brothers and four sisters knew all the crags and gills and only the severest weather kept them from crossing the highest passes in all seasons. Coleridge would recall with affection the seventy-year-old woman who pointed out a mountain track to him, gave him the approximate time in which she thought he, a twenty-three-year-old, would climb it and then told him the time she would do it, adding that she'd "gang like a daisy."[24]

Daniel's two elder brothers Thomas, born in 1762, and William, in 1769, went to school in the church at Threlkeld but, in 1777, the old church was torn down and when it was rebuilt, a separate school was built for the village. Daniel and his next older brother John only went to school in the winter from October to March; they could not be spared from their farm chores in the busy summer months. The Thwaites boys, like other statesmen's children, were far from being poorly educated. Children at church schools were taught their grammar, mathematics and some Latin. There was a well established tradition of learning in the region dating from the 16th century when endowed grammar schools were founded in the fells: at Penrith in 1564, Keswick in 1570 and Hawkshead in 1585. By the 17th century there was a surprisingly high level of literacy given the paucity of reading material. Statesmen's sons 'drove the plough' in Latin at Bampton while at an inn in Ulpha when some college boys asked for their bill in Latin, they received it not only in Latin but also in Greek![25]

In manner, however well educated a boy was, there was no notion of assuming airs of the grandee at the castle; partly because there were few gentlefolk and even fewer nobility in the area, and partly because the independent position of statesmen families was assured in a way unknown in the rest of England. They were careful, self sufficient in that they raised and manufactured their own clothing and food, and had to answer to no one. Even the clergyman, who also often taught in the school and was usually the only 'superior' person locally, was often a dalesman's son and became one of the poorest in the area as a priest, eking out a 'living' of £5 a year with annual gifts of clogs and clothes. Moreover, there were fewer distinctions in dress between northern people; clogs were widely worn in Cumberland during the 18th century, whether by labouring people or the dowager Mrs Senhouse, herself a bishop's daughter, or the Christians at Unerigg Hall. At the first Cumberland Dinner, held in Daniel's birth year in London for notable Cumbrians in exile, one of the verses they sang evinced pride in their plain spokenness and style:

'The sons of refinement reproach us in vain,
Tis our pride that our language and manners are plain,
Old Bess thought them courtly and as they were then
'Ere nonsense and *ton* had made monkies of men.'

However proud these Cumbrians were of their background, there were limits to what they still found acceptable when they returned home. Miss Noble told of how the great Bishop Gibson, Anglo-Saxon scholar and editor of Camden's history, came to see his sister and sat by the fire while she cooked the dinner. He thought her cooking was not quite clean, and said so. "What," she responded, "we must all eat a peck of dirt before we die." "Yes," said he, "but not all at once, Mary, not all at once."

As a result of his statesman upbringing, Daniel was at ease with people whatever their station in life. One account describes him as 'easy of access and lowly towards all with his benevolence' at Blackburn. It was by no means unusual for ordinary Cumbrians, not only notables, to leave their homes to further their careers. There was a long established custom among statesmen families that while all the children grew up to farming, it was the eldest son who usually became his father's right hand man at an early age in preparation for inheriting the farm in due course. The remaining sons were sent away to study a profession or gain an apprenticeship. Where this was not affordable in a family of umpteen sons, the younger sons, at the age of fourteen, would seek all found employment on other farms for wages of £12–14 a year, their aim being to gain experience and financial resources so that by the age of thirty they might have a small farm of their own. Daniel's family, however, did not follow this pattern. His eldest brother Thomas farmed with their father at Lobbes until he married Ann Wilkinson and they moved into High Gate in 1789. At some point Thomas decided on a career change, perhaps an opportunity came to enter the trading world through his father-in-law, and he left farming and went to live in Penrith. With William already away, it was John who took Thomas's place as a farmer and he and his descendents would remain at High Gate and Lobbes throughout the 19th century.[27]

When it was Daniel's turn to be sent away, his father arranged for him to train as an Exciseman first at Penrith and then at Carlisle. Daniel may have been given a place through one of several channels. His sister-in-law Ann, for instance, whose relation Isaac Wilkinson was an Officer with

Preston with its towering
windmills driving its
cotton industry, shortly
before the arrival of the
Railway c. 1840 by
William Westall.

the Excise and, as was then customary, the Excise office was housed in an inn, in this case the Swan Inn, Penrith, which he had taken over in 1777. Another local man in the service was John Banks of Keswick 'the much respected' Supervisor of Excise at Manchester.[28]

The Excise had a large force in Cumberland owing less to the busy port at Whitehaven and more to the long border with Scotland. This meant that Daniel's chosen profession was not without danger. Different rates of duty on commodities, such as whisky and salt, in England and Scotland made border towns hives of smuggling activity. Whether apprehending salt smugglers – when the Longtown exciseman seized a pony loaded with 2 cwt of salt, the smuggler attempted to stab him with a hay fork – or, more regularly, whisky smugglers – as three officers struggled to seize an illegal still and quantity of spirits, one of the excisemen was severely wounded and another, searching for his lost pistol the next day, was attacked by the smugglers, dragged across the River Lyne and kept prisoner until a detachment of Scots Greys from Carlisle rescued him – an excise officer regularly courted injury and death in his work.[29]

Nor after risking life and limb to collect the duties, was the law always upheld against miscreants; indeed the farther away from London, the less likely to be so. On finding that most of the victuallers in Anglesey and North Wales had sold beer and ale for many years without a licence, a newly appointed Supervisor of Excise got 126

people convicted only to discover that he could neither recover the fines nor imprison the offenders. Cumberland also had a long history of refusing to accept any excise control, especially on alcohol. 'Whenever any endeavour is made to Gauge the drinke brewed,' the Collector in Cumberland had reported as long ago as 1686, 'Ryotts are dayly committed on the officers by the inhabitants and encouraged by the Victuallers and Inn Keepers and tho some informations have been brought agst some of the said inhabitants', the sheriff's officers refused to prosecute 'on pretence of feare of their lives.' Justices of the Peace often refused to prosecute; their loyalties were local rather than national and, as is the nature of society in small towns, Justices could well be active in the business themselves or be relatives and friends of those whose trade they were being asked to judge – at least until finally prevented by statue from being directly judges in their own cause. Moreover, at the time Daniel started his training in the 1790s, Samuel Johnson's definition of Excise as a 'hateful tax levied upon commodities, and adjudged not by the common judges of property, but by wretches hired by those to whom the excise is paid', was an opinion by no means confined to the lexicographer. The underlying attitude of the whole population remained one of hostility towards, if not conspiracy to defraud, the revenue well into the 19th century.[30]

The service that Daniel was entering, the Board of Excise, was then quite separate from the Board of Customs, though they were known collectively as the Revenue. Broadly speaking, whereas the Customs collected duty on imports and was largely based in ports and coastal areas, the Excise collected the duty or tax on home-produced goods, though also on some imports, and was scattered widely throughout the land, organised into areas of collection; Daniel at first came under Carlisle Collection. Excise duty had originally been imposed by the Long Parliament in 1643 as a temporary tax measure for the duration of the Civil War, but it had proved so costly that the Excise duties were retained. Vociferous objections to this form of tax, particularly beer duty, led William Prynne to argue in a tract of 1645 that the Excise was illegal; it did his future career no harm for, after the Restoration, he was appointed a Commissioner of the Excise.

Parliament permanently established the Board of Excise in 1683 and granted Charles II one half of the duties on strong waters, ale, beer, tea, coffee, chocolate and sherbet for his personal use, and one half for investment for himself and his heirs in perpetuity. That on his orders, monthly payments of £4000 to the Forces, £300 to the Secret Service, £1000 to his House, £500 to Prince George and £500 to mistress Eleanor 'Nellie' Gwynne gives some idea of the amounts then collected, when the cost of employing an Excise Officer was a mere £50 a year. Not surprisingly, royalty always took a keen interest in 'the duties': the Old Pretender avoided having to resort to pillage during the 1715 Jacobite rising by merely collecting the Excise receipts at Carlisle and, in Daniel's time, George III exhorted Pitt not to forget 'The Duties' on West Indian sugar, which produced enormous sums.[31]

Given the predominantly illiterate population, the recruitment pool for officials was relatively small. Nevertheless, despite the low salaries awarded in His Majesty's Excise Service, the standards for entry had to be high. An officer had to be competent in weights and measurements, documentation, record-keeping and intricate calculations, not to mention being familiar with both the various manufacturing processes upon which duty was levied and legal processes which he had to initiate against offenders. As Thomas Paine, less well known then for being a former Exciseman than for being a radical author twice sentenced to death, wrote on the qualifications of officers 'it is not only necessary that the person should be honest, but that he be sober, diligent, and skilful: sober that he may be always capable of business; and skilful, that he may be able to prevent or detect frauds against the Revenue.'

After a lengthy apprenticeship, in 1794/5 Daniel applied for entry into the Excise Service. Success was determined not by exam results but by patronage. Daniel therefore supplied the all important letter of recommendation, without which his candidature could never be deemed worthy of notice, and a character reference from the local priest. From the Excise Officer who had trained him, he also obtained a letter stating that he was proficient in writing, spelling and arithmetic. Daniel's entry papers have not been found among the surviving Excise records but his patron's word must have carried sufficient authority and influence to be heard clearly at the Board in London. Sometime in 1795, probably when Daniel reached his eighteenth birthday, he received his first appointment in the Excise as an Assistant Officer at Preston in the county of Lancaster.[32]

Location had been central to Preston's development as a bustling medieval market town. Situated on the northern

The bustling market in progress around the obelisk in the centre at Preston. In the background is the Town Hall.

side of the Ribble river and with access to the sea as well as to Yorkshire via the Ribble Valley, Preston was also well-placed on the main route between the north and south through providing easy crossing by bridge, ferry and fords across the great Ribble. When Daniel arrived in 1795 the town appeared more or less the same: a small market town dominated by the large medieval market place where, on a market day in 1801, a visitor, Catherine Hutton, saw 'a thousand carts arranged in order, after having deposited the productions of the country in the streets. At Preston, every article upon sale is exposed to view, and the Prestonians say there is not such a market as theirs in England.' The town was surrounded by fields and willow beds, traversed by an old lane, footpath or bad road. The state of the roads would prove to be a sore point, quite literally, for Daniel and his fellow excisemen.[33]

The Excise service in the countryside was essentially a 'riding' force; each collection was divided into Districts and each District, in turn, was divided into 'rides'. The Assistant Officers, also the Ride Officers, surveyed in and near their District on horseback. 'I know not, in the whole range of language, terms sufficiently expressive to describe this infernal highway,' was how the agriculturist and traveller Arthur Young wrote about the road from Preston to Wigan earlier in the century. 'Let me most seriously caution all travellers who may accidentally propose to travel this terrible country, to avoid it, as they would the devil, for a thousand to one but they break their necks or their limbs by overthrows or breaking down. They will meet with ruts which I actually measured four feet deep and floating with mud only from a wet summer. What must it therefore be in winter?'[34]

Although this route had since been upgraded to a turnpike road to enable a stage coach to travel between Preston, Wigan and Warrington, 'overthrows' and 'breaking downs' continued to bedevil the traveller late in the century. Conducting his Excise surveys on horseback over the length and breadth of his 'ride' around Preston District, day after day in such conditions, must have been at best a wearying and uncomfortable occupation and at worst fraught with attendant hazard for Daniel. Christopher Wilson of Kendal,

who also rode around the northern countryside on business, complained of the days on horseback 'at risk from highwaymen, footpads & pickpockets' and the nights 'in bug ridden country inns.'[35]

In comparison with the large Liverpool Excise Office employing a Collector, an Inspector, four Supervisors, 31 Division Officers, 17 Assistant Officers and 8 Permit Writers, the Preston office was tiny. It was housed at 20 Fox Street in the Customs House and, whereas the Customs Office boasted a Collector, a Surveyor and numerous officers at all levels signalling the importance attached to the Port of Preston, the Excise employed only a Supervisor, one Officer, two Assistant Officers and one Permit Writer. It was, nonetheless, advantageous for Daniel to belong to a smaller staff because he had to supervise more than one trade and was exposed to all aspects of Excise business on a daily basis. London and Liverpool, in contrast, operated a system of more officers and greater specialisation in one trade. It would appear that a country exciseman's work was not especially onerous. The country collections shrugged off their reputation for being lax and inefficient in the eyes of the large city collections. And, even after regulations were introduced in 1803 to increase the official hours of attendance (to 9–4pm in winter and 8–4pm in summer) and to reduce the number of official holidays enjoyed by staff, Daniel still had ample time to enjoy the amusements offered by Preston society.[36]

Preston was a duchy and county palatine with the particular privileges of a Royal Borough first awarded in a royal charter of 1179. This was why, Daniel Defoe explained after his visit in 1725, there were no manufactures and the town was 'full of attorneys, proctors and notaries, the process of law here being of a different nature' than elsewhere. Another visitor in the middle of the century, John Marchant, praised the 'Variety of Company' to be found there. 'Tis a very gay town,' he decided, 'and is called Proud Preston, tho' not near so rich as Liverpool or Manchester.' That the well-bred inhabitants managed to withstand the advance of industrialism and the clamour and dirt of the rapidly expanding manufacturing centres of Manchester and Bolton is clear from Dr Aikin's description in the year of Daniel's arrival. Preston, the doctor wrote, was a handsome, well-built and genteel county town – and genteel was exactly what local polite society prided itself on being. Daniel could therefore divert himself with subscription balls, plays, concerts, books from the two circulating libraries, and in pleasure grounds such as Avenham Walks; he could also attend Preston Race Week, noted for its 'very Genteel' assemblies, and the Assembly Rooms notable for dancing and cards, gossip and tea.[37]

Not for genteel Preston, however, the 'Tonish' excesses of the aristocracy and, to use Reverend Ramsden's words, the 'Glitterings, Dazzlings, Diamonds and so forth' of the beau monde of London, which Prestonians regarded with fascinated disapproval. A modest social eminence was thought more seemly in provincial society. Nor did they allow local ultra-fashionables to escape their mocking censure, as in Anne Parker of Cuerden's comments about a Miss Wall who appeared at a Preston assembly with 'such an Enormous Quantity of Wool False Hair & c upon her Head that I Cou'd not help thinking if it was cut off t'wou'd Serve instead of a Wool Pack in the House of Peers for one of the Bishops to sit upon – poor Miss Wall, 'tis well she does not hear me for she wou'd not like perhaps to have a Bishops Bum placed upon her Noddle.'[38]

This was all very different from the statesmen society Daniel was used to at home. Preston with its lesser gentry and prosperous mercantile and professional families offered a more genteel but also a more hierarchical social milieu. Whittle wrote in his *History of Preston* that ' a regular distance is always kept between the various ranks of society; inferiority is often met, in the public walks, with repulsive countenance and half averted eyes.' Thus, in Daniel's sphere, the head of the Revenue, Richard Pilkington, Collector of Customs, was an Esquire and as a gentleman accepted in polite society; whereas the Collector and Supervisor of Excise, plain Thomas Tunnell, would remain peripheral and his assistant young Daniel Thwaites on £15 a year of no consequence at all.[39]

This did not prevent him from being brought into closer contact with polite society through the volunteer corps. All Daniel's early professional experience was gained under

conditions of war. Pitt, the prime minister, alarmed by the progress of the French Revolution, had declared war on France in February 1793. Patriotism was thereafter the order of the day. Patriotism, promulgated by the press in accounts of military and naval progress accompanied by maps and poems – the masthead of the newly founded *Blackburn Mail* incorporated Britannia, the British Lion and the Wooden Walls of Old England. Patriotism, exhorted from the pulpit to the faithful: 'The contest in which we are engaged has no parallel in the history of mankind,' preached Reverend Thomas Whittaker in 1794, ' every thing dear to us as men, or as Christians is at issue: it is a war of Property against Pillage – of Humanity against Barbarism – of Order against Confusion – of Religion against Atheism – of Allegiance against Rebellion.' Patriotism, demonstrated by charitable subscriptions to support the war effort. Patriotism, celebrated in victories and in royal events – the large number of oak boughs displayed in Blackburn on the anniversary of Charles II's Restoration 'was truly pleasing, as it evinced the detestation entertained of French tyranny, &c by the loyal inhabitants,' explained the *Blackburn Mail*. Patriotism, reverberating throughout the land on Fast Days and Days of 'National Humiliations' in the people's prayers 'imploring God's Assistance on his Majesty's Arms by sea and land, and to avert so great a Scourge as an invasion upon this Island' in 1797. Patriotism trumpeted by regular recruitment parties with much merry-making and sounding of fife and drum as they dispensed largesse: in July 1793 and February 1794, for instance, the principal inhabitants, cockades fluttering in their hats, paraded through the streets of Blackburn as church bells rang and ale, beer, beef and plum pudding were distributed amongst the residents.[40]

Against such a barrage of loyalism few young men, and certainly not Daniel and his Preston cohorts, could withstand the bugle call of the volunteer corps. The Preston, Blackburn and Bolton volunteers were first organised in 1794 as a reserve armed force in case of invasion or local disorder. Although headed by leading county gentlemen, each corps was thereafter comprised of a wide array of officers and men. Whereas the Blackburn Volunteer Troop

contained the cream of the town's Anglican gentlemen and mercantile elite, the Loyal Bolton Volunteer Infantry consisted of bleachers, spinners, retailers and manufacturers. Other commandants simply corralled their own workforce. Jonathan Peel enlisted the workmen of Peel, Yates & Company's print works at Church into his regiment and John Watson used men from his mills to form the ranks of the Loyal Preston Volunteers. Daniel, however, kitted himself out in the uniform of the Royal Preston Volunteers and was commanded by Nicholas Grimshaw Esq of Barton Hall.

Men, officers, young ladies, gentry and local polite society, all could bask in the reflected glory of the dashing volunteers with their intricately braided uniforms, polished boots, gleaming buttons and gold epaulettes. 'We used to march to church in Military order,' remembered Singleton Cooper, son of a Bolton innkeeper. 'We grew in repute and in favour too; for we frequently were invited by the neighbouring Gentry to their Mansions, where on the Lawn in front of the house we used to go through our exercises and evolutions to the seeming great amusement of our inviters, and they never failed to regale us with bread and cheese, and ale.' The officers, naturally, were considered even more worthy of notice and Daniel, despite his junior position at the Excise, was able to mingle in polite society with his fellow volunteers. They were singled out for notice and given toasts at public dinners. When, in July 1798, Lord Derby gave his annual dinner at Preston for the gentlemen of the town, the officers of both volunteer corps were particularly noticed. Daniel's name, however, was not among the list for by then he was no longer in Preston. The Excise Minute books show that in June a reorganisation of 1st, 2nd and 8th rides at Bury had resulted in Daniel being 'dropt' as Assistant to the 3rd Division, Preston.[41]

This was by no means unusual in the service and did not imply that Daniel's performance had been found unsatisfactory. Mobility was part of the Excise remit and excisemen were quite used to being moved about like figures in a never-ending game of chess. One senior officer's promotion to a new collection involved serried moves by at least four or five junior ranks throughout the country. At the same time, regular reorganisation of the divisions and rides to reflect changes in trade, say more printed goods and less paper or more beer and less salt being produced in a Collection, often resulted in officers being surplus to requirements. The saving grace was that they were usually needed elsewhere. In Daniel's case, instructions were given that he 'be provided for on the first convenient Vacancy.' And the first vacancy occurred in Manchester Collections at Stockport 4th Ride where Daniel started work on 20 September 1798. He had only just become used to his ride there when, on 23 May 1800, instructions were received from the Board to send him to Bury where an expansion in the Calico Printing trade meant more work for the local Excise office.[42]

This expansion was fuelled by the extraordinary success of Sir Robert Peel, proprietor of Messrs Peel & Yates, one of the most extensive calico printing businesses in the country. Such was the influence of the firm from 1790–1812 that it governed every institution public and private in Bury. And such were the profits that Peel was personally able to contribute £10,000 [now £½m] to the Prime Minister for the war effort. When it was learnt that the donor was not an aristocratic landowner but an unknown, and thus

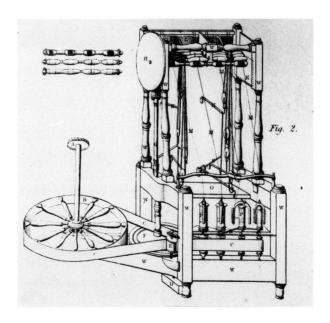

Arkwright's Spinning Jenny. Its invention not only spurred the Industrial Revolution but also contributed mightily to the wealth of the North West.

A pub sign showing the Two Jolly Brewers.

insignificant, tradesman from a little place called Bury, the London *beau monde* was agog and Pitt astonished. That Peel was also an MP had escaped London's notice. Still, shortly thereafter, Robert Peel, Calico Printer received a knighthood; it was his eldest son and namesake who would later become prime minister. The firm continued to expand and figures for 1803 show that it employed 15,000 people, chiefly at Bury and Tamworth in Staffordshire, and paid excise duty of more than £40,000 per annum on prints. It was Daniel's business to see that the duty of threepence per yard on all these printed goods was paid to the Government. To do this he had to visit all the firm's packing rooms where he kept an account of all the pieces packed and then fixed a stamp at the end of each piece. John Lightfoot, an Excise officer in Printed Goods at Accrington during this period, was said to enjoy the complete confidence of the great calico printers in the district. While Daniel was still a junior officer on £25 a year, it is, nevertheless, likely that he came to know the great calico printer of Bury quite well.[43]

Daniel, however, was not destined to remain long at Bury. The opening of a linen printing factory in Bury meant that, with too much work for 1st and 2nd Rides, it was necessary to establish a new ride, 8th Ride, under an officer on £50 a year. To keep within budget, though, the Assistancy to Bury 3rd Division had to be discontinued; once again, Daniel, as the newest and most junior exciseman, was 'dropt'. And, once again, he was quickly appointed to another position but this time he was also promoted, becoming Officer of Stockport 4th Ride, Manchester Collection on a salary doubled to £50 a year.[44]

Stockport was a small market town on the border of Cheshire and Lancashire within easy walking distance of Manchester, about six miles away. Yet Stockport's reputation as an excellent market for cheese and agricultural produce was already being eclipsed by the output of its textile trade during Daniel's second tour of duty there. The change from a domestic industry producing wool and fustian (a mixture of linen and cotton) in the home to a factory based manufacture of cloth had followed the series of exciting inventions that powered trade in the 18th century. Stockport had been the first town in England to establish a silk mill using John Lombe's patented silk-throwing water-powered machine and, by 1770, there were twelve silk machines in profitable production. Competition came after the development of Crompton's mule in 1779 and Cartwright's power-loom and Watt's steam engine in 1785 fuelled the spread of cotton mills in Stockport from one mill in 1780 to twenty-three in 1793. In consequence of the fabulous profits to be made in the cotton trade, more and more silk mills gradually converted to cotton.

Daniel's responsibilities in Printed Goods continued at Stockport but the cottons produced were not calicoes but flowered muslins, popular for aprons, mob-caps and handkerchiefs, and ginghams. One of the mills to be inspected belonged to Samuel Oldknow, the most prominent and one of the earliest mill owners in the area. In 1792 he had erected the first steam engine and produced the first muslin fabric in Stockport. Such was the curiosity aroused by the extraordinary power of this steam engine that the drivers of the London stage coaches apparently used to slacken their speed on passing the mill in order to tell their passengers of the miraculous operations performed therein.[45]

Daniel had considerably advanced his knowledge of the production of goods attracting duty when, in September 1804, he was transferred back to Preston Collection and sent to Blackburn He was twenty-seven years of age and if, as Eric Hobsbawm put it, 'Whoever says Industrial Revolution, says cotton', then Daniel's postings, especially at Bury and Stockport, had given him an insight into the heart of English industrial power. Lowly he might be but living in Lancashire he breathed in the commercial air of men of money, those masters owning businesses, savings and property.

There was a contagious buzz of activity in Georgian England as all around him people were dedicated to making money: from the factory owner, tradesman and speculator to the proverbial butcher, baker and candlestickmaker, all sought success and profit. 'There was never from the earliest ages,' thought Dr Johnson, 'a time in which trade so much engaged the attentions of mankind, or commercial gain was sought with such general emulation.' Young men like Daniel, mobile, ambitious, resourceful and sometimes plain lucky, believed that by their own efforts prosperity would smile upon them as it did upon so many others around them. A great industrialist ordered to be chiselled on his gravestone 'Here lies Jedediah Strutt who without Fortune, Family or friends raised himself to a fortune, family and name in the world.' Walking through Cheapside in London, he reflected in 1767 that 'the sole cause of this vast concourse of people, of the hurry and bustle they were in, and the eagerness that appeared in their countenances, was the getting of Money, and whatever some divines would teach to the contrary, this is true that it is the main business of the life of man.'[46]

The country teemed with swarms of practical men of enterprise seeking to make their fortunes, their pursuit of profit blessed by the master of the new discipline of political economy, Adam Smith, in *Wealth of Nations*. And, as Rubinstein has shown in his studies of wealth, a plethora of cotton fortunes were being made in Lancashire; the two greatest and wealthiest of the early cotton entrepreneurs being Richard Arkwright born in Preston and Sir Robert Peel of Bury, who was said to be worth over £1.5m [now £74m] when he died in 1830. There was no shortage of examples of success stories to fire up the ambitions of budding young entrepreneurs to start up a mill or enter trade for themselves. 'Oh what a pleasure is business!' exclaimed one Sussex shopkeeper but, before either the pleasure or the business could be gained, some capital was necessary to start the process. If, in 1750, it was said that a capital of £20,000 was needed to set up as a banker, £2000–10,000 as a brewer, £1000–5000 as a draper and £10–100 as a butcher, then by 1804 it would cost considerably more, however many opportunities existed for those who could take them.[47]

Yet Daniel had little prospect of amassing sufficient capital to enter this exciting opportunistic world of money. As a plain excise officer his salary at Blackburn remained fixed at £50 a year, an amount Paine thought beggarly for such a position of trust and hard work. He calculated that after tax and expenses were deducted, little more than £46 remained; then, taking into account the expenses of buying and keeping a horse of at least £14 a year, that left £32 or 1s 9d farthing per day. There were no perquisites attached to the work, such as the seizure of contraband goods from which customs officers stationed along the coast could profit. Paine argued the impossibility of an Excise Officer supporting himself, let alone a family, 'with any proper degree of credit and reputation, on so scanty a pittance.' As far as he was concerned, and he spoke from first-hand experience, 'Every year's experience gained in the Excise, is a year's experience lost in trade'.[48]

It would seem from the turn of events in Daniel's life that, at some point, he began to think of a career outside the Excise. The Birmingham businessman William Hutton liked to quote Bacon, 'Each man has his fortune in his own hands', and, after two years in Blackburn, Daniel set about changing direction. In November 1806 he instigated an exchange of stations with Isaac Ross of 5th Division. By doing so Daniel was leaving Printed Goods and specialising in Beer. It is not an unlikely leap of the imagination to believe that Miss Betty Duckworth might have caught Daniel's eye and that they might even have begun a courtship. Whereas matrimony continued to involve wider issues than just romantic love, Sir William Temple's cynical observation that 'Our marriages are made, just like other common bargains and sales, by the mere consideration of interest or gain, without any love or esteem,' was less applicable than it had been in the 18th century. At the turn of the 19th century even marriages of the nobility, where lineage, land and fortune were important factors, took into consideration mutual affection and esteem. This is not to say that Daniel can have been unaware of the attractions of a match with a Duckworth daughter and of the commercial advantages such an alliance could bring him. Suffice it to say that barely had a month elapsed since his switch of Excise specialisation when he wed Miss Duckworth and found himself well-placed to start to raise himself, like Strutt, to 'a fortune, family and name in the world.'

Dray Horses and Drays

Merchants using cart horses to deliver coal.

THE SOUND THAT was continuously heard in Blackburn throughout the 19th century was the clattering of horses' hooves along the cobbled streets. The majority of these horses were work-horses, used to haul carriages, wagons, hansom cabs, omnibuses, trams and brewers' drays. They might simply be depreciable capital equipment to transport goods and people for their owners, but they were the means to a livelihood for all the stable lads, drivers, coachmen, draymen, farriers, tanners, livery manufacturers, glovers, cobblers, harness makers, saddlers, hatters, and vets who worked in Blackburn.[1]

Early mornings must have been exceedingly noisy in the town, what with the shouts of the knockers-up waking the mill hands, the clacking of peoples' clogs as they hurried to work and the rattling of hooves and grinding of wheels as the delivery rounds began. The stable lads led the ambling Thwaites horses out of the stables in Syke Street, across the road, (until the end of the 19th century, that is, when the stables moved to the Brewery site), and into the Brewery yard, where they patiently waited for their carts and drays to be loaded with the day's deliveries. Some were cart horses, used before the age of steam to turn the water and mill wheels, but now for lighter work, such as moving coal, around the Brewery yard. They were smaller in size than the other occupants of the Thwaites stables namely, the dray horses.

These 'Gentle Giants' of the Brewery were the descendents of the battle steeds introduced into England by William the Conqueror. Known as 'destriers', these massive horses, closer to the short-legged Suffolk Punch than the Shire, were capable of carrying a man sheathed in heavy steel armour and chain-mail, weighing up to 400 lbs. As warfare changed in the 17th and 18th centuries, and cavalry required lighter, speedier mounts in battle, demand for the heavy horse came from agriculture, the canals and especially the large common brewers who

needed their enormous casks of porter carried. By the end of the 19th century several breeds, the Shire, Clydesdale, Suffolk Punch and Percheron were used as dray horses. Thwaites chose to use the best known breed, the mighty Shire horse with its white blaze, brown or black body and fringed hooves.

These were the horses resplendent in their black leather harness and polished brass and steel fittings that drew the laden 19th-century drays, reminiscent of old hay wains carried on multi-spoked wheels with iron rims, out of Eanam Brewery every morning to hiss and puff their way up and down Blackburn's hills. The horse-drawn drays brought hops, malt, barley and casks into the Brewery and delivered large oak casks of beer, and crates of bottled beer and

The Thwaites Shire horses, familiar not only in Blackburn but throughout the country.

Star Brewery dray horses King, Tim, Draylad, Old Dan and Star enjoy buckets of beer before delivery time, helped by Patrick Flood (near left) in 1964.

THE HOME OF THWAITE

mineral waters to the public-houses as well as the used hops sold to local farmers for cattle fodder. According to the Brewery History Society, 19th-century drays contained an interesting feature. To sustain the draymen, (ie. the drivers and brewery delivery men) on their journey, slung under the dray was the driver's beer contained in a wooden bucket of a peculiar shape, as if a small cask had been cut in half at its greatest girth and a bottom fitted in where it had been cut: a metal hoop handle was fixed to the smaller end, which was provided with a bung and spigot to enable it to be filled and emptied.[2]

In the 1920s, however, most breweries decided to put their dray horses out to grass and to adopt motor transport. Vaux, for example, which had stabled 120 dray horses in 1911, now retained only three steeds to move broken glass in the Sunderland Brewery. Thwaites, too, moved with the times, and, in 1927, the last of its Shire horses were led out of the Brewery for the last time 'to grass'. Petrol rather than bran or chopped hay now fuelled the dray vehicle. Draymen now drove steam waggons: 'the sparks shooting into the air with the dirty smoke billowing from the short chimney and the red ashes dropping into the ash box below the vehicle,'

DRAY HORSES AND DRAYS

recalled Alex Johnson. Then, they drove ten-ton lorries, called their driver's mate a 'nipper', and often based their hours of work on 'job and finish', as they travelled long distances. Harry Alpin, who worked at Cornbrook Brewery in Manchester, loved every minute of being a drayman, despite drawbacks like vicious dogs, adverse weather conditions, and the odd landlord, evidently reluctant to get out of bed and open the door to accept the beer. 'A free drink was customary at every pub we called at but we often accepted cigarettes instead,' Alpin recalled. One day the brewery bosses sent a circular to all its houses which stated: 'The customary pint is acceptable but the parties must cease.'[3]

By the 1950s, the Shire horses had practically ceased to exist; natural wastage and the slaughter of over 200,000 after the Second World War had combined to reduce the millions of working heavy horses in Britain. When Churchill wrote, 'I have always considered that the substitution of the internal combustion engine for the horse marked a very gloomy passage in the progress of mankind', he was not to know that a young manager of the Soft Drinks department at Thwaites was of the same opinion. David Kay loved horses and he wanted to bring the Shire dray horses back to Eanam. His suggestion that the Brewery use one or two dray horses was rejected. 'Horses? This was 1957, whatever was he thinking about? There was a fleet of lorries to do the deliveries. Whatever was wrong with the lad? They told him to get on with his job and stop talking about horses,' was how Ken Bowden, who ran the Thwaites advertising account, later recalled the incident.[4]

Eventually, in 1959, persistent, persuasive David Kay was allowed to reintroduce two dray horses to the Brewery's local route. As the firm's original stables were occupied by the Estates department, the nearby but derelict stables of Henry Shaw & Co. had to be requisitioned. The place had to be cleared of 'knee-deep weeds, old fireplaces, barrels, bits of machinery, broken bicycles' and 120 tons of coal slack procured during the war for emergencies never experienced; the buildings had rotted and the best one had only three walls and a leaking roof.

Yet David Kay was convinced that the dray horses would not only attract good publicity for Thwaites but would be financially advantageous. He was, in fact, in the vanguard of a growing corporate awareness in the 1960s and 1970s of the benefits of public and community relations. The sight of the Thwaites team of dray horses lumbering through Blackburn or on splendid display at an agricultural show would gladden everyone's hearts at a time when people were becoming more intent upon saving England's heritage. On the financial side, the increased cost of petrol and the scarcity of oil persuaded other brewers to revert to horse power for local deliveries, too. Youngs of Wandsworth, for example, calculated that a four-year-old Shire horse cost about £2,000 a year, compared with £50,000 for a lorry, and did not burn expensive fuel when stuck in a traffic jam.[5]

On Mayday in 1960 the first two Shire horses were led out of the smart new Thwaites stables and yard by two draymen, Harry Crossland and Bill Sycamore, who were on full time horse duty at Thwaites. David Kay also hired as

Draymen delivering barrels through doors set in the pavement from where they rolled into the cellar.

Two of the dray horses on the day Thwaites Shire horses received the Freedom of the City of Blackburn. David Kay is on the right.

horse-foreman Patrick Flood, who would train up several apprentices, including David Clarkson. Three years later, Thwaites had a pair of black Shires; in 1964 they had a team of them and, by 1967, Flood commanded a stables' staff of seven. They looked after the horses and also drove them. The horses' routine was the same then as it remained until the late 20th century when haulage lorries overtook horse power for delivery, but not public relations, duty. Breakfast at 7 a.m. and, other than on a show day, the horses were kept busy delivering barrels of beer to five or six public-houses a day until 3 o'clock. Hours were spent ensuring that

they were beautifully groomed and brushed and their heavy harnesses were well-polished. Their shoes were bespoke and made by the resident farrier; at first Jim Sharples and then the last blacksmith Brian Fitzpatrick, who even made a shoe for presentation to the Princess Royal when she visited the brewery. The horses were pensioned off before the average working age and, as David Clarkson said, the Thwaites horses 'have a good life'.[6]

The return of horse transport was a great success and the people of Blackburn soon grew used to sharing their brewery horses with the rest of the country. The Shire dray

A dray horse, by bowing its head, shows equine courtesy to the Queen on the day in 1977 when she became President of the Shire Horse Society.

horses continue to appear today as Thwaites ambassadors at charity events, shows, carnivals, processions and even on television; their names, from the mighty Major, Cavalier, Colonel and Ambassador, to Classic, Regent, Royal and Captain in the present day, are familiar to a national audience. Following many successes in the sixties, the Thwaites horses continued to win prestigious prizes. At the Shire Horse Society Centenary Show at Peterborough in 1978, Royal was awarded first prize for the single turnout class. Then, Royal and Major won the first prize for best pair of Horses on the Showground and received the 'Jane Smith trophy' which was presented by Her Majesty The Queen, as the Society's President, to Head Horsekeeper David Clarkson, and grooms Charles Beardmore and Eric Longson,

while David Kay, as Deputy President of the Society, proudly watched them. On their return to the Brewery, David Kay reported that 'The horses are back at work today, but we will be turning them out soon for a couple of weeks' well-earned rest in fields full of lovely grass.' The present generation of Shire horses and horsemen at Thwaites has continued to win prizes; they were even awarded the honour of the Freedom of Blackburn. Today, the horses are still looked after by Charles Beardmore, now head horse-keeper, Richard Green the coachman, and groom Jonathan Jones. As one local equestrian admirer, Jack Ingram, said after a visit, 'In the middle of the old cotton town of Blackburn, there is a haven of old world charm in the shape of Thwaites brewery stables.'[7]

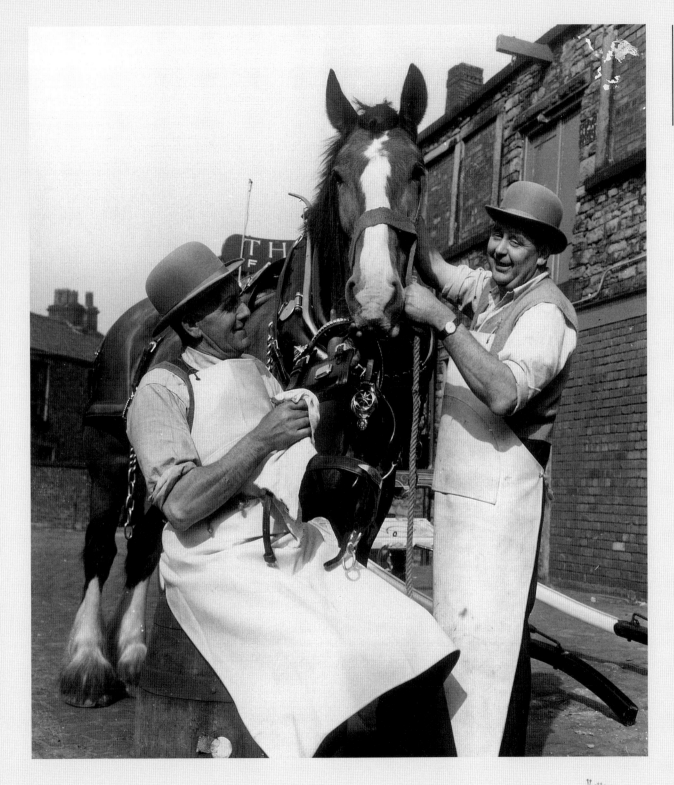

After some years when they had not seen service, dray horses are prepared by Harry Crossland and Bill Sycamore for a return to duty in 1960.

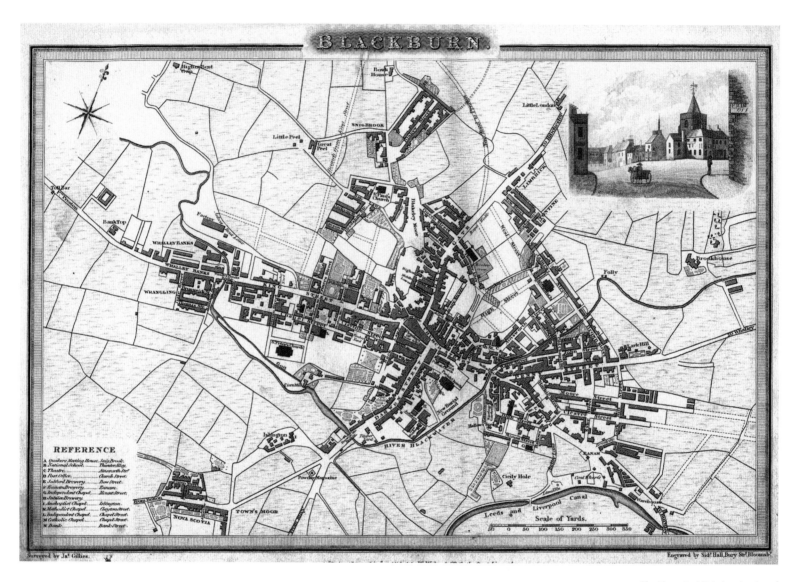

Blackburn in 1824 showing its
growth over the previous 30 years.

CHAPTER TWO

The Eanam Brewery

WHEN DANIEL SETTLED himself into the brewing business in Blackburn, the town was renowned for cotton rather than beer. This was far from being disadvantageous for in 1807 beer was still universally regarded as a prime necessity of life. It formed part of the British diet, the common beverage at every meal from the cradle to the grave. Beer quietened crying babies as effectively as the popular Godrey's cordial; it was given (7 gallons on one occasion) to children on Sunday School treats, to schoolboys at Marlborough for breakfast, and recommended in the 1856 *Every Boy's Book of Sports and Amusements*: 'Tea

we believe to be undesirable, and a pint of really sound bitter will be found to agree much better.' Beer provided energy for workmen: whether agricultural labourers, who believed it was impossible to get in the harvest without copious amounts of harvest beer, or printers who, the American Benjamin Franklin noted with incredulity, downed at work a pint before breakfast, a pint with breakfast, a pint between breakfast and lunch, another at lunch, followed by one more at six o'clock, and then a pint when they knocked off from work, which totalled three quarts a day without counting the evening pints drunk elsewhere. And, finally, beer ensured

Entitled 'The Pious Public-House', this 19th-century print attacked the breweries for encouraging drink in the teeth of evidence to suggest that beer was actually safer than water.

criteria; there was no public supply in Blackburn until 1848 when only a minority of the population received it at a high rental cost, the rest having to rely upon the uncertain quality of pumps, tanks and rivers. In Manchester the water was declared to be 'frequently like ink' while in London the scarcity of public drinking water in the 1820s created the profession of water-carrier and, well into the 1870s, many Londoners believed that water should not be drunk at all unless purified with spirits. Of other non-intoxicants, milk in northern towns was cheaper than in London but even when fresh 'was little used' as of poor, if not tainted, quality; tea and coffee were neither as cheap nor as readily accessible as alcoholic drinks. Although a fall in duty in 1825 allowed coffee to rival beer in price, so that a pint of coffee cost 3–4d and a quart of ale cost 4 ½ -6d, there were not more than about twelve coffee-shops in London in 1821 and none in Blackburn. Whereas Londoners in the 1840s could buy a cup of coffee for 1 ½ d, tea for 2d and cocoa for 4d, they could buy a whole pint of porter for only 2 ½ d. Although the consumption of tea was increasing rapidly throughout the 19th century as the price fell, there remained a strand of public opinion hostile to tea versus beer. 'I view tea drinking,' declared William Cobbett, 'as a destroyer of health, an enfeebler of the frame, an engenderer of effeminacy and laziness, a debaucher of youth and a maker of misery for old age.' In short, tea was the antithesis of beer, which most people continued to regard as essential to their well-being.[2]

The Treasury also regarded beer as essential to the well-being of the nation. And well it might for the excise duties on beer and two of its ingredients, malt and hops, had long played a leading role in sustaining the public revenue; acting, in the economic historian Peter Mathias's words, as 'an impressive fiscal sponge'. Drink revenues were elastic and, therefore, invaluable in war time when the brewing industry played a starring role, providing Walpole with about one quarter of the total tax revenue, and swelling the Exchequer coffers during the Napoleonic Wars when, in 1802, Pitt increased beer duty from 2s per barrel to 10s. Malt tax also jumped from 1s 4 ¼ d in 1780 to 4s 5 ¾ d a bushel in 1803/4, thereby supplying the Revenue with between

a 'decent burial' at the relatively lavish funerals of northern working families and was even commemorated in the graveyard where, for instance, Rebecca Freeland's tombstone read 'She drank good ale, good punch, and wine/And lived to the age of ninety nine.'[1]

Beer and alcoholic drinks were thirst quenchers in an age when other liquids were often contaminated, scarce or more expensive. Water, for example, could meet all three one half and one third of the selling price of malt. Of the total excise revenue for 1805 of £22.5m, beer, malt, hops and spirits provided nearly £15m.[3]

Drinking to the success of British armies and navies thus did more to further the national interest than the proffering of patriotic toasts might imply. At a not untypical such jolly evening in Blackburn, in 1807, the glass was pushed merrily round, which naturally produced a swell of loyal and patriotic songs and toasts including 'The King, Queen and the Royal family – The Prince of Wales – the duke of York, and the British Army – The British Navy and our persevering Admirals and invincible tars – the encouragement of Agriculture in this Kingdom – the town of Blackburn and cotton manufacture' and so on, each downed foaming tankard adding to the national pride (and contribution) of these truly loyal sons of Britain.[4]

Beer's primary place in the national life of Georgian England was indisputable. A long tradition emphasised that it was patriotic to drink beer and, with each victory against Bonaparte, John Bull swaggered around with an ale pot in his hand and barley-corns in his hat. Henry Brougham M.P. praised beer in Parliament as 'the good, sound, wholesome, constitutional beverage of the country.' Popular war time songs pitted English Protestantism, constitutional government and beer against French Catholicism, autocracy and wine. 'What two ideas,' asked Sydney Smith,' are more important than Beer and Britannia?' Beer, more than any other beverage, supported the farmer and the landed interest in good times and bad. Hop growing was entirely dependent upon the brewing industry while Britain's annual barley crops, much of which were used as malt in the mash-tuns of brewers and distillers, provided employment, farming revenues and agricultural rents. The importance of the barley crop, particularly in regions of very light soils where it superseded wheat, was evident both to the farm labourers, who would pursue temperance reformers with the cry 'Wot shall we du wi' 't' barley?', and in the common toast 'Here's a health to the brewer and God speed the plough.'[5]

The prestige attached to the brewing industry in the 19th century, in turn, enhanced the status of the brewer.

Even as a junior partner, Daniel possessed a social status above that commonly accorded a young man in trade and industry. This was a reflexion partly of the success and high rank in society achieved through their profits by the great 18th-century London brewers, such as Whitbread, Truman, Meux, Thrale, Barclay and Calvert who, possessing substantial estates, had entered county society and, often, Parliament. When Dr Johnson was helping the widowed Mrs Thrale with the sale of Thrale's Brewery in 1781, he famously replied to an inquirer 'We are not here to sell a parcel of boilers and vats, but the potentiality of growing rich beyond the dreams of avarice.' While Daniel, in common with most brewers outside London, was unlikely to wallow in any such riches, the knowledge that he could make an excellent living from a successful brewery could only be inspirational.

Daniel's higher status was also a reflexion of the brewer's connection with the agricultural interest; brewing was seen as a long established trade, not a brash new industry, such as cotton manufacturing, and a brewer inhabited the same world of farming and harvests familiar to the landed gentry and upon which they depended. In consequence, in the smaller English towns the social position of the brewer was assured. Well-to-do families were happy to despatch sons, who had failed to enter the navy, army and church, into brewing where they would move in the same circles as magistrates and other leaders of the community and, hopefully, become what *The Times* described in 1827 as a typical brewer-magistrate: ' a man of immense wealth,' possessed of 'a splendid mansion in the country, a park crowded with deer' and enough venison to bribe all whose votes might be useful on licensing day. This happy state was not only beyond Daniel's immediate reach but also ignores the great disparities that existed in the scale and profitability of country brewing.[6]

Of the three categories of brewing, home brewing was, by 1800, in decline. The high consumption of beer in nearly every household in the land, from the great families and big institutions producing large quantities in their own brew-houses down to the farmers allowing their labourers so many pints a day and the cottagers mashing molasses in a tea kettle, meant that the amount brewed privately was prodigious. This amount was thought to have fallen by nearly half between the 1770s and 1820s owing first to the increased malt and hop duties, which made home brewing too expensive for many people, and second to the relative cheapness of commercially brewed beer.[8]

The publican-brewer, in contrast, produced beer to sell in his alehouse, tavern or inn and accounted for most beer production until the 18th century. He brewed enough to meet his customers' consumption, mashing a few bushels or so of malt in an outbuilding every ten days to a fortnight as required. In the south of England, however, the publican-brewer was a dying breed, eclipsed by the growth of the large London commercial brewers, who, in the 18th century, started supplying cheaper, more reliable liquor and, in the 19th century, used surplus capital to lend publicans money to purchase or lease their public-houses in exchange for selling only one brand of beer or porter as stipulated in the 'tied' contract. Excise figures for 1823 show that of 44,292 publicans outside London only about half (22,268) brewed their own beer of which the majority were in the North and the Midlands. In Yorkshire, for example, two-thirds of beer was still brewed by publican-brewers. The ratio in Blackburn was even higher. When Daniel started brewing in 1807 there were said to be fourteen breweries in the town. In fact twelve of these were publican-brewers brewing for retail in their own inns. There is, however, considerable discrepancy in the number of public-houses thought to exist in the town, as one account mentions 'around 92 public-houses (excluding Beer houses) brewing their own beer and ales' at the end of the 18th century. The earliest surviving directory, Holden's Annual Directory for 1811, was probably more correct in its list of twenty-two inns and taverns.[7]

In 1807, however, there were two breweries, the Park Place partnership and Daniel's partnership at Eanam. Park Place appears to have brewed only for home consumption as, according to the Blackburn Mail, its beers could be found 'in the houses of the humble industrious handicraftmen, as well as the cellars of the more opulent.' Confirmation is given by the Brewery in 1794 when it notified the public that an order book would be kept at Mr Stackhouse's shop to supply people who found it inconvenient to walk out of the town in the winter to buy ale and beer. Thus the Eanam partnership took the initiative and deployed, in Charles Wilson's words, 'a sense of market opportunity combined with the capacity needed to exploit it,' to become the first firm in Blackburn to fall into the third category of brewing: commercial brewing.

Daniel was a common brewer, a wholesaler selling beer in bulk to publicans and to private customers able to buy by cask and butt in quantity. He might, in June 1807, be the only one in Blackburn but common brewers had long dominated the brewing industry in London, the 'Common Brewers' of Southwark had been mentioned in the Court Rolls of 1336–8. It was largely owing to the use of hops that a change in the product, in the type of malt liquor brewed, enabled the common brewer to displace the publican-brewer in the production of beer, first in London and later elsewhere. Surprisingly, the native English drink was not beer but ale, a heavy sweet malt liquor which quickly deteriorated so that a publican-brewer had to sell every barrel he brewed within a few days or throw it away. Beer, a malt liquor made bitter by being boiled with hops before fermentation, was brought from the Low Countries to England in the 15th century. Hopping the malt liquor gave it antibiotic qualities that allowed it to keep much longer without spoiling, even in summer heat, which provided a common brewer with a more stable product to brew on a larger scale. From then on, the rise of the common brewer was inexorable. By the mid-16th century, there were twenty-six common brewers in London and by the end of the 17th century nearly two hundred common brewers were producing 1,650,000 barrels a year when the publican-brewers were managing only 12,700 barrels.

In the early 18th century hops again contributed to an innovation in London brewing so seismic that it has been called brewing's own industrial revolution. Porter, the colloquial name given to Entire, in turn an abbreviation for 'entire butt' beer drawn entirely from one cask, was one of the first truly mass-produced consumer goods sold in England. It was also the means by which a select group of London common brewers implemented economies of scale to make massive profits. Porter was a highly-hopped, heavy black beer (really, a weaker Stout) which furnished brewers with numerous economic advantages. The high hop rate allowed the use of inferior malts without detriment to the flavour, to give a saving of nearly 2s per barrel of beer; it produced a keeping beer which could be brewed in large quantities and stored for consumption indefinitely without spoiling but actually improving in flavour; and it could travel distances never practicable before. Porter was, therefore potent, stable, long lasting and cheaper than most extant strong beers and pale ales, which it immediately displaced. By 1800 the porter trade was concentrated in the hands of twelve great breweries with about half producing more than 100,000 barrels annually. Whitbread had first brewed over 200,000 barrels in 1786 and Barclays would be the first with more than 300,000 in 1815.[9]

Although London led the way, the popularity of porter, described as 'the universal cordial of the populace', ensured that porter-brewing spread into the provinces where it was reputedly first brewed in Sheffield around 1744 with Bristol porter appearing in 1780. Nearer to Blackburn, by 1799 Brookes, Rose and Bromfield owned a 'considerable porter brewery' at Liverpool and were sending large consignments to Manchester and other inland towns in Lancashire. When Daniel became a brewer, porter brewing was still confined to the larger towns, as one observer pointed out in 1805: 'The most prevailing kind of malt liquor in the country is strong beer, called in some places ale, and small or table beer; that of the metropolis and all large manufacturing towns such as Manchester, Birmingham, Sheffield, with many seaport towns, Liverpool, Chester, Hull, Bristol, etc., is porter.' Where it was sold in the minor towns it was usually imported from London and these larger towns. Peter Stubs of Warrington never attempted to brew porter and was buying it from Liverpool in 1800, as was Greenalls of St Helens who did not start brewing porter in small quantities until about 1835. Given the weaker demand and modest wholesale base, few common brewers in the smaller market towns risked venturing into porter brewing.[10]

Yet this is exactly what Daniel did in 1807. He would have come across porter when he was working in

From *The Book of English Trades,* published in 1808, this shows a brewer mixing the mash.

Manchester Collections as the Radical weaver Samuel Bamford regularly found it in Manchester alehouses. More significantly, he learnt about the production of porter during his last months as an exciseman when he gauged the brews at Park Place Brewery, which had started to offer porter for sale in 1807. One of the requirements of porter brewing was sufficient space to hold the large vats and butts used for the bulk storage of porter; the design and construction of these vessels had been one of the technical advances introduced in the 18th century. The existing brewery site at Eanam was clearly not big enough for Daniel's ambitious plans. A month after becoming the managing partner, he signed a new lease for additional glebe land and purchased an adjoining lot of freehold land to extend the brewery site at Eanam.[11]

Above A barrel being cleaned as required after each use.
Below right A malt-porter employed to transfer malt within the brewery.

His gamble paid off as porter, weaker and cheaper than strong beer, proved to be as popular a thirst quencher for the mill workers of Blackburn as it had long been for the porters, carters and manual labourers of London. There were only two cotton mills then operating in Blackburn: the Andertons' Spring Hill Mill built in 1797, and Thomas Lund's mill built around 1790 at Wensley Fold on the site of the old spinning factory destroyed in 1769 by weavers irate at the introduction of the spinning jenny. These mills, however, were at the forefront of a burgeoning spinning and, especially, weaving cotton industry that would come to dominate Blackburn for the next century or more. Daniel was enterprising enough to ensure that his brewery was well-positioned to capitalise on what could only be an expanding market for its malt liquors.[12]

As the managing partner, Daniel had absolute control over and responsibility for the everyday executive routine of Eanam Brewery. The best way to supervise operations was, in the time honoured fashion of successful brewing proprietors such as Sir Benjamin Truman, to live in close proximity to the brewery. Daniel and Betty therefore moved into a house at number 32 Cleaver street on the north-eastern corner bounded by Lark Hill street. Here their eleven children were born, beginning in 1809 with Thomas, their eldest surviving child, and ending in 1830 with Alice. From the spacious walled garden, which Daniel had laid out for them at the back of the house and within the grounds of the Brewery, a door opened giving him easy access across the yard to the brewing buildings. Although there was an entrance gate at 31 Cleaver street, the main entrance for brewery business was at the corner of Syke street and Eanam, facing the stables (now the old estates office). The site of the Brewery ran along Cleaver street from the length of Lark Hill street, on the east side, to Syke street on the west, and its south side continued along Eanam and its continuation Brook street (later Quarry street), and occupied 5280 square yards.

Duckworth and Clayton chose a good site for the Brewery. It was closer to the centre of town than their competitors at Park Place and had ample space for future expansion as Eanam was not then developed. Stage wagons belonging to the several firms of local carriers trundled goods through Eanam along the main turnpike road leading eastwards to Burnley, Halifax and Leeds. Just as the smarter "Express" stage coaches, regularly conveying passengers into Blackburn, passed by the Brewery and over the narrow humped back Salford bridge across the river Blakewater to reach the main coaching inns, the Bay Horse at Salford, the Old Black Bull, Market Place, and the New Inn, Church street. Joining this throng of vehicles, stamping horses and barking dogs, swollen on Wednesdays and Saturdays by farmers' carts and people coming to market, trying to get over the bottleneck of Salford bridge were the Eanam Brewery drays on their delivery rounds to the taverns and alehouses in the town centre.

Yet for all its noise and bustle, Blackburn was still too primitive and insignificant a market town in 1807 to attract the prestigious notice of the elite Royal Mail coaches. Despite numerous applications for the privilege of receiving letters sooner and more reliably, as Preston already did, Blackburn's consequence was not deemed sufficient by the Postmaster-General to receive the distinctive maroon coaches trimmed in black with bright red undercarriage and wheels, and each door gleaming with the royal arms and cipher in gold. This should not have surprised the more discerning inhabitants, for Blackburn then possessed little of the refinements of a genteel fashionable town.[13]

Walking through the centre of town, Daniel and Betty met with streets irregularly paved, obstructed by rubbish and sewage, and full of marauding dogs, especially unmuzzled mastiffs, and pigs wandering at large. The appointment of efficient deputy constables, such as George Clayton and John Kay, brought some of the worst offenders before the magistrates. In just one session in 1807, three men were fined 20s each for allowing their unmuzzled dogs loose in the street; three men for leaving their horses and carts obstructing the streets; Henry Sudell's servant for carting ashes mixed with soil from the bog house and spilling them in Queen Street; and James Folds, rather ominously, for 'laying blood and garbage in a passage called Hanging Croft, to the annoyance of passengers.'

Although scavengers were employed to clean the streets and empty the pits, and watchmen and lamplighters to protect the inhabitants at night, the provision of civic services was in its infancy and by no means dependable. A ten guineas reward was offered for information about vandals after street lamps were 'wilfully and maliciously broken' during the night. Even those 'guardians of the night', the watchmen, could fall into temptation, as the local press gleefully reported: 'On Saturday morning, about six o'clock, two of the guardians of the night were discovered lying in a state of intoxication and fast asleep on a midding on Blakeley Moor. Information was immediately given to one of the Commissioners of the Peace who ordered their coats to be stripped and so overpowering was the beverage which they swallowed that this operation was performed without awaking them.'[14]

Blackburn might possess a well-established subscription library, founded in 1787; spanking new Assembly Rooms opened in 1803; two newly erected gentlemen's seats in the neighbourhood, Witton Park and Woodfold Hall; and a Literary Society which met at the New Inn on Monday evenings and, on 18 May, considered the pressing question 'If Five Constables are necessary to guard two *Gentlemen*, how many would it require to guard two *Felons*?' In comparison with other improving Lancashire towns, however, a host of visitors judged it to be 'nothing remarkable' and an 'inconsiderable' place.[15]

Yet Blackburn possessed one very considerable advantage for Daniel and his partners: its proximity to unlimited supplies of water from the rivers, streams and springs that abound, dissect and border the area. The very name Blackburn was given to a shire, the Hundred, a large parish and a particular town derived from a stream, the Blakeburne or Blakewater which ran for two or three miles through them. From Abram's description of Blackburn's geographical position, a picture of 'water, water everywhere' and plenty to drink, emerges. 'The Ribble is the boundary of the Parish on the north side, from end to end; and the Calder, a main affluent of the Ribble, is with its tributary the Hyndburn the parish limit on the east. The river Darwen may be said to belong to the parish through its entire course … it descends rapidly through the town of Over Darwen, is joined at Dobs Meadow by the Sunnyhurst brook, passes through Lower Darwen township, & thus reaches the township of Blackburn, of which it is the boundary to the west. At Fenniscliffe bridge, in Witton Park, the Darwen is replenished by the Blakewater, a stream which descends from Oswaldtwistle, combines to the east of Blackburn with the Little Harwood brook, and flows through the midst of the townships of Blackburn and Witton until it merges with the Darwen … Flowing onwards through the ravine beneath Hoghton Tower, the Darwen is the boundary of the Parish until it discharges itself into the Ribble near Walton bridge.'[16]

Salford Bridge over the River Blackwater in Blackburn.

The one resource essential to brewing operations is water; accordingly all breweries had to possess a good water supply in terms of both quantity and quality. The sale notice of shares in Park Place Brewery states almost immediately, 'The water with which it is supplied is abundant and excellent, and flows in at such a level as to render pumps unnecessary for any purpose whatever.' This was, indeed, a great asset in an era when water was more often unfit to drink or scarce and brewers had to go to great lengths to find and then guard their supplies from contamination. Truman in London had to bore 850 feet deep to tap into the purer water lying below the clay, and many city breweries had to pay for their water. It was

imperative that waters were as pure as possible for any organic traces could produce further fermentations and spoilt beer. When, later, Truman's light London beer became unsound, their Burton brewer thought the street and well water was too polluted for ale brewing and advised them to replace the mains, which had not been cleaned for years. There were pitfalls, though, in the 'cleaning up' process for the unwary brewer. The story is told in the trade of a young and ambitious brewer who, on taking up a new appointment, looked at the running down mains, was horrified to see a thick deposit and had them cleaned straightaway. The brewery's porter had an excellent name but thereafter it lost its flavour and the Brewery eventually

THE EANAM BREWERY

went bankrupt. Daniel and his partners had none of these problems; as Daniel once said, Blackburn was as famous for its water as Dublin was for its Liffey. Furthermore, there were not one but two natural springs of water on the Brewery's site. He could take water directly from the surface of one spring and draw it at the second from the Ward Well, bored not very deep to produce the brewing water, traditionally known in brewing operations as 'liquor'. The Eanam Brewery was thus in the fortunate position of having its own excellent water supply throughout the 19th century and of being able to utilise two additional wells to meet any future expansion in output.[17]

Daniel's business, indeed that of any common brewer, fell into three distinct parts. Very few business records survive before 1897 but, as brewing is a relatively unchanging process, much of the daily routine at the Georgian brewery would be as familiar to medieval brewers as to present day ones. Whatever the period and scale of brewing, the transformation of malt into beer has to pass through the traditional key stages: mashing, hopping, boiling and fermentation. Similarly, when Daniel closed the garden door behind him at the start of the brewer's day and walked across the brewery yard, he entered buildings which, though smaller in size, would be familiar in their purpose to any member of staff at a present day brewery. Furthest away from the house stood a square malting house, containing sacks of malted barley and six foot Hessian 'pockets' full of dried hops. Next, on the side nearer to the house, rose the largest building, erected on the tower principle still applied today. This was the tall, three-storied brewhouse which in the original Regency building soared into a conical chimney designed to make maximum use of gravity as the process of brewing starts at the top and travels downwards through the key stages.

If it was a brewing day, announced to the town by the pungent aroma of malted barley boiling with hops, an aroma that still emanates from Thwaites on a brewing day, two strong general labourers would first hoist sacks of malt to the top of the brewhouse by means of a hand windlass standing in the yard below. The malt was milled by rollers into a coarse powder or 'grist'. Then, the mashing stage

began. The water was boiled and cooled; the correct temperature was judged to be when the brewer could first see his face reflected in the surface of the water as the clouds of steam cleared. Next, the grist was pitched into the water or 'liquor' in a large oak mash tun. The resulting solution, the 'wort', was run off into large open copper pans, which were heated at their base by coal fires. Pockets of hops were gradually added and the mixture boiled for one or two hours. This hot hopped 'wort' then passed through the hop back before being pumped up to an open cooler beneath the rafters of the brewhouse and cooled down over four to nine hours with the help of wooden slatted windows providing ventilation. Once cooled, the 'wort' was dropped down into the slate square Yorkshire fermenting vessels (still used at the Brewery a century later) and yeast was added. Within twenty-four hours the yeast had expanded to form an excessively thick fluffy beard on the surface. The two labourers skimmed off the excess yeast with giant paddles, after which the brew was left to ferment over about six or seven days for ales and much longer for porter. After sufficient fermentation, the brew was siphoned off, or 'racked', into wooden casks – usually the barrel size containing 36 gallons – which were rolled into the Brewery cellars and over the next few days allowed to finish maturing; porter was stored in the large vats – the Park Place ones contained 240 barrels-worth and London vats 1500 barrels – and remained in the cellars for up to a year. Once judged ready for sale and distribution, the casks or butts (containing 108 gallons) were loaded onto the horse drawn flat wagons or 'drays', still used at Thwaites, for delivery to the taverns and alehouses or to private buyers in the locality.[18]

These were the routine operations that constituted the most important part of Daniel's business. Without good ale and porter he could not hope to attract customers and succeed in his venture; nor to meet his partners' expectations of increased profits. Although the general terms of the brewing process were common knowledge and published by brewing manuals, the scientific basis of mashing and especially fermentation would not be revealed by Pasteur for another seventy years. If fermentation was

Old Records

In the year 1790 barley was purchased at £1.1s.0d per quarter. The better quality of barley was invoiced at £1.3s.0d per quarter.

An old recipe for brewing – circa 1790

"98 mea. Malt and 82 m Hops –

First brew of ale at Eanam 10th January, 1790. Boil'd the water – cool'd the same One Hour and five minuets – w'ch water was One Foot Ten Inches deep, in the Tub, there being Malt which I think is mashed too light 98 meas. So that One Foot Nine Inches will be sufficient for the same Quantity of Malt. The Tub being two foot short of full when mash'd. Mash stood on three hours, three hours in taking the Underback 28½ inches deep owing to the Birche, being no too small; it would not run off any faster. When mash'd second time the Tub was 22 inches short of full. Boil'd to wort One Hour and a half. Put in 10lb. of salt the Depth of Wort in the Pan when the Wort One hour and a half. When the wort was all got up w'ch was at the end of one hour was four foot 10 inches in deep. Worked it with 60lb. Barm. Put in when Tun'd 6lb. flour and 4lb. of salt. Tun'd. 27 barrels Ale."

An old recipe for beer found at the Brewery.

bad and beers were either cloudy and acidic or flat and lifeless, Daniel, like other brewers, could only scratch his head in puzzlement. The manuals were no help. Black's 4th edition admitted helplessly, ' It is impossible to describe by writing, the different anomalous appearance which takes place in fermentation, and therefore equally impossible to say what should be done'; brewers were advised when in difficulty to use their smell, taste and, if either were defective, litmus paper. How then could Daniel, an inexperienced brewer, master the intricacies and permutations that bemused scientists and brewers alike?[19]

He had a little technical help. Two 18th-century innovations, the thermometer in the 1780s and the saccharometer (an hydrometer to test the gravity of beer) enabled him to make accurate measurements, though no strict agreement existed about what constituted the precise temperature for, say, the mash heat. He also had some prior knowledge of brewing. Raymond Jepson, retired Excise Surveyor for Blackburn, makes the point that an Excise officer covering a brewery 'knew the place like the back of his hand' and even knew the beer recipes. 'We knew everything that went into it and all the quantities. They might be closely guarded trade secrets; but we knew what they were, we had to know … We used to check them, all the contents of the brews and we could work out the quantities.' Daniel had checked the Park Place brews as well as early Duckworth & Clayton brews, under Thomas Dutton's management, for a good nine months, sufficient time to learn a great deal about their brewing.[20]

Nonetheless, excise vigilance was neither so advanced nor so methodical in the early 19th century as it would become by Jepson's era in the mid-20th century. A complex of detail lay beyond Daniel's ken, the minutiae of brewing, the exact secret recipes and, especially, the skills of buying the barley, malt, hops and yeast were revealed only by close contact with a master of the mystery. On the buying function, the responsibility of choosing the malt and hops from samples, rested the risks of profit and loss because the raw material costs made up so high a proportion of the total annual outlay. Edward Duckworth was likely to be the master who inculcated Daniel into the buying side and entrusted the trade secrets of the art to him. The nature of brewing was such then as to require only one key person to direct operations, usually the managing partner who never relinquished the skills or secrets of the mystery himself, though he might employ someone more skilled than himself. It is probable that Daniel and his father-in-law enticed a skilled salaried workman brewer away from an established position elsewhere, perhaps from a porter brewery in Liverpool or Manchester or even from Park Place. If so, rather than just testing the brew as he had done as an exciseman, on brewing days, Daniel would have got up very early, say at four o'clock, put on the regulation thick white apron, and started to brew with his assistant brewer so as to learn the mystery; he would have gone through the whole

The Brewing Process

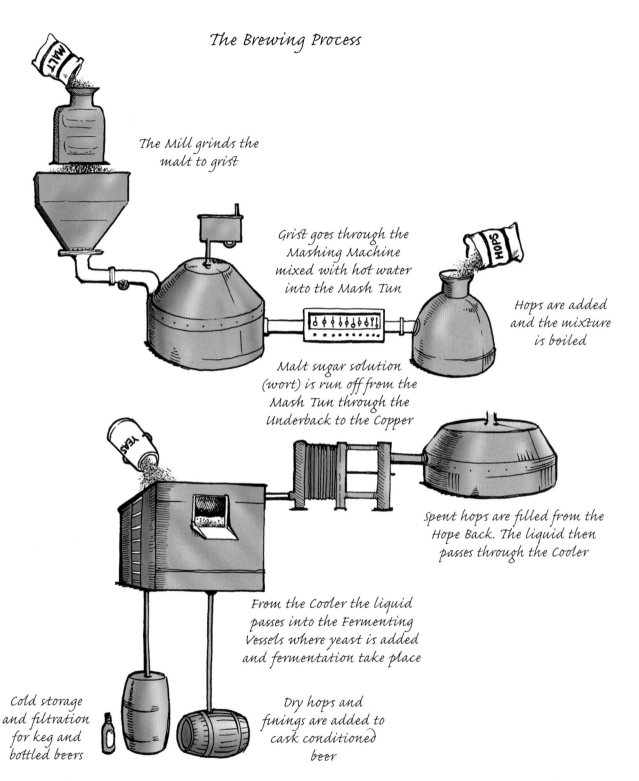

The Mill grinds the malt to grist

Grist goes through the Mashing Machine mixed with hot water into the Mash Tun

Hops are added and the mixture is boiled

Malt sugar solution (wort) is run off from the Mash Tun through the Underback to the Copper

Spent hops are filled from the Hope Back. The liquid then passes through the Cooler

From the Cooler the liquid passes into the Fermenting Vessels where yeast is added and fermentation take place

Cold storage and filtration for keg and bottled beers

Dry hops and finings are added to cask conditioned beer

Clayton having contributed £600 each. When Daniel joined them he only paid £300 in consideration for a third share to William Clayton; Edward Duckworth had waived his £300 'in consideration of natural love and affection' for his son-in-law. Daniel received a third share of the profits he generated as managing partner and paid a third of the £15–13–1 ½ d Ground Rent on the 998 year lease to Reverend Thomas Starkie, the vicar of Blackburn. He also received a salary of £80 a year to manage the Brewery.

Daniel was also responsible for the Books, which provided a record of routine transactions, the bones of the business, and of the special annual balance, the vital organs of the partnership. Many hours of laborious reckoning were passed in the counting house, quills scratching out the columns of figures, the invoices and copies of letters in large Ledgers, as Daniel and his clerk produced the accounts and the correspondence of the Brewery. For the routine business records he kept a General Ledger, listing all commercial transactions, from parcels of malt to tallow for candles and wages for staff; a Victuallers Ledger showing monthly deliveries to publicans and sales to the private trade; a Brewing Book as a log of production of every brew for the Excise; and a small Letter Book containing loose invoices, correspondence with maltsters and other suppliers and with agents in property.

For the partnership he wrote up the Rest Book in which everything, down to the smallest item lying in the Brewery yard, was valued and all liabilities and outstanding debts entered. From this important book, the net worth of the trade might be exactly known, and the annual balance struck every June to coincide with the end of the brewing season and the anniversary of their partnership. Based upon this information, the amount to be 'withdrawn from trade', the profit, was agreed by the partners. In the early years of the partnership, however, the profits were not drawn but retained in the business and this was the means – and the time-honoured one – by which Daniel accumulated capital. As Professor Ashton shows in his history of the Industrial Revolution, 'The records of firm after firm tell the same story … the proprietors agree to pay themselves small salaries, restrict their household expenses, and put their

process for several brewings in his quest to become a successful managing partner. For in those days, partners and proprietors personally directed the brewing operations: it was, according to Professor Mathias, 'courting disaster to allow a gap between experienced skill and final responsibility.'[21]

Where Daniel was on surer ground was in the counting house, which comprised the second part of his business activities. It was the smallest of the Brewery buildings, situated on the right of the entry gates and nearest to the house. He had learnt sound methods of accounting and business as an exciseman; as a novice brewer, he was dealing with sums of money similar to those he had collected from the large cotton mills. The Brewery partnership had a fixed capital of £1200, Duckworth and profits to reserve.' Should, say, William Clayton decide to withdraw his profits or leave the partnership, his share of the assets could be calculated from the previous year's Rest Book, thereby avoiding the possibility of disagreement. The Rest Book summarised the firm's value and, unlike the other ledgers, was carefully guarded from prying eyes by every conscientious managing partner. By paying attention to its contents, Daniel was better able to run his business.[22]

In terms of capital and size, the Eanam Brewery was a medium-sized firm. The sheer range of brewing enterprises, varying from the two-storied brewhouse and four-roomed cottage of Chale Brewery, Isle of Wight, where the owner did his own coopering, to the large establishments of the big London breweries, and the paucity of records, make it difficult to place the early Eanam Brewery nationally. An indication can, however, be gleaned from Ian Donnachie's study of the capital and business of Scottish breweries based on insurance valuations from 1793–1815. The initial capital needed to set up a small brewhouse on either side of the border was small. It could be equipped with a boiler, copper, mash-tun, fermenting vat, cooler, hop-back, pumps and pipes for under £300 in the 1790s, and more than half of Scottish brewers had done so for under £250.

The next group, some 27 breweries, had a fixed capital of under £500 with stock in hand worth twice or three times that valuation. A medium-sized Scottish brewery comparative to Eanam had a fixed capital of around £1000 – 1500 and a circulating capital of stocks of barley, malt, hops, beer and stored empty casks double that sum. One such firm, John Ramsay & Co. of Perth, had a fixed capital of £1250 with an extensive brewhouse, cellars and housing worth over £2000 including stock in 1795. Another country brewery, Ainslie of Duns, had a fixed capital of £1500 and stock in hand valued at £1400 including 450 bushels of malt worth £700, 3000lbs of hops worth £150 and ale worth nearly £350 in 1803. At that time the fixed capital of two firms, just embarking upon their growth, was £2000 at Tennant of Glasgow and £1400 at Younger of Edinburgh. On this evidence the Eanam Brewery was comfortably capitalised for a medium-sized firm.

Although a large proportion of his expenses lay in circulating capital and could be tied up for long periods, Daniel was more fortunate than proprietors of non-brewing businesses. He bought malt and hops on three months' credit but sold for cash; publicans usually settled weekly or monthly. He was, therefore, in a more liquid state financially than most other business owners. In the case of the excise duties, he was not so fortunate. Payment had to be made every 5th or 8th week after gauging at the time of production, so that the amount of capital tied up could be significant on a keeping stock of porter stored for twelve months; the payment in 1810 on a large stock of 50,000 barrels amounted to £22,000.[23]

Large costs were also incurred for the cooperage and the drays. Again, the outlay on casks formed part of the Brewery's circulating capital and their value could even exceed the valuation of a brewery and its plant; at Bass in 1843 the property £8149 and the plant £9876 were valued at less than the casks £17,212 and the staves £5693. The coopers were highly skilled, well paid craftsmen, who not only made the casks and staves but also renewed, repaired and cleaned them. At Eanam Brewery the coopers had their own workrooms in the Coopers' Shed adjoining the brewhouse. Once ready for delivery, the barrels and casks were rolled out of the cellars by the general labourers (a larger brewery had specialised moving coopers to do this), who placed them onto the drays. The clip clop of hooves and jangling of harness, as the horse-drawn traditional dray began its delivery journey, provided one of the immemorial sounds of a brewery yard. Just as the two strong muscular draymen remained symbols of the role of beer in the well-being of the nation.[24]

The upkeep of each dray drawn by two horses with two draymen was expensive but it was a brewery expense on which no sensible brewer ever scrimped. A dray was the best and then the only form of advertisement for a brewery and particularly important for a new brewery, such as Eanam, as a means of popularising its beers. Mathias estimated that a London brewery in 1800 required a stable of at least fifty horses for every 100,000 barrels it sold, when a good dray horse cost £40. Both the size of stable required at Eanam and the cost of a horse in Blackburn were

A brewery stables in 1847. Horses constituted a major cost to brewers who used them primarily for delivery. 50 horses were deemed normal for each 100,000 barrels sold in a year.

considerably less. From the sole surviving drawing of the early Brewery, there would appear to be two drays in use, though, allowing for artistic inaccuracy, there may have been more than four dray horses as well as other horses kept in the stables situated across the road from the Brewery in Syke street. Some idea of the running costs for feed, stabling and upkeep in Lancashire is given by R.W. Dickson in 1815. He calculated the upkeep of three horses for one year as follows: 3 horses at £25 each cost £75; harnesses £12–12–0; 9 bushels of oats for 12 months £29–5–0; hay for 6 months £27–6–0; grass and green crops £19–10–0; wear and tear of horse gear £1–5–0; horse

shoeing £1–11–0; farrier's expenses 15/-; the total being £170–7–6 a year.[25]

When the draymen drove out of the Brewery gates, they were fulfilling orders for Duckworth's (as it was then locally called) ale and porter as solicited by Daniel. The third part of his business was to sell the product to the trade, publican and private. Whereas the brewer John Pryor of Baldock urged his novice son to 'accompany their clerk Robins to the public-houses belonging to the Hatfield Brewery to become acquainted with the publicans,' Daniel was already acquainted with the publicans of Blackburn and of neighbouring villages. As an Excise officer he had regularly surveyed them. A ream of regulations swamped the sale of beer, from adulteration in the cask down even to the publican's pot, and for infringements, such as short measures and unlicensed premises. He was, therefore, not only familiar with the publicans but also already knew a great deal about their trade and beers and about which inns and taverns he would like to supply. It was customary in the 19th century for brewers to lease public-houses from their owners and sub-let them to tenants. Old deeds reveal that Duckworth & Clayton already either owned or held on long leases, properties in the Grimshaw Park area, and in the Brewery area such as the former Eagle Foundry in Starkie street and in Salford. These included the Royal Oak, an alehouse in Salford, the Rose Bud in Accrington and the Red Lion, a tavern in Northgate, all of which were occupied by tenants to whom Daniel supplied beer and porter. The custom of three public-houses on their own would not have enabled the Brewery to be profitable and Daniel, therefore, had to supply many more public-houses than the firm owned.[26]

He also possessed the advantage of being on good terms with the local magistrates through his excise work, a matter of no little import for a brewer. The licensing of inns, taverns and alehouses had been controlled since the 1550s by Justices of the Peace, who after 1729 held annual Brewster Sessions. Public concern waxed and waned over the power vested in the two sitting magistrates who could arbitrarily select and withhold licences and thereby improve or destroy a publican's income. In certain periods and especially in the 18th century the creation and control of licences had waned and been lax. In Durham, for instance, the JP and Rector William Paley was dismayed to discover that the practice 'had long prevailed of signing blank licences, and leaving them to be filled up at the discretion of the Clerk of the Peace.'[27]

The result of a national reluctance to enforce the licensing laws was an increase in disorderly alehouses with London, as ever, leading the way. Shocked commentators observed, as Smollett did, 'the incredible numbers of public-houses, which continually resounded with the noise of riot and intemperance.' Others were, nevertheless, fascinated by the growth of 'night houses 'where every one is permitted to sit tippling and gambling the whole night – apprentices, journeymen, family servants, known thieves, the most abandoned prostitutes, all assemble and mix together.' The 18th-century party continued elsewhere in the country; a village near Leeds boasted between thirty and forty 'little pothouses' which, according to the *Leeds Intelligencer* in 1786, were 'the rendezvous of these nocturnal villains, where they plan their depredations, and where not infrequently they divide their spoil. The landlord connives at their malpractices – it is in his interest so to do.'[28]

The party had to stop, however, after public concern fuelled by landowning and middle class agitation against alehouses and vice waxed into magisterial action. In 1782, the Lancashire JPs gave notice that, although innkeepers had allowed 'great numbers of ill-disposed persons to assemble at their houses and fight cocks, to the great impoverishing of themselves and their families, and to the great encouragement of vice', in future no licences would be granted to them and, furthermore, the magistrates would prosecute and punish them.[29]

The party was well and truly over when William Wilberforce, a Yorkshire MP and recent convert to evangelicalism, joined forces with local JP the Reverend Henry Zouch and resurrected the Society for the Reformation of Manners and successfully lobbied the government. The Royal Proclamation against vice and immorality issued in 1787 was circulated to all magistrates with an official demand for the strict regulation of the victualling trade. There followed a flurry of activity as local authorities introduced new restrictions and regulations for rigorous licensing procedures and the strict permanent control of public-houses. By 1807 a succession of measures had been enacted in Lancashire by county sessions, petty sessions and parish vestries to reduce the number of licences and generally fetter the licensed drink trade.

A vat which would have contained enough for about 3000 barrels worth of beer, each barrel being of 36 gallons. A total of 864,000 pints.

The closer regulatory supervision of public-houses, which, for example, now had set closing times in Lancashire and London, led one victualler to complain 'every house has received instructions as to where shall stand the bar, the customer, the casks, the cocks, the tap-room, nay even the very spot where the proprietor shall eat and drink.'[30]

As the respected proprietor of a brewery and a few respectable public-houses, Daniel's support of a licence inevitably continued to carry weight with local magistrates. This was invaluable in a period when the reform of licensing laws was once more inching its way up the political, moral and religious agenda. In that very year of 1807, over one thousand publicans had lobbied Parliament against the arbitrary powers of the licensing justices, notorious in London for the partiality and suspected corruption of the Middlesex bench. Richard Sheridan, Whig MP and playwright, took up the move for reform and proposed a bill to curb the excesses of magisterial licensing and to allow landlords the right of appeal against suppression of their licences. The Whigs, then in Opposition, regarded the drink interest commanded by the great brewers as a pillar of the old political order supporting the Tory party and keeping it in government. Although the bill was talked out by the Tories, the flickering flame of licensing reform was by no means extinguished; it burned ever more brightly as the decade continued.[31]

Daniel could be thankful that he was in the brewing and not the cotton trade, which blazed with discontent during the first half of the 19th century. Weavers throughout Lancashire, still solely dependent upon their handlooms for a living, led a hand to mouth existence even in prosperous times; they became destitute and faced starvation very quickly in times of unemployment or short time. The economic distress of 1807/8, which led to the collapse of the Watson cotton firm in Preston, saw rising food prices and was exacerbated by Napoleon's imposition of a Continental Blockade that denied British goods access to European markets. In these hard times, with Napoleon's mastery of Europe and military campaigns going badly for Britain in the Peninsular War, the Lancashire weavers deepened their struggle for a minimum wage. 'A wise and just Legislature will e'er long relieve your grievances,' the Bolton Weavers' Committee reassured its starving members. Many weavers could earn only between 6s – 10s a week by working 18 hours a day on six days a week but the 'wise and just Legislature' nevertheless saw fit to withdraw the Bill to regulate wages. Employers had removed their support; Sir Robert Peel, who had earlier supported the Bill, stated in the Lancashire papers that regulation would drive trade out of the country. The unhappy weavers showed their discontent at large meetings in Manchester and went on strike. In Blackburn they gathered on Blakey Moor and a mob collected in Grimshaw Park where, luckily for Edward Duckworth, it chose a neighbouring grocer's to attack. The windows of Henry Copeland's shop in Darwen street were smashed and the four ringleaders caught and convicted at Lancashire Assizes.[32]

Daniel had to contend with his own difficulties, though not with his workforce; for, unlike the putters' out and mill owners, he employed only ten men at the Brewery. In an unpromising trading environment he, at least, had had the benefit of having little competition in building up the Brewery's business. This changed when first Thomas Dutton opened his own brewery nearby at Bow street adjoining Salford bridge, and then, in 1809, George Blelock, a maltster from Preston, founded the Jubilee Brewery at Darwen street. In the face of this increased competition, Daniel's strategy was to enlarge the partnership's property holdings and he bought two public-houses in Penny street, the Plough and the Mason's Arms. He also bought several plots of land, a row of houses and several cottages in Eanam for redevelopment and investment, as the area was thriving; the local paper affirmed that if someone returned after an absence of five years he would hardly recognise the place, so many new houses had been erected there and there was a new stone bridge from the Bowling Green public-house (soon to become a Thwaites house) to Copy Nook.[33]

The long-awaited Leeds and Liverpool Canal, begun in 1770 and, at 127 miles, destined to be the longest canal in the country, joined Blackburn to Leeds in 1810. The wharf, completed beforehand at Eanam along with a large stone warehouse, contained 'a basin so wide before this

A typical brewer's dray with a drayman in livery.

warehouse that six barges, of 40 tons burden each, may lie abreast, and three cranes are erected to hoist the goods into the upper rooms,' marvelled the local press. A vast crowd gathered at Eanam to celebrate the opening of the Canal in June. A procession of twenty-seven vessels, some with bands playing on board and all decorated with bunting, sailed from Henfield (Clayton-le-Moors) to Eanam, accompanied by scores of people on the towpaths. As they approached Blackburn, at every bridge enthusiastic members of the public squeezed their way on board until about 7000 people were afloat. Awaiting them at Eanam were at least 25,000 cheering spectators. 'Such an assemblage of people on such a happy occasion was never remembered in this trading and increasing town by the

oldest inhabitant living,' the *Blackburn Mail* proudly affirmed.

It was a happy occasion for business proprietors, too. Immense benefits flowed from the inauguration of the canal and the completion of the Blackburn to Chorley section linking it with Liverpool. In particular, the carriage of coal which became cheaper and easier to transport in bulk, and relieved the difficulty of replenishing the town's fuel supplies. The Brewery's proximity to the Wharf was also advantageous for sending goods and receiving deliveries of malt and hops; of the twenty-one vessels arriving at Eanam 'Dock' that first week, fourteen carried a total of 380 tons of coal, and five brought 329 loads of malt to Blackburn. The Brewery was also well situated for supplying the bargemen and passenger packet boats with refreshments. 'All classes were jumbled together; groups of men and women dirtily dressed and noisy,' sniffed one passenger, George Head, in 1835. 'The former smoked tobacco and guzzled beer; so also did the latter, besides occasionally picking periwinkles out of their shells with pins.'[34]

Celebrations in Blackburn remained rare, however, in these years of continued economic distress and disturbances. From a brewer's perspective, the presence of extra Militia and special constables to keep the peace during the Luddite outbreaks, which spread through the Midlands, Lancashire and Yorkshire in 1812, demanded increased supplies of ale and porter. Set against this, as a petition opened for signature in the town's booksellers and addressed to the Commons made clear, were high prices, falling wages, disruption of labour and an unprecedented number of business failures; conditions not conducive to an easy trading environment for any firm.

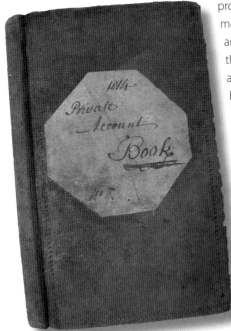

Daniel's strategy was to expand his production cautiously by taking on more properties to secure 'tying arrangements' for his beer; a process that was long established in London and the south and east of England but of shorter duration in the north where the tradition of publican-brewer continued. Daniel bought two properties, the Bridge Inn in 1814 and the Wellington in 1815; both of which were admirably located in King street, the town's most desirable residential street where the mercantile elite, such as the Feildens, Suddells and Liveseys, occupied elegant spacious townhouses. Daniel, however, continued to live at the more humble Cleaver street and

to plough any profits and excess funds into the partnership.[35]

In 1816 he inherited the small sum of £80 on the death of his father at High Gate. Apart from bequests to his four married sisters and two elder brothers Thomas and William, his father left everything, including sums lent out on mortgage, to John, the only one of them to remain at home and work the farms in Cumberland. It was around this time that Daniel welcomed a member of the family to Blackburn. His eldest brother Thomas brought his wife Ann and their six children to live in the town and went into business as a wine and spirit merchant at Eanam Brewery. Although there were already two well established wine and spirit merchants in Blackburn, James Pickup founded in 1792 and Edward Chippendall in King street, and plenty of spirit merchants, Thomas quickly built up a prosperous business, one which nicely complemented the ale and porter sales of the Brewery.[36]

As Daniel gained the company and support of one member of the family, he lost that of another. His father-in-law died on 22 December 1822, 'awfully sudden,' according to the family's notice of his death. Edward Duckworth had retired to bed in good health at half past ten and shortly after, while talking with his wife Grace, his voice faltered and he died, 'a kind husband and a tender and affectionate parent.' His will reflected a benevolent care of his family's interests. He had owned considerable property in Grimshaw Park, still detached from Blackburn by open fields, and, after leaving his residence, bakehouse and grocery business and two properties to his wife, and, in turn, to his unmarried daughter also Grace, he divided the remainder of his Grimshaw properties between his two married daughters Ellen Greenwood and Mary Yates. When it came to the Brewery, he divided his share of the profit account, £550, as well as his original capital of £600 between these three daughters.

He evidently retained complete confidence in the abilities and prospects of his Brewery partner and son-in-law, also one of his co-executors. Edward left his remaining daughter Betty nothing but his one-third share and interest in the Brewery Concern, including all the equipment, ready money, money at interest and all the Public-Houses and other property. Conscious that the sudden withdrawal of £1150 and loss of a partner might have a deleterious effect on the Brewery's cash flow, he stipulated that the £550 sum should not be paid for twelve months and the £600 for twenty-four months after his death and without incurring any interest.[37]

Daniel had played the dominant role in the partnership since the renewal of the original agreement in 1814. Duckworth was almost seventy when he died and William Clayton was sixty-six and, it transpired, not averse to relinquishing his share of the partnership after his friend's death. First, however, Daniel had to meet the calls due on the Duckworth estate. An item in the private account book belonging to John Wilkinson reveals that on 15 January 1824 he lent Daniel £500 at 4 ½ per cent interest; a sum that remained outstanding until 15 January 1828 when £200 was repaid. By then the Eanam Brewey was solely a Thwaites concern; Betty retained her share and Daniel had bought Clayton's share to add to his own original one. Daniel had also paid his sisters-in-law the £600 due from the Duckworth estate.

As Betty took no active role in the running of the Brewery, Daniel remained in sole executive control at Eanam. It was around this time that he first employed Joseph Yates, who was either the younger brother or son of Robert Yates of Duckworth Hall who was married to Betty's sister Mary. John Wilkinson was also involved in the financial affairs of the Yates family. Wilkinson was the brother of Leonard Wilkinson, who was Daniel's friend and solicitor, and he acted as a private banker investing and lending out excess family funds. According to his accounts, Robert and George Yates had borrowed £150 from Daniel in 1817 and had a debt of nearly £2000 outstanding on the Wilkinson books. In 1824 Joseph Yates raised a mortgage for £2000 on his estate at Duckworth Hall which by 1829 had increased to £2508. As only one of Wilkinson's account books is extant it is not know when, if ever, these debts were repaid. Joseph joined Thwaites (as it now became known locally) as a traveller, a superior position within a brewery. As the sole proprietor, Daniel discussed the purchase of malts and hops and the quality of the beer with his skilled assistant brewer, though he had the final say; he took all the decisions on finance, property acquisitions and licensing. And he now delegated the responsibility of maintaining the growing tied trade and of opening up the free trade through daily contact with publicans to Joseph Yates. It was well that he did free himself to concentrate to a greater degree upon the first two parts of his business, as he was inevitably caught up in the changes that swept through the industry during the period from 1816 into the 1830s, testing years for the nation as well as for brewers.[38]

The end of the Napoleonic Wars at Waterloo in 1815 had been rightly and well celebrated but the general euphoria quickly evaporated in the face of post-war depression and royal and political ineptitude. Corn laws, which kept food prices high; unemployment as demobilised servicemen flooded the labour market; falling wages with the end of large government textile purchases; the Tory government's unwillingness to contemplate a minimum wage and other economic improvements in the lives of manufacturing workers; the coronation of George IV, who refused to allow his queen to attend and instigated a Bill of Pains and

shivering and starving neighbours. 'Alas, poor weaver, thy fond hopes of better days always proves abortive,' despaired William Varley, a weaver of Higham near Burnley. Better days remained a pipe dream when the trade and commerce of the country were stagnant and even the prosperous faced ruin. Speculations in cotton caused a collapse in the market in 1825 and the failure of several Liverpool and Manchester firms. By that summer the Bank of England was drawing in its issues and London bankers were refusing to help struggling county banks. By the end of the year the country was 'one scene of confusion, dismay and bankruptcy.'[40]

A banking crisis engulfed the country in the new year of 1826 as a series of strong runs on northern banks took its toll, producing one failure after another. 'Oh what distressing events are daily taking place in the trading & banking World!' exclaimed Mrs Whittaker on 12 February to her son William, the new vicar of Blackburn. She told him first of the bankruptcy of Dixon & Taylor of Huddersfield who 'sent Merchandise to every quarter of the continent & did business to a very great extent,' and then, that 'Lancaster is at present in a fever of excitement at the failure of Dillworths [sic] Bank … a respectable Banking House' in which their friend Mr Beetham had £400 'most likely his all in the Bank, hard earn'd savings from his situation at the grammar school.' Thwaites local bankers, Cunliffe Brooks & Co. stood firm in the crisis, as did most breweries. An earlier victim of the difficult trading environment was George Blelock, whose bankruptcy closed the Jubilee Brewery until taken over by William Clark, without great success; it was eventually sold to Bannister Eccles who incorporated it into the Jubilee Mill. No one running a company in Blackburn could afford to be sanguine and that Thwaites and Duttons survived is a testimony to their strict attention to business and steely nerves. From Liverpool, the successful merchant John Gladstone gloomily admitted that year,' in all my experience for above forty years as a man of business, I never could look forward with less satisfaction and more dread.'[41]

Others with much less to lose had even more to dread. 'Famine & nakedness are sad companions to this severe

Penalties against her to obtain a divorce; and, one amongst many countrywide strikes and demonstrations, the Peterloo massacre when an enormous and peaceful crowd gathered for a reform meeting was suddenly charged by sabre-brandishing Yeomanry on the instructions of jittery authorities, leaving eleven dead and 400 injured. Such was the litany of events that discredited the institutions and authorities, and succeeded in arousing a popular agitation for reform among the labouring people of England. As one local historian wrote 'Lancashire, once a stronghold of Toryism, in a decade had become the most radical county in the land.'[39]

It was, as always, the weaver who bore the brunt of economic distress; few brewing staff ever underwent such deprivation, certainly none at Thwaites Brewery where jobs remained for life and Daniel never had to put the tiny workforce on short time or cut wages. The Brewery staff could feel fortunate, indeed, when they daily encountered winter,' William Whittaker wrote on 28 January. Abram states that the severe trade had thrown about two-thirds of the cotton work folk into 'a state of absolute indigence' by March. Although the Weavers Society of Blackburn petitioned the Home Secretary in April and manufacturers appealed to Huskisson, President of the Board of Trade, to introduce legislation for a minimum wage so as to prevent unscrupulous mill owners paying as little as possible, the Government refused to act; Huskisson shrugging off their 'vain and hazardous attempt to interpose the authority of the law between the labourer and his employer in regulating the demand for labour and the price to be paid for it.' Thus, when Bannister Eccles turned on the new power-loom weaving machines in his Dandy factory, the hand loom weaver saw the last of a miserable existence shattered by the iron frames. As weaver Thomas Duckworth recalled 'they fancied the power-loom was going to crush them to death.' Fear and hunger drove the weavers, supported by other working people, to take matters into their own hands.[42]

On 25 April William Whittaker hastened to send his mother an account of 'the frightful & distressing events' in Blackburn and reassure her of his safety. 'I rejoice exceedingly that *you* are neither a *magistrate* nor *manufacturer*,' she replied the next day,' but one cannot withhold a large share of compassion from the misguided but miserable & starving population, whose sufferings irritated to frenzy – are madly endeavouring to destroy the means by w^h the rich are enabled to give them relief – but alas hunger only feels, & has no power to reason.' The day before, a mass meeting of weavers had convened on Enfield Moor and, after listening to several speeches, a mob of men armed with pikes, bludgeons and a few firearms, set off for Accrington where they wrecked all the power-looms at Sykes Mill and at three other factories before marching to Blackburn. En route they met a troop of Queens Bay Dragoons. Lessons had evidently been learnt from Peterloo for, far from charging into them, the soldiers emptied their haversacks of sandwiches among the hungry crowd and rode off. By the time the mob entered Blackburn, reports about their purpose had preceded them. Shops hurriedly

closed and gates were locked, including those of the Brewery. This was wise, as the men marched through Eanam, passed the Brewery and continued on to Salford, looking for refreshment. The landlady of the Bay Horse Inn, by then held on lease by Thwaites, did not escape their attentions. They forced their way in and compelled her to serve a large quantity of drink and give them all the bread in the house. From there, fortified by alcohol, they smashed 212 power-looms at the Dandy factory and another twenty-five at Haughton's mill in Grimshaw Park before being forcibly stopped by soldiers and special constables.[43]

Blackburn remained in a state of siege and alarm over the following days as riots broke out in surrounding areas. Abram estimated that some 768 power-looms were destroyed and the damage amounted to over £11,500 in the Hundred of Blackburn. Whilst the riots allowed weavers to vent their desperation, they did little to alleviate their distressing conditions. The commercial depression increased, if anything, and in 1827 it claimed one of Blackburn's most generous benefactors, Henry Sudell of Woodfold Park. He was brought down by losses made in cotton speculations with debts amounting to £132,000. In August he was declared 'a Bankrupt, to the universal grief of the inhabitants' and left Woodfold for ever.[44]

Brewers might have escaped relatively unscathed from the riots and financial crises of these troubled years but they, too, had experienced unrest and scrutiny in their business. They were under attack on several fronts during this epoch from free trade reformers campaigning to achieve 'free licensing' in the beer industry; in the course of which brewers' commercial operations were examined by parliamentary enquiries and the ensuing revelations discredited the brewing trade. The *Select Committee on the Police of the Metropolis* (1816–17) produced evidence of licensing abuses and the true extent of the tied trade based upon instances of collusion between the large London brewers and magistrates. Henry Bennet's subsequent bills to amend the licensing law failed but the free traders persisted in their anti-monopoly campaign and their petition bearing 14,000 signatures resulted in the *Select Committee on Public Breweries* (1818). By this time half the public-houses in London were tied to the large brewers.[45]

Amongst the complaints examined were those of price-fixing and adulteration. Market leaders in London apparently met regularly at Brewers' Hall to fix retail prices. Moreover, high prices of duties and materials had led to the widespread use amongst small brewers and publicans of adulterants such as copperas, wormwood, coculus indicus, vitriol and opium so as to increase strength and flavour. The Excise, having prosecuted fifteen smaller brewers between 1815–18 and seventeen publicans for adulteration, suggested it was a natural consequence of the tied trade because publicans had to pay off their debts to the brewers. Even the Scottish chemist Professor Andrew Ure recalled that the amount of opium added to the beer sold on one early Clyde paddle steamer was so excessive that he could have carried out a post-mortem on its passengers without their realising what was happening. The great brewers were exonerated from charges of profiteering and adulteration but the Committee found that tied houses were sometimes forced to take inferior beer from the very London brewers who supplied better beer to free houses. 'Your Committee cannot reprobate in too strong terms so disgraceful a practice,' castigated the Report. Lord Liverpool's government took no action but the disclosures reflected badly on the whole industry and lingered in the public mind.[46]

Although two compromise Acts, produced in 1823 and 1824, failed to change the *status quo*, Escourt's Licensing Act (1828) implemented some of the free traders' ideas by limiting magistrates' discretion; the Act allowed an appeal to Quarter Sessions against their refusal to grant, transfer or renew a licence and the sale of beer off the premises was entirely freed from their control. Brewers, opposed to any further reforms except any that would reduce the high duties on their beer, breathed a collective sigh of relief at what they took to be a final settlement of political interference in the licensing trade.

Relief was premature as beer remained at the forefront of the political agenda for several reasons. The first concerned gin. Spirit duties were much higher in England

than in Scotland and Ireland. In the hope of curbing an increase in smuggling, the Government reduced spirit duties not in England but in Scotland from 6s 2d per gallon and in Ireland from 5s 7 ¼ d to 2s 3 ¾ d, which caused the MP Hume to announce in the Commons in 1824 that he would continue to smuggle Scottish whisky into his own house 'for if such foolish laws were made, they ought to be broken.' The following year duties on spirits were reduced in England from 11s 8 ¼ d to 7/- per gallon, still much higher than the other two countries, and lowered the cost of the spirit licence from 5 to 2 guineas. The public quickly took advantage of the price cuts and spirit sales rose sharply, as did the number of spirit retailing licences. At the same time, the number of licensed premises in London being lavishly refurbished in the style known as 'gin palace' had steadily increased. Brian Harrison points out that the gin palace was created by a retail revolution which aimed to supply London's huge population more efficiently and had transformed London chemists, hosiers and tea-sellers. (The actual term 'gin palace' was not used until 1824). Fears of an impending gin mania, redolent of the 18th-century 'Gin Craze', were, nevertheless, linked by public opinion to the spread of the gin palace-type public-house. Hogarth, in his celebrated prints, contrasted *Gin Lane* where, in his words, 'Idleness, poverty, misery and distress', are 'the dreadful consequences of gin-drinking' with *Beer Lane* where 'all is joyous and thriving. Industry and jollity go hand in hand', and so did the ruling classes in the 1820s. They were shocked by the excesses of gin drinking among the poor and labouring classes, and against the increase in the number of licences granted by magistrates.[47]

In Blackburn the general state of morals and manners raised such an outcry that the *Blackburn Mail* urged leading citizens to exert their best energies to promote a reform in the community. The vicar and churchwardens wrote to the licensing magistrates before successive Brewster Sessions with requests to entertain no further applications, and in 1825 affirmed 'not the least necessity exists for granting any more licences' in the town. They also desired 'the total abolition of Tap-rooms' which 'would prevent much intoxication particularly on Sunday Mornings,' when people by law were meant to be in Church. This was a message repeated in Blackburn Police reports and the *Blackburn Mail* emphatically praised the magistrates for enforcing the laws against drunkards, profane swearers and Sabbath-breakers.[48]

The solution for those worried about gin and spirit drinking lay in beer, Brougham's 'moral species of beverage', respectable and wholesome in contrast to disreputable gin, Carlyle's 'liquid Madness sold at ten pence the quartern.' The trouble was that gin was cheaper to drink than beer. The price of beer remained high as the prices of other goods fell, and the double duties on beer and malt added as much as 160 per cent to the cost of brewing materials. When brewers complained of stagnant, if not declining, output burdened as they were by the duties, as figures from 1815 onwards show, the government merely pointed to the high profits made by the large London brewers, which had been disclosed in the 1818–1830 enquiries to be 10–12.5 per cent. Yet there was no denying that a reduction in beer and malt taxes would lower the price of beer, and allow it to compete more effectively against 'harmful' spirits.[49]

The second reason beer remained at the forefront of the political agenda lay in the long agricultural depression that had plunged the country villages of southern and eastern England into a rural distress as acute as the industrial one found in the towns of northern England. The heavy burden of tithes, poor rates, duties on hops and barley, taxes on farm horses, sheepdogs and leather fell on the agricultural community; tenants could not pay rents and landlords could not meet their engagements without collecting rents. William Jacob's comment was typical of many when he observed in 1817 that 'at no period in the memory of man has there been so great a portion of industrious agricultural labourers absolutely destitute as at the present.' By 1830 the endurance of the wretched labourers had reached its limit. As the power-looms came to Blackburn so the threshing-machines came to the cultivated villages of Hampshire, Berkshire and East Anglia. They brought riot and incendiarism, rick-burning and a bogeyman, Captain Swing, to terrorise the neighbourhoods and anonymously smash the machines. Throughout that severe winter, Parliament was inundated with petitions and addresses from the county meetings held in south-eastern England, begging for the relief of agriculture by reducing taxation. The country gentlemen specifically advocated the repeal or reduction of taxes on malt and beer and the unrestricted sale of beer. They wanted cheap beer so as to support agriculture.[50]

The Government, to everyone's surprise, responded with alacrity. Lord Liverpool had been succeeded by Canning, who died in office in 1827. The present Tory prime minister the Duke of Wellington was, above all, a man of decisive action. His government was unpopular, his party was divided by the passage of Catholic Emancipation and amendments to the Corn Laws, and the serious ill health of George IV threatened an imminent general election. Wellington wanted to help the country gentlemen, bedrock

Bobbing: it was not unusual for beer to be adulterated by the publican in order to avoid payment of the Malt Tax. Here a block of salt is lowered into the butt provided by the brewer and with the subsequent addition of treacle and other ingredients two, even three casks could be made from the one.

of the Tory party, and legislating on beer would revive the agrarian interest, assuage the free traders, offer relief to the labouring classes and be unopposed by the Whig opposition. The Cabinet, therefore, proposed the free trade in beer. A committee on the Sale of Beer by Retail was appointed on 4 March 1830 but the Government, without waiting for the report, published a Bill three weeks later.

'How the deuce this Beer Act ever passed we cannot very well comprehend,' exclaimed the bemused *Chartist*, given the number of magistrates and brewers in Parliament. They were outnumbered and the Beer Act was passed in July 1830, after the death of George IV. Its main provisions were to empower any ratepayer to sell beer by retail on or off the premises on payment to the Collectors of Excise of two guineas per year for a licence; to repeal the duties on strong beer (10s per barrel) and cider; and to open between 5 a.m. and 10 p.m., except on Sundays during the hours of divine service. In every other respect the conditions for beer houses, as they were called, were similar to those of other public-houses.[51]

The initial response was a national celebration. When even the Bill had been received, 'with more cheering and greater applause than any proposition' that Alderman Waithman had ever heard before in the Commons, it was hardly surprising that ordinary folk celebrated the Act by

getting drunk. 'I was obliged to get out of my gig three times from people coming along, waggoners drunk, when I was returning from shooting on the very day of operation of the bill,' complained the Mayor of Arundel. At Kings Lynn, all the devotees of Sir John Barleycorn celebrated and drunkenness was rife in the streets. A fortnight later, on 24 October 1830, Sydney Smith observed, 'The new Beer Bill has begun its operation. Every one is drunk. Those who are not singing are sprawling. The sovereign people are in a beastly state.'[52]

They were also determined to apply for their beer house licences. In Liverpool 800 beer houses opened within the first three weeks of the Act and over 24,000 licences were taken out in England that year. William Howitt, who wrote about rural life, described them as 'kept by people without capital, often without character.' Some of the beer sellers had been persuaded by brewers' agents who, eager to capture this trade, advanced them the licence fee and supplied them with casks on credit; one brewing firm opened 200 such beer houses in the Birmingham area. Other beer sellers had probably taken the opportunity to legitimise their unlicensed covert hush shops and dram shops, at Oldham 200 remained in 1839, as against 343 licensed public-houses and beer shops. The beer shop's premises were usually meagre, often in the back rooms of

Three Public-Houses side by side on the west side of New Street in Preston; from left to right the White Bull, Swan Inn, Golden Ball. The row was redeveloped in 1893.

THE EANAM BREWERY

cottages located in courts or down narrow alleys in poor neighbourhoods or even in tiny sheds erected for the purpose, as their customers generally could not afford the higher prices of a public-house.[53]

Magistrates and clergyman immediately took the view that they were centres of disaffection, crime and drunkenness. 'Houses of this description sprung up in every corner of the land, by the roadside, in every city, town, and village,' the *Bristol Journal* reported in 1834, 'have become the resort of individuals of depraved, abandoned, and desperate character.' By then, opposition to beer houses had become so great that Lord Melbourne's Whig government had been persuaded to set up a select committee in 1833 to examine claims that beer house keepers were a feckless 'slippery' set of people, and beer shops the cause of 'a very great deal of drunkenness; a very great increase of idleness; a very great deal of extravagance' and encouraged poaching, whoring and gambling. There was, in fact, little hard evidence for much of this, except for the charge against an increase in drunkenness. The chief constable of Leeds calculated that drunkenness charges had increased over three times in the thirty months following the Act. In Blackburn a large proportion of crime was for drunkenness. The vicar, writing to his bishop in 1835, blamed the beer houses for the state of the town's working classes: 'Their immorality in every respect, their gross, filthy habits, their ruffian-like brutality beggar all description. The Sabbath breaking and drunkenness are dreadful. The beer shops have increased the latter to a frightful extent. They have done more injury to the cause of morals and religion than anything that I am aware of.' The Government sponsored an Act in 1834, which stipulated that 'on' the premises beer house licences would only be granted on production of certificates of good character signed by six ratepayers in the parish.[54]

The results of these Acts for northern brewers, such as Daniel, were mixed. From their perspective the legislation was based chiefly upon the London trade. Lord Derby reported that the Lancashire beer interest remained lukewarm about opening up the beer trade and displayed 'a considerable degree of alarm and apprehension.' John

A barmaid pours gin, widely condemned as "mother's ruin".

Hail ! smiling nymph, of *spirits* gay, | Of witching beauty is thy form,
Although you're often *wineing*, | Thine eyes of heav'nly blue;
With pleasure we shall hail the day | I'd care not should the world prove
When Hymen's wreath you're twining .| If you to me were true.   [false,

BLACKBURN RIOTS. MAY 1878.

Pryor, the Hertfordshire brewer, was convinced that 'throwing open the beer trade and granting licences to who ever may require them' was an 'unjust and sweeping measure [which] would ruin publicans, victuallers and many small brewers, and seriously injure all of them.'[55]

It was a view generally supported within the trade. For even though a law that facilitated the consumption of beer was welcomed, and beer sales did increase – Benjamin Greene's advanced by 50 percent the following year – brewers had to be prepared to write down the valuations placed on their public-house properties. They expected that there would be a great increase in beer houses, which would depreciate the value of their 'tied houses.' This was the dichotomy that explained the mixed response from brewers.[56]

Daniel, like other brewers keen to exploit opportunities and keep a competitive edge, immediately reduced the price of beer and porter on 11 October, the day the Act came into effect. Local newspapers bear witness to the brewing industry's scramble to assure their customers of fair prices. Without the duty, beers could be cheaper. In general, prices were reduced by 3d per quarter for porter. The fears of a flood of beer houses devaluing property prices and ruining trade were never realised. Blackburn was already amply supplied with public-houses, Daniel owned quite a number of both freehold and leasehold ones, so that the beer houses that emerged were neither in the more prosperous Eanam area nor in fashionable King street. They were opened at first in the very poor areas where Thwaites and Duttons were less inclined to trade. By 1849, however, there were more beer houses than public-houses. The Police Superintendent reported that Blackburn contained 112 fully licensed houses and 176 beer houses. To the question, should this have worried Messrs Thwaites and Dutton, the answer is, no. The revolution so feared by brewers and publicans and desired by free traders never happened. What did happen was that common brewers supplied the better beer houses as they did the public-houses, and that they ended up, by a variety of tying arrangements, controlling the sale of beer.[57]

Beer house keepers were unable to produce a reliable beer. To buy a decent set of brewing utensils, to purchase regular supplies of malt and hops months in advance to obtain good prices and to be able to store beer in their small rooms were often beyond their means and capabilities. The minimum quantities of beer they brewed were often of a poor quality, produced without the benefit of saccharometers and good malt. A Lancashire overseer thought the beer house brewers sold 'a very thick and new brew.' Added to which their price advantage amounted to no more than 1d a quart compared with beer supplied by common brewers.[58]

Canny Blackburn beer house keepers therefore turned to Messrs Thwaites and Dutton for supplies of beer. While no figures are available for the amounts they supplied, figures do exist for a common brewer in Leeds. Henry Bentley produced 3000 barrels for around 140 customers in the first year of the Beer Act, an enormous increase. In the first fortnight of the Act, thirty-one new accounts were opened by beer houses and so many deliveries were made and in such small quantities that Bentley's beer briefly had to be rationed. Some of these accounts were closed when they went unpaid and the beer shop went out of business. The reality was that independent beer house producers built upon the rock of free trade were easily beached by inadequate capital and credit resources and unable to pose any danger to the production and sale of beer by the established common brewer. The point was made by a magistrate who recalled that two common brewers had predicted that the Act would curtail their hunting activities and probably ruin them. Two seasons later, however, their sales were up by more than a third and they appeared 'with new coats and better horses.'[59]

The Eanam Brewery entered the Victorian age having survived war time, riot and depression, conditions that brought down other breweries. Daniel was sixty when Queen Victoria ascended the throne. Her coronation was loyally celebrated in Blackburn on 28 June with a vast procession of civic officialdom, surrounded by 10,000 schoolchildren. As bands played the National Anthem copies of the words and music were sold in the streets at 1d each. Next in the procession came Mr Walkden's typographers with a printing press; the iron founders and mechanics; the young men at Mr Railton's working a steam engine and distributing coronation medals to the crowd as they passed. One hundred mounted members of the Royal Ancient Order of Foresters; Messrs Parkinson & Yates's men, surrounding a working steam engine blowing steam out at the crowd, twenty feet long it was mounted on a carriage drawn by eight horses; 800 members of the Loyal Independent Order of Odd Fellows 'looking neat, each person having their insignia, and the apparatus belonging to the lodges making an imposing appearance; the Joiners' Society brought along their model of a church and a house, 'they looked well.' And many more tagged on to the end of the procession, as it wound its way through the streets of the town, to the cheers and waving of crowds lining the route.

Breweries, mills and places of business provided drink and food for their work force and a day's holiday in honour of the young queen's accession. In the afternoon the Eanam Brewery, in common with other buildings, was illuminated by gas and Daniel Thwaites, brewer of Blackburn, took his place at the official dinner for 120 gentlemen of the town at Cloth Hall in Fleming Square, when 'toasts, sentiments, glee singing and speeches were made in abundance.' Afterwards the gentlemen joined the ladies at the Ball held in the Assembly Rooms, where swirling waltzes replaced the stately minuets and gavottes of an earlier era.

Six years later, however, Daniel fell ill and died on 23 October 1843. The notice placed in the paper was more formal than the one he had helped to write for his father-in-law, in keeping with the more sedate Victorian public *mores*. 'In all the transactions of life, Mr Thwaites maintained the character so universally accorded to him, of the most strict and undeviating probity, and will long be remembered by a numerous circle of acquaintances, as a man in whose heart there was no guile, and whose whole conduct was influenced by a spirit of Christian charity and benevolence.' There is no mention of his large family nor of his business; yet both depended upon him for their prosperity and survival. From his entry into the partnership thirty six years ago, the Brewery had remained at the centre of his existence and he had built it into a solid business, nothing outstanding but a sound one. He left three sons to succeed to the partnership but without his experience and direction their future and that of the Brewery remained uncertain.

The memorial in St John's Church, Blackburn to Daniel who died in 1843 and his wife Betty who died in 1853.

The Public-House in 1807

*'No Sir, there is nothing which has yet been contrived by man by which
so much happiness is produced as by a good tavern or inn.'*
Samuel Johnson.

A MAN SEEKING such 'happiness' in the parish of Blackburn in 1807 had a choice of four sorts of drinking places: in order of status, the inn, the tavern, the alehouse and the illicit drink shop. Taverns, plentiful in London, sold only wine and there was but one in Blackburn, St John's Tavern by St John's church, perhaps, as a medieval pilgrim pointed out, because 'Taverns are for the rich and for lovers of good wine.' By the 1800s, however, those rich enough to afford a tavern's higher prices, even in London, mostly preferred the added luxuries and facilities of the inn.

Although the inn was then synonymous with the grand coaching inn, a large, fashionable establishment offering the

The bucolic ideal in the country inn, this, The World's End, painted by Thomas Rowlandson in 1803.

more prosperous traveller extensive accommodation and stabling for horses, together with decent food, wines and beer, in Blackburn nearly all the victualling houses were then called inns. This was common practice in Lancashire where the distinction between inn and alehouse was somewhat blurred – to the confusion even of JPs, 'I do not know which must be inns and which must be alehouses,' admitted one bemused magistrate. The Blackburn directory aimed to help. It lists in 1811 some twenty-two victualling houses of which five are 'Principal Inns', thirteen are 'Inns' and the remaining four are without title and thus 'alehouses'. The principal inns, such as the Bay Horse and the Old Bull were, in effect, coaching inns and posting-houses and as such received the mail coaches; the plain inns, such as the Spectator Inn and the Plough and the White Bull possessed fewer stables so fewer coaches could be accommodated and more carriers baited there.[1]

The inns, whether principal or plain, formed the elite of English victualling houses. When a posting visitor or a more prosperous resident – the Eanam Brewery partners dining with their attorney Leonard Wilkinson, perhaps – arrived on the premises of a large inn, they expected to be well served, and they usually were. Posting inns always kept at least two post-boys ready, booted and spurred, and with their horses harnessed from eight in the morning to seven in the evening, waiting for the traditional cry "Horses on!" When Prince Puckler-Muscau told his servant to call for horses, 'in less than a minute they were harnessed before the door, and in fifteen driving like the wind.' Guests found abundant comforts inside these inns, even if they were

An Inn kitchen with "Doctor Syntax, in the middle of a smoaking hot political squabble, wish(ing) to whet his whistle". The nature of the room is seen from the hams hanging from the ceiling. By Thomas Rowlandson.

furnished with a good deal of dark oak, as at the Bay Horse with its dark-panelled rooms and passages filled with leather trunks and packages; this inn was, nonetheless, 'the resort of some of Blackburn's wealthiest men.'[2]

Elsewhere, visitors such as the Dutchman staying at the White Hart at Harwich, found such comfort and elegance everywhere that he thought 'if the rooms of the public inns are like this, what must the apartments of the nobility be like.' When he rang the bell, it was answered by a person dressed like a gentleman. 'I make this man a bow, taking him for the host, and dismiss him to send a waiter to me. "I am the waiter, sir," he replied. He then disappeared, and within five minutes served up a most elegant breakfast. There was a teapot of a kind of black earthenware, which I have since learned to be of Wedgwood make, with a low relief of classic figures; the cream pot was of silver, the cup and saucer of Staffordshire ware, but, oh, how large the cup! The tea caddy was of neat lacquer work, and in the divisions, I found excellent green and black tea with scalloped silver spoon for ladling out the exact measure. There was a china plate with toast, top and bottom, upon a china bason, and another with slices of thin bread and butter, also a bason of very fine loaf sugar. All this was brought to me on the neatest tray. I made the tea myself to my taste. Another waiter then brought in a copper scuttle shaped like a Roman helmet. I felt very comfortable, such was the elegance of the fireplace, the polished steel grate, the fender of polished steel, and the poker, shovel and tongs, with vase tops, with which it was such a delight to stir the fire.' It was not just breakfast that was produced with

The widow Mrs Vernon a publican-brewer in Cheshire photographed in 1931. The last publican-brewer in Preston continued into the 1960s.

such alacrity. Count Pecchio observed that at every inn, 'dinner, or supper, is always ready, a fire is burning in every room, and water always boiling for tea or coffee. Soft feather-beds, with a fire blazing up the chimney, invite to repose; and the tables are covered with newspapers.'[3]

The third category of drinking place, towering above inns and taverns in number and popularity though not size, was the alehouse. It occupied smaller premises, sold beer, and, only later on, spirits, and offered basic food and lodging. Since at least the 16th century, each parish had an alehouse just as it had a church, indeed, they often nestled side by side on the village green or at the centre of a town. By 1807, however, the term was used interchangeably with

that of a 'public-house'. A notice in the *Blackburn Evening Mail* on 4 November announced: 'Robert Calvert, deceased late of Blackburn, alehousekeeper assigns his estate; as a result the public-house known as the White Bull, near Salford Bridge in Blackburn will be let along with the stable, brewhouse and other out buildings, backyard and convenience.' This advertisement provides further evidence of the blurring of terminology in Blackburn, as the White Bull was better known even then as an Inn. By the 1800s, with taverns and smaller inns in decline and popular alehouses in the ascendancy, the larger alehouses were eager to adopt the more superior name of Inn; too eager in the eyes of some customers. A Kentish parson was quick to remind that the village of Barming's self-styled Bull Inn was just an 'alehouse – it cannot be called an inn.'[4]

The alehouse or (plain) inn was an ordinary private dwelling house adapted with a few alterations for the drink trade. A two-storied building with ground at the front to allow carts, drays and coaches to drive up to the door, it could be white-washed, stuccoed or timber-framed. Country alehouses in Lancashire were often very rustic. The radical Samuel Bamford described Old Joe Wellin's at Middleton as 'an old thatched timber and daub house, which one entered down a step, through a strong low door with a wooden latch' and frequented by 'rough fellows.' Inside, customers of a smaller Blackburn alehouse drank in the adapted kitchen or 'house-place' where an array of bright pewter pots, plates and dishes stood on the mantel shelf above a wide open fireplace. Hams, flitches and bundles of herbs hung from the beamed ceiling. A corner of the room had been partitioned off and secured by lock to form a beer store or tap room. In the middle of the room, men, never women, sat around a three-legged table upon which stood pots of ale or porter. Some of the men smoked from the free clay pipes, churchwardens, supplied by the landlord and refilled them from a box of tobacco. There was commonly a plate of bread and another of cheese from which customers could help themselves.[5]

The more well-to-do customers of larger alehouses and inns, such as Daniel's Spectator Inn and King's Arms, sat in the parlour, which was better furnished with benches, chairs and mahogany tables. At the London public-house kept by Simon Place from the 1780s, the benches were 'covered with leather and stuffed.' The one common feature, shared by the kitchen tap room and the parlour, was a fire in the open hearth. In warmer weather people drank standing by the open front door or seated on benches outside, near the entrance. Enjoyment of the sunshine was not infrequently marred by drinkers relieving themselves against the alehouse wall. Mounting criticism in Manchester led to landlords erecting 'flags' or urine stones in front of their houses to shield customers from the public gaze.[6]

Finally, a man could decide to frequent an unlicensed drinking place. This was more often to be found in isolated villages, towns and larger urban centres, such as Manchester, than flourishing country villages. Some were alehouses that had lost their licences or not yet obtained them, while others were determinedly illicit hush or dram shops selling spirits. In Lancashire, several alehouses opened near the mills and, to circumvent the law, the landlords gave away the beer and charged an equivalent price for a piece of straw. Samuel Bamford discovered and described an illicit hush shop near Bury. The room contained a good fire of turf and wood burning opposite the door. In the centre stood 'a kind of low table, formed of an inner door which had been lifted from its hinges, and placed on bricks and logs of wood to serve as a table, and on it two candles in clay sockets were burning. About a dozen pots, of nearly all sorts and shapes were on the table; each pot containing ale, or what appeared to be so. The room was dimmed by tobacco smoke; but we could discern not fewer than some eight or ten men, seated in various parts of it, some on stools, some on piled bricks, some on logs of wood; whilst others occupied empty firkins, mugs capsized, or any article affording a seat.' In the next room were other men and 'the blows on their table, and the tremendous cursings, told us they were at high words about a game of cards.'[7]

The Plough Inn at Kensal Green. It shows how many pubs were converted from relatively modest homes.

Whether illegal or legal, all these victualling houses were family run businesses. When drinking in any of the public-houses, the customer was looked after by the publican, who exuded goodwill, his business sense masked by an ability to entertain with stories and jokes and to jolly everyone along. He made sure his beer looked and tasted good and that everyone had something to drink. Some landlords kept a special chair or place from which they directed proceedings. Simon Place attended to the parlour, 'his seat which was directly opposite the door was always reserved for him.' The victualler's licence stood as a badge of his alehouse's respectability and he ensured that no arguments or fights broke out to spoil the enjoyment of other customers and attract the attention of the constabulary and the magistrates. At the other end of the scale, new customers to a hush shop were welcomed with suspicion. "Well, what dun yo' want?" said a brawny, dark bearded fellow to Bamford. "Wot are yo', and weer dun yo

come fro,' was demanded sternly; several of the company rising and repeating the questions. The dark man then shouted for his mother, the landlady, who was afraid that Bamford was an informer or exciseman.[8]

On arrival at a respectable public-house, customers received friendly greetings from the landlady, usually the publican's wife or widow. She served them with drinks and marked up their consumption on the score for a final reckoning or for credit. She was often helped by her children in the smaller houses, her daughters clearing away the mugs and cleaning up and her sons helping their father with cellar work. In bigger houses, a servant girl or two carried out these tasks and a pot boy kept the pewter pots polished, filled mugs and jugs at the hatch for home drinking and ran outside with orders of jugs of beer for neighbours.

In Blackburn, where most people knew one another, a family atmosphere pervaded the inns and alehouses and inspired devotion from regulars to a particular public-house. The 'quality', the gentry and gentlemen, frequented the parlours of principal inns around the King street area and were happy to pay the higher price charged for their quart of ale by the fireside. Despite a growing evangelical disapproval of public drinking, clergymen were not to be easily discouraged from entering even the rougher sort of alehouse. That respectable Norfolk parson, James Woodforde, in 1790 visited Yarmouth, where he went to 'a pot-house on the quay with my brother amongst some jolly tars.' In 1809 the clientele of an alehouse still included the middle classes, traders, merchants and professional men who not only met for business but also for pleasure. One trader later recalled how he 'left his house and family every afternoon and night to smoke his pipe and enjoy his glass or glasses of grog among his pot companions in the parlour of a public-house.' The parlour room, at say the Spectator Inn, also attracted aspirant skilled workers, clerks, tradesmen, craftsmen and artisans, who generally experienced increased prosperity during the Regency era.[9]

The more basic tap room in, for example, the Hare and Hounds, Furthergate, which contained no parlour, and the Sun Inn, Rawtenstall described as 'a very old house' in a Thwaites' valuation of 1895, attracted the weavers and spinners, labourers and semi-skilled workers, who formed the largest category of public-house customers. Here the drink was 1d or ½ d cheaper than in the parlour, and the furnishings like those of the kitchen home-place. The floor was usually sanded or covered with sawdust to absorb the drips of spilt ale. The air was thick with the fug of tobacco smoke mingled with smoke from the open hearth. In comparison with small, cramped cold houses, the tap room provided warmth and, later, lavatories, and male company, especially hospitable to those plagued by economic difficulties. By 1807, however, some respectable public-houses were turning up their noses at the poorer people. The critic Sydney Smith complained in the *Edinburgh Review* that many publicans and their wives 'want the corrective of competition to prevent them from treating humble and ill-dressed people with the most sovereign contumely and contempt.' This attitude was less prevalent in a small town

like Blackburn or its outlying villages when most incomes were so heavily tied to one industry, cotton. There was, in any case, still a marked tendency for the working community to stick together by trade when it came to choosing a drinking place, easier to do in those days when townsfolk lived close to their place of work. An observer noted in 1805 that, ' the first rank namely the japanners rarely associated in their hours of relaxation with the workers of copper, brass, iron etc; the latter frequent common pot-houses, the former get into the third and fourth inns and club rooms.' The close union between trade and public-house is evident in such names as the Weavers, the Spinners Arms and the Mason's Arms.[10]

In addition to offering their customers a place to sit at leisure and enjoy a drink, to read the newspaper, to eat and to sleep, public-houses provided them with a meeting place. When prominent cotton merchants attended the 'Exchange' in Blackburn, they used the Old Bull Inn,

A child employed as a pot-boy to deliver pint and quart jugs of beer to nearby homes or workplaces.

standing before the main entrance at 'high change' between 3–5 p.m. on a Wednesday to discuss market fluctuations. In the same way, doctors came to meet patients; coroners to hold inquests; traders and merchants to negotiate contracts; solicitors to assign deeds; supporters of cock-fighting, dog fighting and ratting to watch the latest contest; pugilists to wrestle in the yard and men to place wagers on them at public-houses. All the sales of property in Blackburn took place at the principal inns and tenants paid their rents at the Old Bull. Many public-houses had a pay-table where workmen received their wages; the landlord took the mill owner's banknotes and used his own float of small change to pay the weavers and spinners. The temptation for workers to spend their wages on drink was a strong one. Their drunkenness on a Saturday night provoked mounting criticism of the pay-table system. Liverpool's mayor decreed that wages should not be paid on Fridays and 'they should on no account be paid at any pubic-house.'[11]

The *Blackburn Evening Mail* was founded in 1793 after Mr Waterworth held a meeting of prospective subscribers at the Bay Horse Inn. Years later, workmen discovered pieces of type lying under its floorboards; the compositors

presumably putting the paper to bed in the more spacious premises of the Inn. Many publicans provided friendly societies and clubs with a special club room for their meetings. There was no specific charge for the room but, in return for its use, members were expected to pay a 'wet rent', an amount on drink sufficient to satisfy the publican. In the case of the Lancashire artisans' botanical societies, the proportion of dues spent on drink averaged 4d, though the Tyldesley Botanical Society extracted a 'wet rent' of 6d and 3d for the book fund from its members' monthly fee. At the Prestwich Society, 'after the more serious business of the meeting had been disposed of', the assembled company remained on into the night drinking and singing. One member even composed "The Botanists' Song" commemorating how 'science circles with the glass'; and another claimed his specimens always looked 'best through a glass.' By 1811 the meetings of 'Weaver-botanists' had spread throughout Lancashire. Bamford later recalled that, as botanical gatherings in public-houses were so well established, during periods of political agitation, such as 1817–18, radical reformers held political meetings under the pretence of being botanists.[12]

There was considerable radical activity in public-houses during the Napoleonic Wars. Radicals formed debating clubs and congregated in the tap room, parlour or club room of public-houses, while constables, informers and spies came there to keep watch. Non-radical regulars sat in their local alehouse unaware of the political ferment surrounding them. Radicals had to hold covert political meetings because of the Two Acts of 1796 forbidding seditious meetings, followed by the Combination Acts of 1799–1800 outlawing trade unionism and political activism. In 1794 a public-house near Royton had been gutted by a mob after providing a venue for Radicals. While some publicans were radical activists, others succumbed to magisterial arm-twisting. Victuallers in Manchester issued a group notice banning radical meetings on their premises and, as late as 1820, Mancunian public-houses displayed signs bearing the words 'No Jacobins admitted here.' Certain landlords even informed on radicals and allowed their alehouses to be used by spies. As a result, people in

A gooseberry gauge used in competitions in public-houses.

1807 had learnt to be circumspect about their political views while drinking. A Bolton man spoke of how 'you might sit in a public-house and wait till the crowd had gone and you would not have heard one word about political matter; if a person had introduced a subject of that kind he would have been considered a Jacobin.'[13]

Constables also attended public-houses on official business. They used them for lock-ups in the absence of a formal custodial station (the police did not yet exist) in Blackburn. It was customary to commandeer the cellars of local inns as a place of confinement for prisoners awaiting trial. Customers of both the Britannia Inn (a Thwaites house) and the Golden Fleece (a Duttons house) in Penny street might have been a little nervous to discover that criminals

were held in chains beneath their feet. In 1805 John Hall, landlord of the Fleece, drew up a scale of charges for such involuntary guests, pricing their stay at 1s per day and 1s 6d per night.[14]

More voluntary guests also fell foul of the law by drinking on Sundays at the time of Church services. As did people in an earlier age, such as Samuel Pepys in Cambridge on 26 February 1660. While waiting for Mr Pechell who had gone to church, Pepys and a friend were at the Rose tavern 'where we sat and drank till sermon done; and then Mr Pechell came to us and we three sat drinking the King's and his whole family's health till it begun to be dark.' In 1807 many houses still followed this custom and ignored Sabbath closing hours – sometimes at their peril as one Grimshaw Park landlady discovered. Kay the constable, suspecting a breach of the law, approached the alehouse whereupon she locked the door in his face. As the *Blackburn Mail* reported, she 'gave the company time to send off like alarmed rabbits, and hide themselves under beds, and up the chimneys etc.' Kay was not so easily deceived and, upon at last gaining entry, he 'ran from hiding place to hiding place, and in a short time brought to light' four men. They were fined 10s and the landlady faced prosecution and, perhaps, the revocation of her licence at the next Brewster Sessions. Blackburn took its Sundays seriously; five more men were charged for not attending church and for 'having

assembled for *sport* and *pastime* on that day.' They denied the charges but compounded their guilt in the eyes of the magistrate by saying they were only 'clubbing or joining for a drink.'[15]

The quiet enjoyment of a pot or two of strong beer was less frequently disturbed by the hubbub of people being locked up in the cellar than it was by the disorder of drunk customers in the tap room and parlour. Drunkenness remained as ubiquitous in Lancashire as it had always been throughout the whole of England. As Roy Porter points out, Englishmen excused their vices as virtues and 'indulged them with brio'. They liked to get

A not unusual scene of some drunkenness as the Pugilist Club make merry in an upper room of a pub in this picture by Samuel Collings of 1789.

THE PUBLIC-HOUSE IN 1807

excessively drunk and were traditionally quite unable to resist the lure of 'a spree', a good drinking session. From Restoration London, where Pepys struggled to curb his drinking: he goes with friends to the Dolphin 'and there we did drink a great Quantity of Sack. And did tell many merry stories, and in good humours we were', and all too often ends up with another hangover: 'my head not very well and my body out of order by last nights' drinking – which is my folly.' To Restoration Lancashire, where Roger Lowe wrote in his diary, 'Roger Naylor and Richard Twisse came, and would have me goe with them to Alehouse. I went, and very mery we ware. I must not spend a 1d, but yet I did.' Drunkenness abounded. The *Gentleman's Magazine* listed ninety-nine ways of calling a man drunk, from the genteel 'sipping the spirit of Adonis' to the vulgar 'stripping me naked.'[16]

Drunkenness was the regular, satisfactory condition of most of 18th-century England with Defoe stating, in 1702 that, 'an honest drunken fellow is a character in a man's praise.' While the drinking prowess of the three-bottle-a-day man was respected, that of the six-bottle man was considered supreme. Statesmen of the day, Pitt, Fox, Grey and Sheridan were all said to be six-bottle men and if Fox was suddenly wanted to speak in the House of Commons, he was often hauled from club or tavern 'in such a condition that he required a long application of wet towels to his head before he was able to go to his place and speak.' Drinking was also competitive. 'I was always ambitious,' admitted man-about-town William Hickey, 'of sitting out every man at the table when I presided.'[17]

Sobriety was also successfully avoided by the less privileged. 'Drunk for a penny, dead drunk for tuppence; straw free,' advertised the gin-shops during the 18th-century Gin Craze. The tradespeople of rural Sussex were no less abstemious as Thomas Turner recounted in his diary in 1750, 'we continued drinking like horses, as the vulgar phrase is, and singing till many of us were very drunk, and then we went dancing, and pulling wigs, caps and hats, and thus we continued in this frantic manner.' If in the 18th century all the decent people of Lichfield got drunk every night, 'and were not the worse thought of',

the weavers and spinners were no less forward in Regency Lancashire. Travelling through Lancashire, Richard Ayton was deeply impressed by the love of strong ale exhibited in the public-houses, which he called 'the great schools of the county' where the manners, habits and opinions of the people were fashioned. 'It is no unusual thing for a man,' he wrote in 1813, 'to retire altogether from his home and live for a fortnight at a public house; during the whole of which time his only concern is never to allow himself to get sober. When he has expended all his money, he will return to his employment and toil away resolutely and cheerfully.' Some of the most skilful factory hands were 'fellows who would not quit their drink while they had a sixpence left, and who would only work that they might return to drink again.'[18]

From the publican's perspective, while heavy drinking was good for his takings, all too often it led to fights and general brawling which could damage his furniture, drive away custom and incur magisterial attention. It also made the theft of pewter pots, blankets, liquor, and cash easier when the publican and his family and servants were distracted by disorderly behaviour. By the 1830s, thefts from vicualling houses in Preston comprised the third largest category of robberies. Closing time must have been greeted with relief by landlords on such occasions. The exact time of closing varied to county and depended upon local magistracy and petty sessions. Public-houses closed at 8 p.m. in Essex, at 9 p.m. in West Kent, 10 p.m. in Lincolnshire and 11 p.m. in Lancashire. The publican traditionally called out to his customers "Time, please". At John Shaw's Punch House in Manchester, however, closing time was a rigid 8 p.m. and exactly on the hour, he proclaimed "Eight o'clock, gentlemen; eight o'clock." If his customers continued to linger, he would call to his servant woman Molly to bring his horsewhip, and crack it in their ears and near their bodies. Should this fail to dislodge them, Molly was ordered to bring her pail, with which she speedily flooded the floor, and drove the customers out with shoes full of water. There is, though, no record that any of the public-houses serving Thwaites beer had to resort to such measures at closing time in 1807.[19]

The Cooper

OOPERING, like brewing, is an ancient craft with its own guild, the Worshipful Company of Coopers, and much of the daily routine at a cooperage, as at a brewery, would be as familiar to a Biblical cooper as to a 20th-century one. A cooper traditionally also worked as a carpenter and it is thought that Joseph and Jesus combined both tasks in their Nazareth carpenter's shop. And the tools kept in the cooper's shop at the Thwaites museum today would be familiar to coopers throughout the ages. As Bob Gilding wrote in 1971 of his visit to a 17th-century German cooper's shop, 'given a set of staves and truss-hoops, and with someone to turn the grindstone on which to sharpen the tools, I could easily have produced 'a cask there.'[1]

The cooper was a familiar figure throughout Britain as nearly every village once had its own cooper to produce the housewife's wooden buckets, the pails in the horse's stables and the casks in which goods, such as ale, china ware, nails, herrings and gunpowder, were packed. As a highly skilled craftsman, a cooper was a respected member of the community, a man who commanded good wages for the construction of casks and other wooden containers. 'On that fair stood the cooper, my brother, with a cart-load of cooper's ware of all descriptions, selling them to the lady wives of the farmers, and to the farmers in the top boots and spurs, and passing jokes with them,' remembered Alexander Somerville in 1850. 'To be the cooper's brother in Oldhamstock's fair was to make me be looked upon with respect even by some of those youths who once used me ill'.[2]

If a general cooper received respect, a brewery cooper inspired veneration as a member of the cooper elite. A brewery cooper was an immensely skilled craftsman. In the first place, he had to work to exact measurements; a wine and spirits cask could be made to the nearest gallon or so but a brewer's cask had to be produced to the

nearest pint. In the second place, he had to produce goods to a higher specification than general coopers; the casks built at Thwaites and at all the other breweries were the only ones to have the insides shaved completely smooth to prevent bacteria forming in the crevices and ruining the beer. The foreman cooper used to run a silk handkerchief around the inside of the barrel to test it and if the handkerchief caught, then the cask was sent back to the cooper to be shaved again.

During the 19th century, the cooper's shed at the Eanam Brewery was divided between 'wet' coopers and 'dry' coopers. The 'wet' coopers worked at blocks to make the casks of oak to a specific size, from the largest barrel holding 54 gallons to the smallest kilderkin containing 18

Facing page The cooper: a skilled craftsman for many centuries he made barrels out of oak.

Above Coopers at work in the early 20th century.

gallons, and to hold the beer without leaking. The 'dry' coopers paid little attention to size, producing 'inferior' ware, such as pails to hold butter, and they worked at benches. To complete their inferior status, 'dry' coopers were on day work; they started at seven, watched the time, lingered – if they could without detection – over their breaks and finished promptly at darkness or by five. Lording it over them were the 'wet' coopers on piecework; they strolled in and out of the Brewery when they chose and took long breaks. When they stalked through the cooper's shed to use the grindstone, any 'dry' cooper or apprentice using it immediately stopped and scurried away. If ever complaints were made about their hours, and attempts were made at Shaw's Brewery in London to rein in these masters of the cooper universe, then the biggest 'wet' cooper there always answered that he was celebrating his birthday. He had four birthdays each week and the fifth day was 'hog day', the day on which the pieceworkers booked out their completed work.

While many a lad aspired to join these exalted cooperage circles, most were ineligible unless their fathers' already wore the coveted leather-apron uniform. This rule was strictly upheld by the Lancashire coopers' society and the Thwaites apprentices were always sons of members and their numbers carefully controlled. According to John Dunlop, writing in 1839, the apprentice paid five shillings on entry and one shilling to each cooper in the cooper's shed. He then paid ten shillings at a bothering, 'which is a foolish and barbarous ceremony', also known as the 'Trusso' ceremony, where the apprentice was inducted by being ducked in water, 'beat and made the sport of the rest in a very rude manner.' The 'Trusso' was, even in the 20th century, 'a painful experience.' For John Charnley, an apprentice at Thwaites, his 'Trusso' in 1965 consisted of being rolled in the cask, doused in water, feeling no doubt as London apprentice Bob Gilding did: 'the heat of the cask, the pounding of the trussing adze [a heavy hand tool with a steel cutting blade used to dress timber] on the truss hoops, and the one minute up, one minute down of the ride in the barrel, with dizzying spin, and the sawdust and wood ash sticking to perspiring flesh at the end.' At some breweries, in addition to the induction 'Trusso', an apprentice had to pay a fine and provide a gallon of beer every time he completed a new kind of cask.[3]

The last Trussing which took place in 1970. Bob Dodds for many years a cooper at the company puts a congratulatory hand on the new apprentice's shoulder.

The cooper's shop at Thwaites Brewery must have been bewildering for any new apprentice. There was the greeting ritual to overcome, whereby unless the correct phrase was used, the apprentice was either ignored or picked up by the hair of his head and deposited outside with the door shut in his face by the largest cooper. The utterance of the magical words 'Good morning gentlemen all,' however, immediately produced a reply to the nervous apprentice's enquiry about how much iron would be required by each cooper that day.

Then there was the noise of the cooperage, a concatenation of sounds booming across the brewery yard. From the sawmill came the scream of the circular saw as it ripped through the staves; from the workshop rang the rat-a-tat-tat of the cooper's hammer on his driver, broken only by the clang of the handsaw hitting a nail or stone embedded in the timber; then there was the thunk of the trussing adze beating down the truss hoops onto the cask; and the loud crash of the flogger (a flat metal bar shaped at one end into a handle) driving the important top hoop down onto the cask. While coopers learnt to accept this deafening pitch as part of their working life, they relished the comparative silence of their breaks. Should any man, apprentice or master, interrupt such an interlude, a piece of timber or a loose rivet would as likely be lobbed in the direction of the offender.

An apprentice at Thwaites, as at any brewery cooperage, also had to learn to light the cresset fire and to withstand the tremendous heat in the cooper's shed. He had to start a fire in the cresset (similar to a brazier) and, if lit correctly, the fire would not smoke, but a new apprentice often lit the shavings from the bottom, causing the cresset to smoke copiously so that the coopers cried out "Smoke-o-o-o" until the novice corrected the fire. As one cooper wrote in 1825, 'I have known frequent instances of working from three in the morning till ten at night, the smoke during nearly the whole of this time being so intense in some workshops, that a man can scarcely be perceived, although only the distance of a few feet from you; and they are frequently obliged to run out to breathe a little fresh air to prevent suffocation. Some times in the course of the day they are surrounded by three or four fires, the heat of which is so great that a person unaccustomed to it could not possibly stand it for more than a minute.'[4]

The barrels and casks were fired over the cresset until warm and pliable enough to be trussed into shape by the cooper's manual dexterity. This was an exercise fraught with danger for the unwary apprentice, for not only had the warmth to be tested by the back of the hand – as the heat of a baby's bath is tested by an elbow – but with too fierce a flame, a sudden draught or the wrong-sized cresset, the cask could, and often did, catch fire. Then the first experienced cooper to spot the flames shouted out "All-a-fire!" and ran to remove the burning cask for, regardless of singed hair and eyelashes, the 'tub' had to be saved. Physical strength was an essential ingredient of the cooper's craft. Larger 'tubs' could only be trussed whilst still over the fire so, in addition to the physical exertion required to bend the 'tub', the cooper had to contend with the heat of the fire inside it.

Not surprisingly, coopering was thirsty work. 'This addiction to continuous drinking … was accounted for,' Henry Mayhew explained, ' by their work being very laborious, while the heat is often so great that they acquire a distaste for solids during the hours of labour and stay the cravings of the appetite with draughts of beer.' Brewery coopers were in the right place for unlimited amounts of refreshing beer and they received it as a customary allowance. Coopers elsewhere were not always so well looked after. 'They will have as much beer as they please; if we only happen to be out of beer for ten minutes all the yard is in a ferment,' complained one employee faced with a disgruntled cooper's shed in 1825. Coopers could also avail themselves of 'waxers' and 'bulls' – the cooper's terms for his unofficial drink, obtained by pouring a quantity of boiling water into a cask that had recently been emptied of wines or spirits, leaving it to stand and then draining off the resultant brew into a drip 'tub', which usually stood at the back of the cooper's shed. They helped themselves to amounts of 'bull' at will throughout the day and night, though they seldom overindulged.[5]

This was partly because they could also cook something tasty to eat on the cresset fires in the chimney corner, the natural social centre of the shed; a piece of hoop-iron bent into a 'V' shape and placed on top of a cresset made a natural toaster or barbecue for fish. One cooper even liked to place an enamel plate on the hoop-iron and cook bacon and eggs for breakfast. It was also partly due to the pride a 'wet' cooper, in particular, took in his craft and the underlying strength of his independent position; paid for the work he produced, not for the hours he kept, he had his own set of tools and his own special 'berth' or space in the cooper's shed. The piecemeal wet cooper at a brewery like Thwaites was always very much a master of his craft. In 2003 Les Hindle, a long-serving Mathew Brown cooper, who moved to work on the back set at Thwaites, retired and donated his treasured tools to the Thwaites Brewery's Museum. 'I didn't have much use for my tools anymore so I thought it would be nice for other people to gain an insight into what was once a thriving trade,' Hindle explained. Another example of his coopering days can be seen in the bar area of the Visitor Centre at Thwaites where all the barrels used as tables were crafted by him, a fitting legacy of the cooper's daily work 'rolling out the barrel.'[6]

The head brewer, Mr Philip Timson, (above) shares a pint with the new cooper. The indenture document (below) is proudly displayed, presumably before a bath.

CHAPTER THREE

Daniel Thwaites Jnr 1817–1888

I N THE UNSETTLED early years of Queen Victoria's reign, years which became known as the 'hungry forties', it was particularly important for proprietors to ensure as smooth a succession as possible in their businesses. Two years before he died, Daniel had set his affairs in order and had written his will. His first concern had been for his 'dear wife' Betty's comfort in her widowhood and he had provided her with an annuity of £240 a year [about £12,000 today] charged to his three sons as well as such of his goods and furniture as she wanted. He had also placed £3000 [about £150,000 today] in trust for each of their eight daughters so that they received the interest and dividends as income twice a year for their 'own sole and separate use' independently of any present or

future husbands. In so doing, he had assured his daughters' financial security when by law all their property and money would otherwise pass directly to their husbands upon marriage.

When he came to provide for his three sons, his plan had long been that they should take over the Brewery, thereby ensuring a seamless succession and its survival as a family business. He had, therefore, bequeathed the Brewery, stock, plant and everything connected with it, and all the adjoining cottages, premises, stables, buildings and land at Eanam to them. In addition, he had left specific bequests of freehold public-houses, land and houses from his property portfolio to each of them. He had appointed Betty, Thomas

Above The market place at Blackburn looking South with the new Town Hall flying the flag in 1860.

Thomas, Daniel and John were not close in age. Thomas, the eldest child, was eight years older than Daniel, the sixth child, who in turn was seven years older than John, the tenth child. In March 1817, four months before Daniel's birth, Edward, the brother closest in age, died aged two. The Thwaites family was nonetheless considered fortunate in health; in that epoch of high infant mortality, eleven of the children not only survived into adulthood but also lived into their sixties and well beyond. It was inevitable in such a large family, where Thomas was a young man of twenty when Alice, the baby of the family, was born, that the elder batch of children saw little of the younger ones. Daniel and his younger sister Sarah bridged the divide as the middle children and, until his marriage, he remained in close contact with all of his siblings.

Regardless of their place in the family, the children shared the same standard of education and upbringing. There was no national system of schooling but, as their parents could afford the fees for a private academy, none of them had to attend the local Dame school where, for a few pence a week, children were taught to read and, possibly, a few rudimentary sums; the uneven lessons were frequently interrupted by other demands on the dame's attention, such as selling milk or attending to customers in her shop. The eight girls, instead, went to one of the many Board and Day schools for young ladies run on the lines of Miss Parker's, which promised parents that the 'utmost exertion will be used to give Satisfaction to those who may be inclined to Countenance the understanding' of teaching reading, English Grammar, Needlework, Geography and Music; French and Drawing Masters could be engaged for an additional fee if required.

Such was the demand for schools in Blackburn that, according to Baines, there were in 1824 no fewer than sixteen private schools there and, in 1826, George Edmundson, a Quaker master, opened another, the Lower Bank Academy for boys. Daniel and, later, John were educated at this school, described by the historian Whittle as in ' a very salubrious situation, & is well-adapted for a school to educate young gentlemen.' The school was first established at the top of Branch Road at King street and

and Daniel as trustees for John, still a minor, and he had directed them to apply the income and profits from John's share to his maintenance, support and education until the age of twenty-one or 'for putting him out to business' and generally advancing him in the world.

Daniel appeared to be a sensible parent, and to appreciate that unforeseen circumstances might cause his sons to wish to leave the family partnership but, in that event, he had directed in his will that they would not be able to withdraw any capital from the Brewery; instead, they should be paid a yearly rent commensurate with their interest in the partnership. In this way, presumably, he hoped to fence the continuity of the Brewery under the managing partnership of Thomas and Daniel. It had been his particular wish, and he could state it no more clearly than this: 'I strongly recommend but do not enjoin that both during the infancy of John and after he shall have attained 21 years my said three sons carry on my said business jointly and in equal shares in such manner as I have heretofore done so long as they can agree so to do, but particularly until John shall attain 21 years of age.' Thomas and Daniel were thus left in no doubt about their father's purpose when he died in 1843; and, like most sons of that era, whatever their own yearnings, they respected and followed their father's wishes.[1]

later moved to Duke's Brow. It divided its pupils into three categories: boarders paying 30gs per term for board, washing and English lessons; weekly boarders paying 30gs a year; and day scholars paying 6gs a year plus 1 guinea a quarter and 1s per quarter for pens and ink. Daniel's education was more rigorous than his sisters' as he had lessons in English, mathematics, Latin, French and could even add Russian, with Greek and Italian available for an extra 4gs each per annum. This school provided the sum of Daniel's education as, shortly after his sixteenth birthday, he left to start a commercial training, though the details are nowhere stated. He, nevertheless, had more schooling than some brewers' sons; Edward Greene, for instance, left Bury Grammar School when he was just thirteen to enter his father's brewery.[2]

Although Daniel's formal schooling ended in 1833, he had habitually attended Sunday School from a young age with his brothers and sisters. Their parents had been married in St Mary's, the ancient parish church, but preferred to worship at St John's where the Thwaites children were baptised, the family rented a pew and had a burial vault. The church had been built in the classical style in 1789, substantially financed by Henry Sudell, and was for some years the only Anglican church in use while a new parish church was under construction to replace the dilapidated and dangerous St Mary's. Church services at St John's were announced by the pealing of the parish church bells which, after St Mary's demolition, had the merit of ensuring the survival of its lovely old bell tower. After Sunday services, the gentlemen of the congregation met to discuss local, social and political affairs and, as they grew up, the Thwaites boys accompanied their father and came to know the leading local families, such as the Feildens, Hornbys, Lunds, Carrs and Hindles, who worshipped at St John's during the vicariate of William Whittaker.[3]

The brothers came of age during a period of heightened political awareness among the working people of Lancashire. An exciting, if dangerous, epoch of mass protest, when, a Bolton man recalled in 1833, 'you cannot sit ten minutes in any public house in this town or any other I am acquainted with without hearing men discussing politics and other measures of government, and often as rationally as if they were legislators, though probably they could not write five sentences.' As the brothers stood outside St John's after divine services, walked back from school, ran errands to the Market Place and helped their father at the Brewery, around them swirled the talk of reform; reform of the corn laws of the political system which, despite the Reform Acts of 1832 and 1835, excluded those who did not own property from the electorate; and of the hated Poor Laws. Pressure for reform came not just from radicals, chartists and workers but also from Tories, free trader manufacturers, and clergymen concerned by the inhumanity of the new workhouse system.[4]

The political force of reformers' demands was felt by the authorities in the course of the Chartist agitation. Chartism took its name from the petition, 'the People's Charter', which was presented to Parliament by six Radical MPs and six working men in 1837 seeking political reforms: universal male suffrage, voting by secret ballot, equal electoral districts, annual Parliaments, payment and the abolition of property qualifications for MPs. Chartism was never a monolithic movement but rather an umbrella covering diverse groups with a host of causes that appealed to working people throughout the country. In Lancashire, the movement was principally fuelled by concern with the new Poor Law Act. The unpopularity of Lord Melbourne's Whig government had surged among northern workers after the change in the poor laws; 'pregnant with evil' was the opinion of John Walter, MP and editor of *The Times*, and 'calculated to produce a revolution in the manners and habits of the British people.'[5]

Whilst reform of the Elizabethan system was overdue, the hasty measure that replaced it in 1834 abolished outdoor relief for the unemployed and widows, children and the elderly unable to support themselves. The Act established instead the institution of the workhouse, deliberately designed to be unpleasant for those forced to shelter within its forbidding walls. In Blackburn, the burgeoning population had grown to 27,000 in 1831 and was still largely dependent upon the cotton industry. In 1837/8, again suffering from a downturn in trade, Blackburn

The "village politicians" sit around a table at a rural inn, discussing the affairs of the day. c. 1850.

became a turbulent place, as weavers and spinners feared the imminent embrace of the town's workhouse. Blackburn had not welcomed the new Poor Law. When it was first implemented in 1838 the editor of the Tory paper the *Blackburn Standard* noted 'the event was celebrated by a riot in the workhouse, the paupers declining to acknowledge the grateful blessing of that humane and interesting measure. The strange infatuation of persons who cannot perceive the benefits resulting from a separation from a wife and child cannot we apprehend be too deeply deplored.' When faced with this system at times of economic depression, the working public of Lancashire was easily converted to Chartism by people they knew in this first mass working class movement.[6]

News of planned Chartist meetings and mammoth rallies was easily spread by journeymen artisans visiting

public-houses, such as the Holy Lamb in Northgate, which were on their 'tramping route' to seek work, and known to be the haunt of likeminded reformers. Local Chartists made inflammatory speeches, William Beesley, for instance, declaiming that 'if the rights of the people are much longer withheld, bloodshed and anarchy must inevitably follow.' After a meeting of about 50,000 people was held on 24 September 1838 at Kersal Moor in Manchester, a spate of torchlight meetings followed in surrounding towns; in Blackburn, supporters of Chartism and anti-poor law campaigners joined in a large demonstration on Blakey Moor.[7]

When, in May 1839, the Charter was rejected by Parliament, the movement took a more radical turn with calls for members to defend liberty by the use of arms. As rumours spread of this militancy and armed rebellion, panicky magistrates and landowners requested military protection from the Home Secretary Lord John Russell. There were permanent barracks at Manchester, Stockport and Burnley but not at Blackburn, though employers, vicars and landowners had long lobbied for the erection of them, especially after the riots in 1826. The Thwaites boys' father and uncle Thomas Thwaites had then joined other leading citizens in a letter of 1829 urging the Archbishop of Canterbury to memorialise the Government on their behalf – but to no avail. Even though the Ordnance purchased 20 acres of land between the Canal and the Burnley road at Furthergate and near to the Brewery, nothing was ever built there. Blackburn only had a small number of troops in temporary barracks and had to rely upon reinforcements arriving in time from elsewhere. Lord John Russell finally moved against the Chartists that summer; some ringleaders were arrested and magistrates were authorised to arrest armed Chartists. General Napier, appointed to command the Northern District with 5000 soldiers, took a dim view of local magistrates. 'Alarm! Trumpets! Magistrates in a fuss! Troops! Troops! Troops! North, South, East, West! I *screech* at these applications like a gate, swinging on rusty hinges, and swear! Lord, how they make me swear!'[8]

One of the most dramatic Sunday services the Reverend Whittaker ever held in Blackburn was when he, too, made a stand against the Chartists. As part of a concerted effort, Chartists had organised a series of Sunday demonstrations. On 4 August, large groups of working men crowded into parish churches in Blackburn, Bury, Chorley, Preston, Leigh and Manchester to hear the texts they had challenged the vicars to preach. The men occupied all the best pews as well as the free benches to the rear and in the galleries, thereby upsetting the normal rules of propriety used by the Church to maintain social order, and peacefully protested against the ecclesiastic support of the government's oppression, as they saw it, of working people.

In Blackburn, the Reverend Whittaker rose to the occasion and preached from James 5:1–16. 'Go to now, ye rich men, weep and howl for your miseries that shall come upon you.' The congregation was so large, about four thousand people were crammed in, that Whittaker's wife and children had to sit on the altar steps. The demonstrators failed to live up to the expectations of either the regular church-goers, full of self-congratulation in withstanding such danger, or the specially sworn-in constables, waiting to cope with the anticipated riot. Other than by the presence of several men holding 'a pike ornamented with the head of a Tory' and a few more wearing their caps in church, the Chartists gave no indication that they were irregular members of the congregation. They listened implacably as Whittaker attacked all their political demands, commented on their 'not quite seemly' manner and guise, and told them they were 'grossly deceived, most infamously and imprudently deluded' by the contemptibly small body of agitators led by one or two dissolute individuals. At the end of the long sermon, the Chartists departed peacefully. Whittaker was pleased with his sermon, which proved so popular that he had it published; it sold extremely well, passing through eleven editions within six months. As a copy lay amongst the Thwaites papers, it is likely that Thomas, Daniel and John were not only familiar with Whittaker's famous Chartist sermon but had also read it.[9]

Blackburn had escaped the full force of Chartism; elsewhere there were serious riots that summer and 20 people were killed in Newport, Wales in November. Although arrests and transportation of the leaders decimated the Chartist organisation, the severe trade depression revived the movement under the leadership of Feargus O'Connor. In May 1842 an enormous second petition containing 3.5 million signatures was presented to Parliament, and again rejected. Coming in a year of wage reductions, widespread unemployment and general economic depression in the industrial parts of the country, this result was all too likely to provoke further disturbances.

Daniel was by then working with Thomas and their father at the Brewery when reports filtered through to Blackburn that a massive demonstration was being planned, which might also attract the support of the anti-corn law league dissatisfied with the Peel government's decision not to repeal the Corn Laws. Fears grew of a 'turn out' of hands at the mills, which would have Chartist support, and more riots. The Thwaites family and other local employers had only just recovered from the riot and destruction of property inflicted in April by supporters of the losing candidate in the General Election. William Turner, a Whig, had lost by one vote, and, when the result was confirmed by a parliamentary scrutiny, 'an angry and violent crowd' had pulled up cobble stones in the street outside the Bull Inn, used by the victorious Tory party, and pelted its windows and doors. A book seller was trampled to death and other property damaged in the ensuing riot; further violence elsewhere was contained only by the arrival of a detachment of the 60th Rifles.[10]

In June, as the Chartists pasted up posters calling for 'Bread not Barracks', Colonel Wemyss, commander of Bolton, observed that a 'very different feeling prevails among those who have property at stake.' As it did in Blackburn where, without the security afforded by a large Barracks, employers and landowners urged the magistrates to increase the number of special constables to protect their property. Although Chartist attacks were anticipated at the mills, owners of other businesses were equally nervous. Even if the Eanam Brewery escaped unharmed, the Thwaites men knew that their public-houses offered an easy target for rioters. Orders were therefore given to board up windows and lock doors and gates once the alarm was sounded by the parish church bells. Nerves were not steadied by the presence in Blackburn of Feargus O'Connor himself on 30 June to rally support; an event downplayed by the *Blackburn Standard*, which assured its readers that there were only about 500 people there and, perhaps more perceptively, that the crowd 'would evidently have been better pleased if the Orator had given each a loaf,' rather than a speech.[11]

The threat of twenty-five per cent wage reductions at mills in Ashton and Manchester in July provided the swell to a wave of strikes surging through the mill towns of Lancashire in early August. Touring mobs of 'turn outs' trawled through the mills, forcibly drawing out the plugs from factory boilers to stop them working and create a general strike among the workers. The Plug plotters reached Bolton on 11 August and went from mill to mill and

stopped them. On 13 August men, armed with bludgeons, started to gather in Blackburn, intent upon obtaining 'a fair day's wages for a fair day's work', and reports were received that mills had already been plugged three and four miles away. While not unexpected news, the force available to repel a mob, rumoured at thousands, consisted of ninety-six soldiers of the 72nd Highlanders and a very small number of constables. The magistrates therefore hurriedly swore in, as 'special constables', a number of respectable inhabitants to join the posse of soldiers, police and magistrates rushing to meet the strikers now advancing towards Furthergate on the Accrington road and on the Brewery's side of the town.[12]

As in the riots of 1826, once the peal of church bells sounded the alarm, Blackburn quickly looked like a town under siege: shops instantly closed, all business was suspended and owners protected their property as best they could. Over the next week, Blackburn reeled under the tumult of what Miller called 'the insurrectionary torrent' of strikers and Chartists turning out the hands from the mills; skirmishes with police and soldiers; strikers throwing stones; several readings of the Riot Act and soldiers firing at the crowds, swollen by the turned out mill hands who usually joined the strikers; and soldiers taking prisoners. Despite proprietors directing some of their hands to resist, the plug plotters largely succeeded in bringing the mills to a standstill in Blackburn; just as they were doing in all the mill towns in Lancashire, Yorkshire and as far north as Paisley in Scotland.

Nevertheless, the damage to property was contained in Blackburn by preventing the strikers from entering the town and, if they did, by arresting the ringleaders as quickly as possible. As one JP, John Fowden Hindle, observed on 15 October, these prompt actions 'had the effect of striking sudden terror into the minds of the rioters, of paralysing their plans and inspiring the peaceable inhabitants of the neighbourhood for many miles round, with courage and a fixed determination to offer the most vigorous resistance to mob violence.'

None felt more resolute than the young men of the town, sons of the leading proprietors, who eagerly offered to defend Blackburn. As the magistrates, including Feilden, John F Hindle and William Hornby, informed Sir James Graham the Home Secretary, 'The respectable classes of Society in the Town and neighbourhood are disposed to give us every support and, at our request, a number of them have voluntarily organized themselves as a protective force. They divide themselves into small parties and perambulate the Township during the whole of the night … ' This voluntary, unofficial militia consisted of men over 21 years and belonging to respectable propertied families; it is therefore probable that among the young Feildens, Horbys, Lunds and Hindles embarking on this adventurous mission to keep 'the Peace of the Town' were Thomas and Daniel and some of their Duckworth and Thwaites cousins.[13]

Contained by the show of military and voluntary strength, the strikes soon petered out. The government, which had faced the probability of a northern-led insurrection, was generous in its approval of the measures taken by the magistracy in Blackburn compared to weak conduct elsewhere. Sir James Graham informed Queen Victoria that, 'The Mobs are somewhat overawed by the vigor with which the troops have acted at Preston, at Blackburn, and at Bolton, where several Prisoners have been taken, where the troops in self defence have been compelled to fire, and where several Persons have been killed and wounded among the Rioters.' The Queen, in turn, conveyed her approbation, writing, 'At Preston the lesson (& a severe one it was) has done good – for it is worse to let these Riots get ahead than to *act* with severity at first.' By the last week of August the hands had returned to work and Blackburn had returned to normal. The Chartists had been unable to press their advantage to achieve political reform; after the rejection of a third Charter in 1848, the movement disintegrated.[14]

The dramatic plug plot strikes did little to improve conditions in Blackburn and trade worsened. Whereas in 1842 Whittle wrote 'Sad distress prevailed', in 1843 it had become 'Great distress'; so great that soup kitchens were opened, the one in Old Square, part of Market Place, supplying 800 quarts daily. And there was little to lift the

spirits in the townsfolks' surroundings. Within the course of the Thwaites boys' childhood, Blackburn had become darkened by a smoky squalor. Catherine Jacson dismissed it as 'a black dirty place where all the more unlovely features of an altogether manufacturing town everywhere displayed themselves'; in 1825 a place where, even in the summer, Mary Whittaker worried about her washing: 'my white dresses cannot be washed in the town owing to the quantity of soot constantly falling.' On his arrival in 1843 William Cooke Taylor felt pulled 'into the dark and troubled vortex of manufactures' where deprivation was stamped onto the 'pale and emaciated features' of 'the poorer sort of people' as they hurried to and from the mills, their clogs like a kettle drum roll on the cobblestones of the narrow, ill-lighted streets.[15]

The year 1843 was therefore not the most auspicious year for Thomas and Daniel to become proprietors of the Brewery. They were surrounded by industrial strife, political agitation over the repeal of the corn laws, depressed trade and scenes of misery. The Brewery buildings, so new in 1807, now needed updating and the pool from which to replenish their workforce was extremely limited. The politician John Morley, born in 1838, recalled that the condition of Blackburn in his boyhood was 'something very like savagery.' The overwhelming majority of the local population was still uneducated and illiterate. A handbill published to announce the opening of the Mechanics Institute in 1844 stated that Blackburn was the most backward town in the country. In London, eighty-nine men and seventy-six women out of every hundred could read and write; in Blackburn, out of every hundred only thirty-nine men and eleven women could write their own names.[16]

Yet, in spite of the unsettled environment, Thomas and Daniel had course for optimism as they settled their father's estate and took up the reins of proprietorship to drive the Eanam Brewery forward. The probate value of his estate was slightly less than £50,000 [£2m] but this figure did not include land (real property), any settled estate and, more importantly, the actual business (rather than stock) valuations. Even allowing for the requirement to service

A map dated 1848
showing Eanam Brewery
now at the centre of a
much enlarged
Blackburn.

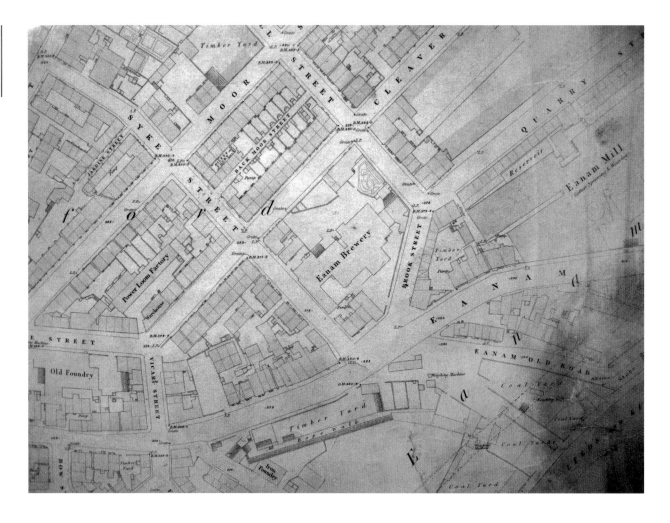

their mother's annuity and to provide their sisters' income
from the £24,000, a capital sum against which the brothers
could lend as mortgage, Thomas and Daniel were in a
comfortable position. Their father had steadily extended the
Brewery's business and ploughed back the profits to
enlarge the fixed capital to £36,000 and provide a larger
circulating capital to support the increased production of
beer. For, notwithstanding the economic depression,
brewers generally were continuing to profit from the
lowered prices and increased consumption stemming from
the removal of beer duties and 'free' licensing. The average
annual output of beer rose from 14.6 million barrels in
1830–5 to 16.1 million in 1850–4, while *per capita*

consumption of beer grew from 21.7 gallons to 22.5 gallons
over the same period; both the output and consumption
would continue to climb upwards throughout the century,
bringing prosperity to many Victorian brewers.[17]

Furthermore, Thomas and Daniel were well-placed to
benefit from the two national developments that
contributed to the increase in the scale and prosperity of
brewing during the second half of the 19th century. The
first was that the rapid growth in population in England and
Wales was most marked in the urban working class,
traditionally the largest consumers of beer. The increased
demand for Thwaites beer was reflected in the population
figures for Blackburn: growth in the parish from 39,899 in

1811 to 71,711 in 1841 and in the town from 15,000 to 36,629 over the same period.

The second development was the creation of a national railway network. 'We are all possessed of a Railway Mania,' wrote the Lancashire landowner General Gascoyne on 11 February 1825, and Daniel joined in as an early investor in railway companies. The economic advantages were evident at the outset of the opening of the Stockton and Darlington railway, constructed as a coal-carrying venture in 1825; the price of coal at Stockton fell from 18s to 12s per ton and the demand for coal for export increased rapidly. 'The Locomotive Engine is now at work on this line,' wrote one of its proprietors a month later, 'and I am rejoiced to say she excites the astonishment and admiration of the country.' It was not until 1833, however, that the line offered a regular passenger service, by which time the impressive Liverpool and Manchester Railway had been opened with great ceremony by the Prime Minister on 15 September 1830; an event which saw Huskisson the MP for Liverpool accidentally killed on the line and which inspired the poet Tennyson's lines encapsulating the sense of progress embodied by railways: 'Let the great world spin for ever down the ringing grooves of change'. The success of these two railways inspired other railway companies to proceed so that, by 1843, there were 2000 miles of track.[18]

Although George Stephenson had sent three railway engineers to inspect Blackburn in 1840, it was not until 1843 that a group of prominent local businessmen issued a prospectus to pitch for investors in the formation of the Blackburn and Preston Railway Co., stating 'Within a circumference of about eight miles, of which Blackburn is the centre, there is a population of above 450,000 persons … That district comprises several considerable Towns and Villages, and some of the most extensive cotton mills, calico printing works, and other trading concerns in Lancashire … This district is also situated in the immediate vicinity of extensive coal fields, and inexhaustible quarries of free stone, flags and slate, some of which, owing to the expense of carriage, are now nearly unproductive to the owners, as well as comparatively useless to the public. This part of Lancashire is destitute of Railway Communication.'

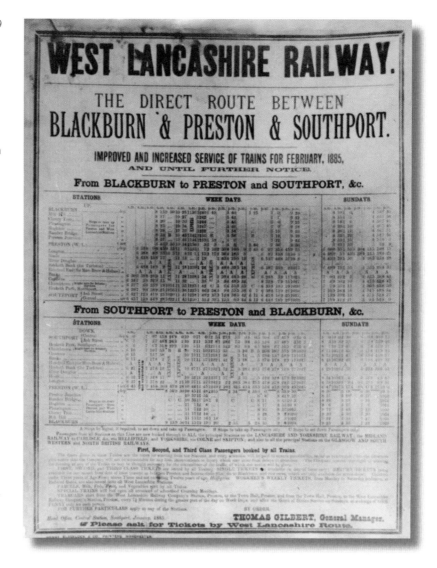

The promoters succeeded in getting an Act passed on 6 June 1844 and then amalgamated with the Blackburn, Burnley, Accrington and Colne Extension Railway known as the East Lancashire Railway [ELR] in 1846.[19]

One Whit Monday 1 June 1846 the Preston to Blackburn Section was inaugurated. 'Glorious First! Weather most serene and splendid,' a passenger, Charles Tiplady, enthused. 'On this day a new era in the history of Blackburn commenced by the formal opening of the Blackburn and Preston Railway Line.' On the return journey to Blackburn,

The Preston to Blackburn Railway became a reality in 1846 and by 1885 the services were many and frequent.

the *Blackburn Standard* reported that, as 'on the outward journey, on every bridge, by every road-side, and at every available point of view, the population had turned out to see the iron monster and its tail shoot by. At half-past seven the train drove into the Blackburn station amidst the loud applause of the numerous spectators. The bells were ringing merrily, the flags were flying and the scene was stirring and memorable.'[20]

On this 'iron monster' rested hopes for the future progress of the town and 'a new course of prosperity' which, in the event, were not to be disappointed. The addition of another railway – the Blackburn, Darwen and Bolton Railway formed in 1844, which then continued the line on to Clitheroe and became the Bolton, Blackburn, Clitheroe and West Yorkshire Junction Railway in 1850 – linked Blackburn with the major trading centres of northern Britain, using a method of transport that was cheaper, quicker and easier than any known before. The popularity of railway travel is shown by the statistics: between 1842 and 1847 the annual number of passengers in Britain rose from 23 million to 57 million. In Lancashire, working people started to use the railway for cheap day outings to the coast: with the result that there was not a bed to be had in Blackpool where, in the summer, 'railway carriages and the station were placed at the disposal of persons to sleep in, but in addition to this a great number had to walk the beach all night.'[21]

Fights broke out not only amongst those desperate for a berth at the seaside but amongst the hardworking, hard drinking navvies, who built the lines, and also between the railway companies themselves. The ELR and the Lancashire and Yorkshire [L&Y] railway companies fought over the collection of tolls from passengers carried in ELR trains over the L&Y line from Clifford Junction to Manchester, in what the newspapers described as 'a most extraordinary and unprecedented scene' on 12 March 1849. The ELR was caught the following year waging a battle over running rights through Blackburn tunnel and station to Daisyfield, which the BC&NW Jct Railway had been granted by Parliament, and the ELR simply blockaded the tunnel until forced by threat of retaliation elsewhere to remove the obstructing engines, stones and over 200 navvies.[22]

Not surprisingly, there was considerable local opposition at first to the merger of these last two warring companies. Charles Tiplady was one of the shareholders who attended the meeting of ELR directors to consider the proposal on 7 June 1857. 'We had a free pass [on the railway] I was in company with Mr Thwaites' he wrote in his diary. While he opposed the amalgamation, he does not say whether Daniel did. In the event the two companies merged and, in 1854, the new railway company was swallowed up by the Lancashire & Yorkshire Railway Company.[23]

'I perceive the railways have set all the Towns of Britain a-dancing,' Carlyle wrote in 1850, 'Reading is coming up to London, Basingstoke is going down to Gosport or Southampton, Dumfries to Liverpool and Glasgow, while at Crewe and other points, I see new ganglions of human population establishing themselves.' And amongst those 'a-dancing', newly mobilised and emancipated from geographical constraints were the country brewers whose market was no longer circumscribed by the high costs of existing road transport and the slowness of the canal transport. Beer was no longer confined to the distance travelled by the dray horse but could now easily travel anywhere in the country. In beer terms, with the age of steam came the age of Burton ales and Guinness stout. With competition increasing at a national level in the supply of good beer to the free trade, ambitious brewers had to ensure their breweries were able to adapt to the changed market. Daniel wanted to install a steam engine and reorganise the Brewery. He was forestalled, however, by Thomas's decision to leave the partnership.[24]

Thomas had married shortly after his father died and through his wife Mary had come to know her family connection, William Ashburn. After working as an agent for Henry Sudell and managing a small cotton mill in Langcliffe, Ashburn had moved on to a better position as Manager for William Eccles at the large Commercial Mills. Ashburn was 42 years old, ambitious and experienced; he was ready to run his own cotton mill. Thomas at 35 had gained commercial experience at the Brewery, and possessed capital, assets and good business connections. Nothing could be more satisfactory for Ashburn than to ask Thomas to join him in a business partnership. Thomas was clearly attracted by the opportunity to make his own money independently of his Brewery inheritance. Despite the vicissitude of the cotton trade, fortunes were still being made by Lancashire cotton men. While Thomas had a third share of the Brewery, he was unable to access this capital until John came of age; until then, by the terms of their father's will, if he left the Thwaites partnership he would receive only a yearly rent for his interest in the Brewery fixtures and premises.[25]

There were, however, other assets which he was able to realise in the interim period. Under the terms of his father's will he had received a larger share of the freehold property portfolio than his younger brothers. Daniel had inherited three public-houses and a house and land at Eanam and John's share was four public-houses, two houses and land in Union Street and a row of houses at Saint Albans. Thomas, however, received only two public-houses but numerous properties and plots of land in Moor Street, at Daisyfield and Bottomgate, as well as his father's farm, house and contents at Ramsgreave, a small village about three miles north of Blackburn. Thomas retained the Brewery related properties for the time being but he sold Ramsgreave farm to help fund the building of a new cotton spinning mill.[26]

He may also have been able to realise another asset. Five years earlier, on 7 January 1839, a great storm had lashed Blackburn from 2am until 7pm. It was, in fact, a hurricane which had blown down the pinnacle of the old parish church and numerous chimneys. Amongst the buildings Whittle lists as damaged were the Wellington Inn (Thwaites), which had 'nearly to be rebuilt;' the Craven Heifer, 'which was dismantled;' Henry Shaw's malt house at Copy Nook 'suffered severely' and 'Mr Thwaites' brewery, on Carr Lane had the chimney injured: the engine was disabled most severely; this engine crushed forty loads of malt every day and was a sad loss.' Whittle does not elaborate on which Mr Thwaites but it seems unlikely that this Thwaites brewery belonged to the other branch of the family; after the brothers' uncle Thomas died, his sons, another Thomas and Wilkinson, continued his business as T & W Thwaites, wine

and spirit merchants, at 56 Victoria Buildings in Blackburn, and are never recorded as becoming brewers. It is more likely that it was Thomas and Daniels' father, who purchased a small brewhouse so as to train and start Thomas in the business and to supply the new residential area of Preston New Road. The severe storm damage sustained in 1839 may have put an end to the operation on the grounds of cost; the records do not divulge whether Thomas or his father then sold the site or if Thomas disposed of it in 1844 to fund his new mill.[27]

Although Thomas left his capital in the Brewery he retired as an active partner on 8 November 1844; an event announced officially in the *London Gazette*. He then formed a new partnership, Messrs Thwaites and Ashburn, and built a spinning and weaving mill at Bottomgate. Business was so profitable that they looked for larger premises. Whittle recorded that, in 1852, 'a new cotton spinning mill is about to be erected upon a very large scale by Messrs Thwaites and Ashburn', the Paradise Mills. By this time Thomas, the prosperous millowner, had long settled Mary and their three sons Daniel, John and Thomas in one of the 'first rank' town houses, built in 1838, at Number 13 Richmond Terrace by St John's Church. As his brother John had come of age in 1845, the three brothers agreed to a division of the capital based on a valuation in March 1846. Daniel and John purchased Thomas's inherited public-houses and some of the development plots and Thomas also withdrew £13,000.[28]

When Thomas left Eanam Brewery, Daniel, now the senior partner, set about restructuring the partnership. He and Thomas had never felt the need for a formal agreement and Thomas's retirement had been an entirely amicable arrangement; John, in his 21st year, also entered the partnership on the basis of an informal understanding in 1844. Daniel thought it necessary, however, to enter into a formal legal agreement when he invited their cousin and employee Joseph Yates to become a partner in Daniel Thwaites & Company. The new

Label for T. & W. Thwaites, which started at Eanam Brewery and supplied Thwaites with wines and spirits until the 1890s.

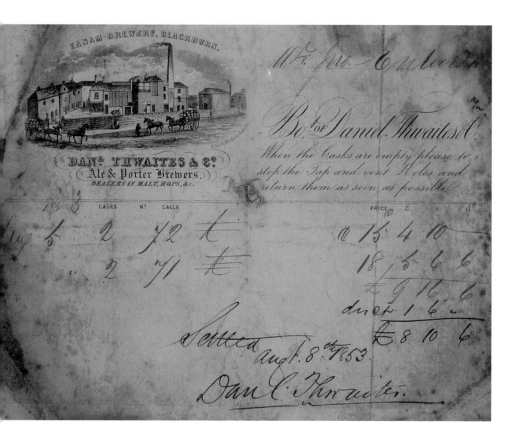

and this sum was entered into the co-partnership's Book as a debt owing to them; until the partnership paid it off they would receive £5 per cent per annum interest. Similarly, the partnership would pay them £800 a year rental for the use of the utensils and occupation of the premises. They would keep a horse and groom charged to the partnership and the Thwaites family also had the use of any of the Brewery's horses. Daniel also introduced some changes to the accounting practices. When it came to the firm's bank accounts, the deed stipulated that the trade cash account was to be settled and balanced on Thursday mornings and the balance paid into the bank, and all cheques were to be signed by Daniel on behalf of the partnership. Instead of one Rest Book, however, each partner had their own book made up mutually and signed weekly by each of them; and instead of a June accounting, the yearly partnership account was to be made on 31 December.[29]

Once the partnership was satisfactorily settled, Daniel could continue to modernise the plant and buildings, and extend the premises within the site and install the latest model of steam engine. His spending plans were inevitably constrained by the prospect of Thomas's probable withdrawal of capital within the next few years. Daniel was careful not to over-extend the business during his testing first years without the support of either his father or his eldest brother. As Henry Michell, son of a Surrey brewer, wrote on taking on the brewing business in 1835, 'I very soon found the difference between looking forward to having a business of my own and the reality. Oh with what fear and trembling my feelings alternated between hope and despair, sometimes I thought I was going to make a fortune in a hurry and then things looked adverse and I fancied nothing but ruin stared us in the face'. Business success for both Henry Michell and Daniel and John Thwaites was earned through hard work, strict cost accounting, prudent investment and enterprise.[30]

It was fortuitous for the Thwaites partners that the economy not only improved but that, in 1845, it was also at the beginning of an upward trend lasting nearly thirty years, propelled by maturing industries; the repeal of the corn laws in 1846; the Customs Law which abolished duties on

partnership deed provides a glimpse of the Brewery business on 9 November 1844. Joseph Yates entered the partnership partly to relieve Daniel and John from some of the work of managing a brewery and partly as a reward for his 'faithful services' to their father and themselves over many years. They trusted him completely and he was, therefore, not to be a mere junior partner but 'in consideration of the mutual confidence they repose in each other,' a co-partner for a term of fourteen years. While Yates continued as the Traveller, to solicit orders and to collect the payment of accounts due to the firm, Daniel and John took responsibility for three departments: first, making all the purchases with the assistance of such clerks and servants as necessary; second, keeping the Books of Account; and third, managing the production and manufacturing of beer.

Daniel and Johns' circulating capital of stock in trade (i.e. barley, hops, beer), drays and barrels amounted to £16,000, live animals and nearly all meat and manufactured goods and reduced duties on cheese, butter and other goods; cheap imports; and the creation of the railways. A combination of higher wages and cheaper food left urban working people better off and with more to spend on their traditional pastime, drinking. Moreover, the passing of the Ten Hours Act in 1844, limiting working hours for women and children of 13–18 years, and of the Factory Act of 1850, initiating the Saturday half-holiday for women and children and, in practice, for most workmen, provided a regular time for leisure and enjoyment, which many working people celebrated in the public-house and on cheap railway travel. The Saturday half-day was also adopted at Eanam Brewery for the small workforce. Breweries remained small employers of labour, Daniel employing some sixteen men and two boys whereas, at the mill in 1851, Thomas employed three hundred and sixty hands.

Daniel and John also had to adapt to developments in the beer market during the middle years of the 19th century. The change in beer drinking was undoubtedly facilitated by the railways and promoted by the popular Great Exhibition in 1851. Thousands of Britons converged upon London in fleets of special excursion trains organised by a former Baptist bible reader and wood-turner, the newly-established travel entrepreneur Thomas Cook. Wandering through the glass temple of Crystal Palace, a shrine to machinery and innovation, people were amazed at the array of manufactured consumer goods, including the novel, fussy, ornate furnishings and interior decoration on display. The good behaviour of the crowds surprised the organisers and polite Londoners who had expected drunken brawls from the rough provincial masses surging into the enormous refreshment hall. Amongst those selling beer there was Michael Bass of Bass & Co., who had obtained permission from the commissariat to lay on bitter beer in draught. The result, described by a business writer in 1886, was that 'All the world and his wife were tempted, they tasted and were conquered; and if the Prince Consort's Universal Exhibition did not introduce the period of universal peace, it brought about universal bitter beer.'[31]

Bass was one of the Burton on Trent brewers who

succeeded in marketing a high quality pale ale on a massive scale between 1850 and 1875. A Burton brew combined flavour, strength and reliability with a light, clear, sparkling appearance. It showed to good effect the new cheap glass drinking vessels that were first produced after technological innovations in the glass industry in the 1840s and had replaced the traditional pewter and treen tankards and mugs by the 1850s. Although the town had long been known for its brewing, it was not until the 1830s that its pale bitter beer, first produced for export, became popular with the middle class drinkers in London and the large cities. Burton beer was never cheap, selling for 6d to 8d a quart, but it offered quality and quickly became a 'status' drink for the expanding artisan and shop-keeper class in the railway age.[32]

For Burton benefited hugely from the creation of a national railway network, with the Midland, the LNWR, the Great Northern and the North Staffordshire railways all eventually running through the town. The railways enabled the two largest firms, Bass and Allsopp, to distribute their beer cheaply – freight charges were reduced from £3 for about 5 barrels to 15s – and quickly – foregoing the three week canal route for a 12 hour rail journey to London. These breweries were also pioneers in the art of marketing; they used their trademarks, Bass's red triangle and Allsopp's red hand, to create nationally recognisable brands, and agencies to develop sales in the free trade. Thus, Bass, for instance, saw its output of 145,000 barrels in 1855, *doubled* within the next three years; by 1876 Bass and Allsopp would be producing over 900,000 barrels annually.[33]

Burton beer, so 'novel, bright, fresh and pale', is described by the beer historian Richard Wilson as 'the high-fashion beer of the railway age,' and, as with anything fashionable, others wanted to produce their own version. Soon, brewers from London and the North established breweries in Burton; and every brewer in the country was attempting to brew their own Burton-type bitter ale with natural calcium-laden hard water or, after the 1870s, chemical treatment of the liquor. Making a good Burton-type ale, as Wilson says, became the *sine qua non* for that generation of brewers who reaped the rewards of the great increase in beer consumption in the 1860s and 1870s. After Edward Greene, the East Anglian brewer, died in 1891, the *London Star* noted, 'He was one of the first country brewers to discover that beer need not be vile, black, turgid stuff, but brewed a bright amber-coloured liquid of Burton type which sold at a shilling per gallon, and made a fortune.' Just as Daniel's father had been an early northern producer of porter, so the younger Daniel now produced Thwaites own 'amber-coloured' pale bitter, his best bitter. Like any brewer of enterprise in the 1860–1870s, when *per capita* consumption in England and Wales increased from 31.6 to 40.5 gallons, he saw sales of this and his other beers increase splendidly.[34]

The decade of the 1850s was one of growth for the Brewery and increasing prosperity for the Thwaites partners. This was reflected in developments in the family and the personal lives of the partners. Their mother Betty died in 1853 and was buried alongside their father in the family vault in St John's Church. Their children erected a fine marble memorial tablet on the west wall of the church, and dedicated these words to their parents:

'A tribute of love and affection and respect to the memory of Daniel Thwaites of Blackburn who died 23rd day of October 1843, in the 67th year of his age, and to Betty his wife, who died 23rd April 1853, in the 69th year of her age. Betty was a loving mother to her large family.' The tablet can still be seen on the wall of St John's, though the church is now used as a charity centre.

After their mother's death, the family made plans to move from the house in Cleaver Street. Four of the sisters were already married and living elsewhere. Mary had been the first of the family to marry and was living with three young children at Langho where her husband Dr Philip Kershaw was the Director of the private Billington District Madhouse (now called Mytton Fold Farm). Betsey had married William Ward, just before their father's death. Ward was a well-liked local vet, his surgery was in Lord Street, and he treated the Brewery horses. Although fifteen years older than Daniel, the two men were good friends and shared an interest in hunting and farming. The Wards and their four young children lived in Wilpshire where Ward also farmed 112 acres.

Ellen and Esther had also married men of substance. Ellen's husband James Sturdy was a prominent local solicitor and mill-owner and was involved in local politics as a town councillor. In 1813 Thomas and Jane Sturdy had christened their son James Barlow Stewardson Sturdy; an infant in whom, as Abram delicately phrased it, Dr Barlow took a paternal interest. James was, indeed, the illegitimate son of Dr James Barlow, an eminent physician and surgeon who had performed his first caesarean operation in 1793. Barlow had married and separated from his wife in Chorley in 1795 and thereafter passed himself off as a bachelor in Blackburn, where he was considered 'something of a rake'. He recognised James Sturdy publicly as his son, educated him and settled him in a firm of solicitors. When James and Ellen married, Barlow gave them a house, Spring Side, situated on his land at Preston New Road and opposite his own large house, Spring Mount, completed and occupied by him in 1826, shortly after the construction of the Road. On Barlow's death in 1839, Sturdy, his sole heir, inherited both houses as well as other property in Blackburn and the bulk of his wealth. By the mid-1850s, the Sturdys and their three daughters were comfortably ensconced in Spring Mount not too far from her newly married youngest sister Esther.

The only member of the family to marry into Blackburn's cottonocracy, Esther's husband Thomas Lund was the grandson of Thomas Lund, who owned the old Wensley Fold mill said to have been the first building in Blackburn to be lighted with gas, transported from Manchester in bladders. In 1822 grandfather Lund built the large new spinning mill, also known locally for its time signal; every night at nine o'clock the night watchmen fired off the Wensley Fold "Blunderbuss". The Lunds were a large, wealthy, well-established family and settled Esther and Thomas into Lovely Hall, Salesbury, complete with a retinue of servants. Thomas was a magistrate, cotton manufacturer and, according to the census, a 'farmer of means'. He joined Daniel and John in taking an active interest in local politics, hunting and railway investments.[35]

With their sisters and brother Thomas so comfortably settled, the rest of the family felt that they, too, could afford to migrate to a more salubrious residential district. Cleaver

Street had relinquished its reputation as a select street and grown into a built-up, poorer area since their childhood; it was no longer deemed a suitable address for the four unmarried sisters Grace, Sarah, Ann and Alice. The neighbourhood in which the Sturdys lived on the western outskirts of Blackburn surrounding Preston New Road was then considered most desirable. It was within easy travelling distance of Eanam Brewery yet still offered an attractive rural aspect to the affluent Blackburn families not yet interested in or able to purchase country estates. Daniel, therefore, decided to build in this fashionable area, known as the West End of Blackburn, and entered into negotiations with William Feilden, who owned much of the land surrounding his Witton Estate, for several plots of land there: a large one for himself at Billinge Scarr, south of Preston New Road and near the former Carr Brewery; a second slightly smaller one on the opposite side of Preston New Road for John; and a smaller one nearer to the Lunds, and the Lower Academy at Dukes Bow, for his sisters.

While plans were being drawn up and builders contracted to carry out the work, the Thwaites siblings went to live at Beardwood Cliffe, a large newly constructed 'villa' set in its own grounds and conveniently situated between Daniel and Johns' building sites. Coincidentally, Daniel's older cousin Thomas Thwaites (of the 'Wine and Spirit' branch), who lived at 'West Bank', had built Beardwood Cliffe for his sons William and (yet another) Daniel, who were being groomed to inherit the flourishing T&W Thwaites business and were a generation younger than the Brewery Thwaites. These two branches of the family were, nonetheless, extremely close and saw a great deal of each other. It was, therefore, most convenient for Daniel and his siblings to live at Beardwood as an interim measure.

No sooner had they settled in, than cousin Thomas Thwaites, returning by rail from Baccup to Blackburn on 7 May 1857, was taken ill and died in the railway carriage, to the great distress of his family. His unmarried brother and partner Wilkinson Thwaites, James Wileson a land agent, and Daniel were executors of his will, guardians of his orphaned children and trustees of the substantial trusts of the £20,000 settled on each child. Daniel was shortly left in sole authority as both Wilkinson and Willson died the following year. William and his brother Daniel came to live at their house, Beadwood Cliffe while their two sisters remained at West Bank, which they inherited.[36]

It was also in 1858 that the fourteen year partnership of Daniel Thwaites & Co. expired and, for unstated reasons, was not renewed. Joseph Yates departed, he was considerably older than his fellow partners and had probably reached an age when retirement was either a necessary or an attractive prospect. The same could not be said of John Thwaites who was only thirty-four years-old. John would appear to prefer riding to hounds with the Pendle Harriers or being out on the moors with dog and gun for a good day's shooting than to applying himself to the routine of ledgers and brews at Eanam Brewery. And there would also appear to be funds ample enough to allow him to lead the life of a country gentleman, for he never worked again. By all accounts he was 'generous and warm-hearted' and 'the most hospitable of men'. He bought his bride Prudence Freke-Evans of a family long settled at Wateringbury in Kent, to live at Troy, the mansion he built in the 'West End' of Blackburn and where they brought up a family of seven sons and seven daughters.[37]

The official announcement of the dissolution of the partnership, published in the *London Gazette* on 25 February 1859, stated that it was by mutual consent. Although John retired from active involvement he became, in effect, a sleeping partner; his capital remained in the Brewery earning him interest and producing a comfortable income. He also retained ownership in a share of the property portfolio for which he received rental income. Daniel, however, was now in sole charge of the business which he ran with the help of a manager, Joseph Smith, and of a property adviser, Henry Gornall, a conveyancing solicitor of Revidge Road. Daniel had now been a partner for fifteen years and during this period he had grown the firm and shown himself to be an astute, ambitious and experienced brewer.[38]

Although in the 1840s he had directed his energies almost exclusively to the Brewery – and, living in Cleaver Street, little in the Brewery yard had escaped his notice – in

Daniel Thwaites had a passion for hunting which he enjoyed with his local hunt the Pendle Harriers.

town had been subsumed in the Improvement Commissioners, devised under the 1841 Improvement Act. These worthy gentlemen had been busy paving some streets for the new market place, repairing some old drains and constructing the town's first substantial public building, the market house opened in January 1848. They had even contemplated improving the inadequate supply of water but then left it to private enterprise; many of them appeared on the provisional committee of the new Blackburn Waterworks Company, and profited accordingly.

Beyond their improving scope lay the piles of ordure festering in every street, and the cesspools blocking the river Blakewater, the common sewer of the town. The river was 'the black, murky, slimy, filthy, sink of abomination,' angrily wrote a reader to the *Blackburn Standard* in 1846, 'that, like a poisonous serpent, seems to envelope the town in its sinuous and deadly folds.' Blackburn, as its name indicated, was in the early 1850s even blacker from smoke and coal dust and dirtier from dung and rubbish than it had been in the 1800s. Daniel and his sisters had to tread as guardedly in the streets as their parents had done; the pigs might have disappeared from the main roads but dead cats and dogs floated in the river and the filth and stench had increased a hundred fold since their childhood.[39]

Charles Dickens could have based the inimitable depiction of a dingy northern manufacturing town in his novel *Hard Times*, serialised weekly in the magazine *Household Words* starting in April 1854, as easily on Blackburn as he did on Preston and Birmingham. 'Coketown,' he wrote, 'was a town of red brick, or brick that would have been red if the smoke and ashes had allowed it: but as matters stood, it was a town of unnatural red and black like the painted face of a savage. It was a town of machinery and tall chimneys, out of which interminable serpents of smoke trailed themselves for ever and ever, and never got uncoiled. It had a black canal in it, and a river that ran purple with ill-smelling dye, and vast piles of buildings full of windows where there was a rattling and a trembling all day long and where the piston of the steam-engine worked monotonously up and down, like the head of an elephant in a state of melancholy madness.'[40]

the 1850s he began to relax his work routine sufficiently to allow time for recreation and for public life. He shared a passion for hunting and horses with John and started to ride to hounds regularly with the Blackburn hunt, the Pendle Harriers run by his landed friend John Chamberlain Starkie of Huntroyde. In the autumn of 1850 he also joined a group of some of Blackburn's leading businessmen to lobby for a local governing council.

The town was one of the largest in the country to remain unincorporated, and as it rapidly increased in size, so did the problems of sanitation, law and order. The twelve Police Commissioners, appointed by statute in 1803 to oversee the paving, lighting, watching and cleansing of the

In such a mid-19th-century town, there was infinite space for improvement and it says much for the industry and enterprise of the Victorians that they embarked on widespread civic 'clean-up' programmes. Brewing, like any other industry, contributed to the smoke and dirt of a town. Yet the process of brewing required a high standard of cleanliness, in the utensils, water and people; people bringing dirt into the brewhouse, dung on their clogs, filth on their clothes and hair, threatened the quality of the brew. Added to this was a belief among educated people, who had lived through riots and Chartism, that cleaner water, streets and houses was a way of bringing stability and a social and moral discipline to working people. 'If the poor are badly fed and badly lodged, it is now found that they generate fevers and pestilence; grow vicious and demoralised, and become dangerous to the peace, order, and safety of the country.'[41]

The best way to start the clean-up was with the authority and funds of local government, hence the move among influential men in Blackburn to obtain a charter for incorporation. At a public meeting of ratepayers held at the end of November 1850, the proposal for a petition for a charter was carried, though William Hornby feared the rates would be doubled under a corporation. The committee appointed to carry it forward wielded all the authority of wealth and property; its members were Daniel, Charles Tiplady (stationer and printer), Hornby, Raynsford Jackson and John Livesey (cotton manufacturers), Thomas Dugdale (surgeon), William Hoole (headmaster), Robert Hutchinson (mill owner), James Boyle (confectioner), Christopher Parkinson and J. Parkinson (wholesale grocers), Thomas Ainsworth (attorney) and George Dewhurst (reed maker). They had little difficulty in gaining signatures for the petition of 28 November 1850 to the Queen in Council for a charter of incorporation for the borough.

Incorporation of the Borough of Blackburn was duly granted in 1851 when William Hornby became the first mayor and cousin Thomas Thwaites an alderman. The first municipal election was held on 1 November 1851 when all three Thwaites brothers stood as candidates for the thirty-six councillor seats, six in each of the wards. The election

was vigorously contested and the Conservatives won a majority. Daniel was elected for Trinity Ward and John and Thomas for St. John's Ward. Despite the enthusiasm for reform in Blackburn, the new council moved slowly to implement improvements. Drainage works began in 1856 but the main outlet sewer was not completed until 1861 and there was no Board of Health created, as in Over Darwen. Above ground, the town gradually presented a more genteel appearance in the 1850s; the construction of a town hall, new villas along Preston New Road, better working-class housing and, most welcome of all to the public, was the opening of Corporation Park on 19 October 1857, which brought 'a breath of the countryside' to brewery, mill, factory and shop worker, to poor labouring families who paraded along the walks on Saturday afternoon and Sundays at their newly found leisure.[42]

It was in May 1852 that Daniel also became a magistrate. One of the arguments made for building a town hall was to provide court rooms. 'It was a reproach to the town that there was neither Police-office nor Sessions-room in it,' James Pilkington MP had decided. 'It was disreputable to a town of 40,000 inhabitants that it could find no better room for the administration of justice than one which was some 12 or 14 feet square.' The informal Regency ways of making do with a room at the best Inn were beneath the earnest Victorians; justice must be meted out with requisite formality. When Daniel sat on the Bench in 1858 it was in the impressive panelled courtroom in the new Town Hall. Sitting with fellow magistrates John Sparrow, Thomas Hart and John Baynes, he heard, what to Tiplady, was 'the sad affair' of how Alexander Emmott, secretary of the local Philanthropic Burial Society had embezzled £133–7–4. The bench sentenced him to repay the amount plus a £20 guinea fine and costs or face imprisonment.[43]

By becoming a magistrate, Daniel had taken a first step up the ladder of county office and acceptance in county society. The magistracy had traditionally been the preserve of the gentry and clergy. Before the 1830s, social qualifications of oath, land and manners counted, and effectively excluded manufacturers and merchants so that his father would have been ineligible. Even in 1840, Lacy, the illegitimate son of an aristocrat, was favoured above an industrialist, as a Duchy official explained. '*The better admixture of blood* is evident, for he is not only highly respectable in character but a man of *good manners*, which is more than I can say for nine-tenths of our justices.' The landed dominance was, however, being steadily eroded in Lancashire by the effect of political reform, admitting Whigs and Radicals, and industrialisation and population growth creating the need for new justices. Daniel moved easily onto the bench as brewers continued to be viewed as a social cut above cotton manufacturers and, by 1851, even the barriers to cottonocracy had been removed. In Blackburn Hundred, of the forty-nine justices appointed between 1846 and 1851, twenty-four were textile manufacturers.[44]

As a magistrate, Daniel received an important boost to his local status and power. He was now a prosperous forty year-old bachelor with all the consequence of improving wealth and a splendid new mansion, Billinge Scarr. Lancashire society could only concur with Jane Austen's famous intimation that 'it is a truth universally acknowledged that a single man in possession of a good fortune must be in want of a wife.' And Daniel, like *Pride and Prejudice*'s Mr Bingley, was a young man from the north of England who was also captivated by a young lady in southern England; and Daniel's proposal was accepted with little delay. Miss Eliza Amelia Gregory lived quietly with her widowed mother in the village of Hendon in the county of Middlesex. Her father George Gregory, headmaster of Repton School in Derbyshire, had died when she was eight years old. Eliza, like Austen's Bennett sisters, was educated for marriage but left without a fortune to fascinate the suitors deemed suitable by her brother George Gregory. He lived nearby at Brent Bridge House and it was through his wife's connection with Blackburn that Daniel became acquainted with Eliza.[45]

George Gregory considered himself a gentleman of consequence. A scholar at Repton, he could not look to his father's estate (under £100) for advancement, and possessed no obvious position and an uncertain income. Yet, in 1839, he had been sufficiently attentive as to capture in marriage an eighteen-year-old co-heiress, Miss Mary Jane Fowden

Hindle, the elder daughter of Captain William Fowden Hindle of Ollerton Hall in Cheshire. Thereafter, Gregory had devoted himself to the estates of his wife and her younger sister and co-heiress Miss Sarah Hindle. Assiduous in his duty to promote their interests, he never hesitated to borrow against and speculate with their rents and capital, manage and purchase land, and enter into protracted, expensive legal proceedings.

In the course of this exacting stewardship he entered into negotiations with Daniel in 1855 for the purchase of one hundred acres of Hindle land. Mary Jane Gregory and her sister had inherited their fortune from their grandfather John Fowden Hindle, a gentlemanly cotton merchant in Blackburn. Shortly before his death in 1831 he had purchased Sudell's Woodfold Estates. He provided handsomely for his children, leaving £60,000 in trust for his three daughters; £20,000 in trust and an income of £500 a year for his second son William Fowden Hindle; £100,000 in Consols, Woodfold Hall, a townhouse in King Street and the cotton business to John Fowden Hindle Jr his elder son and heir. John Fowden Hindle Sr directed his three trustees to retain power over William Fowden Hindle 'at all times' and never to allow him access to the capital. In the event of John Fowden Hindle Jr dying without issue, the family estates and capital account were to bypass William Fowden Hindle and be given in trust to his daughters Mary Jane and Sarah. When John Fowden Hindle Jr died unexpectedly in 1849, not only was he the only surviving trustee of all the family trusts but he was also found to be insolvent from over-extension in the volatile cotton market. The complications arising form the various trusts, creditors, accountings, deceased trustees, court cases and disputes within the family proved troublesome for all the Hindles and kept a battalion of lawyers happily engaged on their behalf over the following two decades.[46]

At the centre of these disputations, set in parkland surrounded by the Mellor hills and valleys of Ribblesdale, was Woodfold Hall. This stately Regency house, which still stands today, encircled by about eight hundred acres, had already witnessed the downfall of two owners, Sudell and Hindle Jr before being rented to a succession of tenants. At the time of

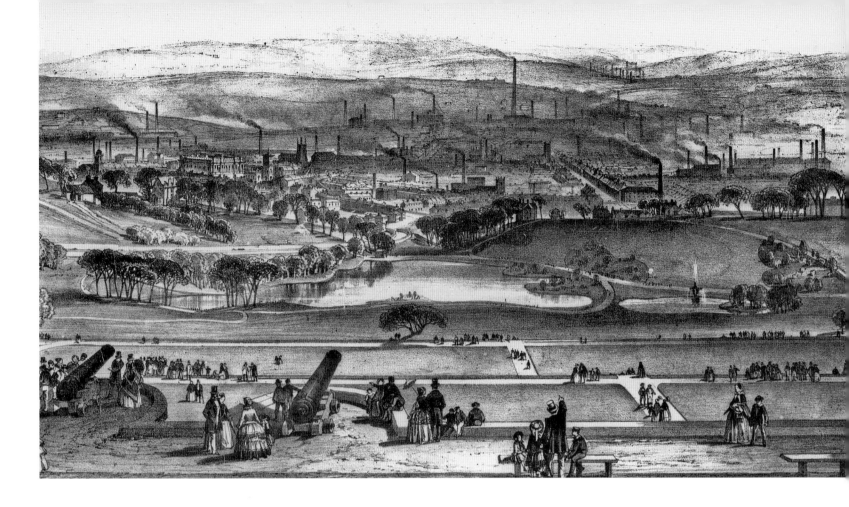

Hindle Jr's death in 1849 it was forthwith let until 1854 to the Preston banker Henry Fleetwood for £300 a year. In 1855, when Daniel was contemplating moving out of Cleaver Street and before Gregory found another tenant, the two men discussed a possible sale of one hundred acres of estate land with or without the Hall. Price was all to both parties. 'However unless I can get a better price for the land from Mr Thwaites than it would fetch by *auction* and also a better price for the house than the *value of the materials*, what inducement is there to dispose of the very cream of the Estate in this manner,' Gregory asked his Blackburn solicitor, Henry Brock Hollinshead on 30 November 1855. 'I can only sell if I can sell well.' Gregory declared he would not entertain an offer of less than £10,000 for the house and stabling which, adding in the timber and land, would make a total price of £30,000, 'and at this price to a Gentleman having

business in Black[n] & an income sufficient to live at Woodfold it would be indisputably cheap.' This was the offer Gregory told Hollinshead he would make to Daniel and 'I dare say he will admit that there is no other Woodfold Hall within 3 miles of Black[n].[47]

Before Daniel was able to concur with, or baulk at, this high valuation, Gregory had changed his mind about a sale, largely because the trustees disputed the power of sale during the continuing Hindle litigation. Daniel's fellow magistrate, the cotton merchant John Sparrow was the next tenant of Woodfold Hall. After Daniel married Eliza at St Mary's parish church of Hendon on 28 December 1859, he brought her to live at his new house, Billinge Scarr. The calls made by the newly married couple upon the Thwaites family and relations and friends in the area included one to the Sparrows at Woodfold Hall. Unfortunately, John Sparrow

A view of Blackburn and the Corporation Park in 1857 on the occasion of its opening.

Daniel Jnr and his wife Eliza Amelia in later years.

fell on hard times in the early 1860s and had to leave Woodfold. This by no means precluded the Thwaites couple from paying further visits there as the next tenants were none other than his sister Esther Lund and her family.

Daniel took a closer interest in Woodfold after Gregory's property machinations led to a quarrel with Sarah Hindle. Gregory had been obliged to use her funds to purchase Lumb Bank Farm at Pleasington in 1857. She had married her cousin Ronaldo McGildowny around 1860 and, in the course of arranging matters, had discovered the use of her funds without her proper consent and, naturally, disputed the purchase. Gregory would not give her a proper accounting of his stewardship and the McGildownys consulted their lawyers. Elizabeth Hindle, the sisters' mother, took the McGildownys' part; she had never trusted Gregory and, in writing her will in 1857, had stipulated that her

trustees were to keep in their care her bequests to her only granddaughter Mary Gregory 'so long as her father George Frederick Gregory shall live' and only to deliver them at his decease. To prevent a complete ruction in the family and a forced sale of Woodfold after Sarah's death in 1864, Daniel was persuaded to buy the McGildowny half share in the Woodfold Estate.[48]

It was during these early years of marriage that he also bought a house in London, at Queen's Gate, Kensington. There Eliza bore him a son and heir, Edward George Duckworth Thwaites on 20 March 1861; to their grief, he died on 10 August at Billinge Scarr and was buried in the Thwaites vault at St John's Church. After this, Eliza passed more time in London and Daniel purchased a larger London house, Addison Lodge in Addison Road near to the Gregorys, who now lived at Number 21 Addison Road, adjacent to Lord Holland's lovely Jacobean Holland House in Kensington. In those days, Kensington was considered by Londoners to be a village in the country. A turnpike even lay between Westminster and Kensington, with green open meadows bordering the muddy lanes. The Duke of Argyll, who lived nearby on Campden Hill, thought the spacious gardens of Argyll Lodge healthy for his children and marvellous for the bird life. Addison Lodge was Eliza Thwaites' favourite home, perhaps because her baby, a healthy daughter they named Elma Amy Thwaites was born there in May 1864.

The tranquil air of Kensington was much more conducive to the well-being of mother and child than the distressing atmosphere pervading Blackburn in the early 1860s. The civil war being fought in America between 1861 and 1865 brought in its wake a cotton famine with dreadful privations for the people of Lancashire. The mills processed raw cotton imported from the southern Confederate states of America; these supplies were stopped by the northern blockade of southern ships. The outcome of every battle affected the prices of cotton; 'General Lee's defeat in one caused a fall of 3d per lb in cotton, then a southern success brought an upswing of more than 3d,' according to Henry Gibbs, a Manchester cotton merchant. Before the end of 1862, supplies were so scarce that the price of raw cotton had advanced 300 percent. The scenario in every cotton town ran along these lines: spinning stopped – looms were idle – workers were put on short time or turned out – supplies of yarn ran out – mills closed – workers were starving – firms started to fail – soup kitchens were opened – relief tickets were handed out for clogs and coal to the unemployed. Articles appeared in the national press on the Distress in Lancashire with appeals for subscriptions, and public meetings were held locally on "Emigration or Starvation."[49]

'General trade disastrous in the Extreme,' wrote Charles Tiplady, not usually given to hyperbole. Soup kitchens were in full operation near the Brewery in Cleaver Street and short time was almost universal in 1861. 'Many heavy failures affecting several firms in this town & neighbourhood – But we live in very trying times'. Among the heavy failures was the firm of Messrs Thwaites and Ashburn. In what should

have been a year of civic splendour for Thomas as Mayor of Blackburn, he suffered such heavy commercial losses that the Paradise Mills closed, the Richmond Terrace house had to be sold, the family had to move to a small house, and all his assets had to be liquidated. Daniel and John rallied round with financial support and places at the Brewery for two of his sons, James and John. Daniel also made a £300 donation to the Relief Fund for cotton operatives. The times were, as Tiplady wrote, 'very trying', especially for the Thwaites family: the sudden death of Esther Lund was followed by the failure of Thomas Lund's cotton firm in 1866 and then, in February 1867, the death of James Sturdy JP and former Mayor.[50]

Daniel, however, continued to prosper. He purchased the Snig Brook Brewery from James Cunningham, which produced 10,000 barrels a year. He also continued to build new public-houses and buy additional sites in central areas, especially corner sites. During this period Eanam Brewery expanded production to provide 100,000 barrels a year by 1878. Brewing was a booming industry as demand for beer rose in line with the gross consumption of all intoxicants

The Thwaites Coat of Arms granted to Daniel Jnr on his marriage in 1859.

between 1860 and 1880. In 1869 25.1 million barrels of beer were brewed, 4.6 million more than in 1860. By 1871 consumption had risen by a further 1.3 million barrels and the years 1870–1876 were exceptional for the rising working class incomes and increase in drink expenditure. The boom in Lancashire mill and mining towns was deplored by the middle classes who found 'miners indulging in Champagne wine' and frowned upon the workers buying sealskin waistcoats. Although Daniel, like other northern brewers, was investing in the tied houses, a large part of the barrelage still rested on the expansion of the free trade, encouraged by discounts and increased by the exertions of his two well-paid Travellers.[51]

The business also had to adapt to the drink industry's return to the political spotlight. Various pieces of legislation were introduced by Gladstone's Liberal government. The 1869 Wine and Beer House Act gave licensing power back to the magistrates and was intended as a measure of control over the more unsavoury beer shops. It was followed by the Intoxicating Liquor Licensing Act of 1872,

'The Lancashire Distress' depicting the soup kitchen in Crooked Lane, Preston.

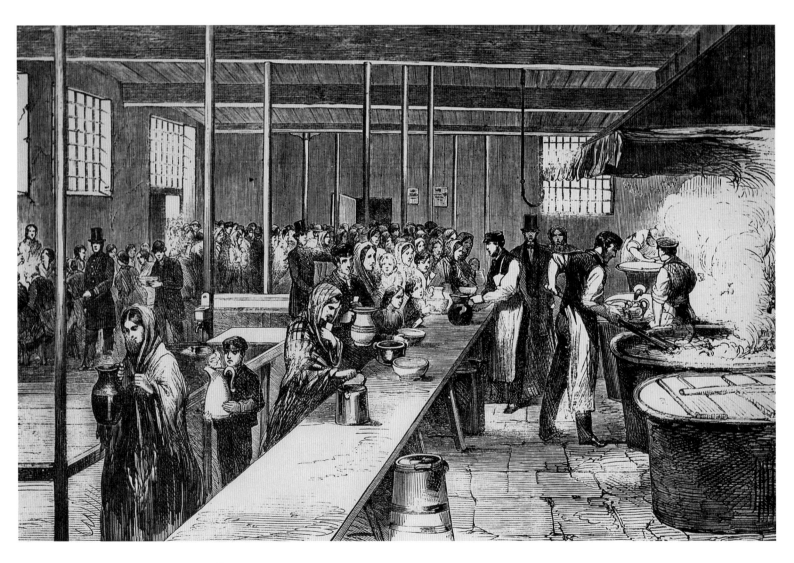

which introduced higher licence fees, licensing inspectors, a reduction in opening hours, restrictions on the sale of spirits to those 'apparently under the age of 16' and increased penalties for licensing offences. The Act was generally unpopular and licensed victuallers were vehemently opposed to it as an attack on property and the freedoms of the common man.[52]

Political interest in the brewing industry was being stoked by the Temperance movement which had undergone a long gestation since its birth in northern towns, especially in Preston under teetotaller Joseph Liveseys' leadership in the 1830s. In Blackburn, where the movement had begun as a local branch of the British and Foreign Temperance Society (B.F.T.S) in London, the Reverend Whittaker had brought a customary moral energy to his role as president of the interdenominational committee. The Eanam Brewery had little to fear from the BFTS's proceedings as it made little headway in either reducing beer-drinking or drunkenness in Blackburn. More challenging to the beer trade was the development of the teetotal movement, which adopted the reclaiming of drunkards as its leading objective and turned itself into a revolutionary social and moral crusade. Blackburn's temperance society was the first to adopt a 'pledge' forbidding entry to drinking places and all alcoholic drinking; it became the model for the Preston society in 1832.

As the effects of the 1830 Beer Act were seen to increase not only the consumption of beer but also drunkenness, the movement stopped regarding beer as the healthy alternative to spirits and actively opposed the sale and drinking of beer. The term 'teetotal' was apparently coined in Preston by Dick Turner, a former drunkard whom Livesey had reformed, and who had a stammer. The term became popular among radical abstainers who refused to make a distinction between the evils of beer and gin.[33]

The force behind the temperance movement's crusade was the United Kingdom Alliance, which was founded in Manchester in 1853 and directed its energetic activities to parliamentary action at Westminster; by the 1870s, it had

succeeded in making the temperance question a pressing political issue. The 1872 Licensing Act was a Liberal measure and it led to an important shift in party attitudes to the drink question with the identification of the Liberals as the pro-temperance party. This, naturally, had certain attractions for the Conservative party, which was moved to align itself

The Struggle, the periodical that fought the "mighty evil of intemperance … the bane of thousands of families".

increasingly with the drink interest. At the Preston by-election in August 1872, the Conservative candidate declared that the Licensing Bill was 'the silliest bill' and that the teetotallers and prohibitionists would do away with the foaming tankards and roast beef of merry England. The Conservatives won a decisive victory over a good Liberal candidate; the Liberal attorney-general attacked the Tories for making political capital out of the Licensing Act which Gladstone liked to believe had been carried 'with the general assent of the House.'[54]

The drink issue was of importance to Daniel, not only as a brewer but also as a Conservative politician. In January 1874, Gladstone called a general election. Blackburn sent

A bust of Daniel Thwaites Jnr now in the Thwaites museum.

two members to Parliament but only Henry M Feilden (Convervative) sought re-election, as Edward Hornby (Conservative) had already notified the local Committee that he wished to stand down. The long innings of various Hornbys and Feildens as sitting members since 1832 had meant that very few other candidates ever had a chance to stand. Daniel harboured parliamentary ambitions, had been an active supporter of the local Tory party, and was on good terms with Feilden and Hornby and his father William Hornby. He, therefore, seized this opening with alacrity and signified a willingness to put his name forward. While soundings were taken in all the local Tory clubs, the Liberal opposition sought to undermine him by circulating rumours that his unpopular and peremptory candidature was causing a split in Tory ranks.

After being endorsed publicly by the Hornbys: 'Daniel Thwaites is my friend, a gentleman of high position, wealth and generosity, and I have known him for 30 years', Daniel was adopted as the second Tory candidate, and he and Feilden issued their manifestoes on 27 January. Daniel favoured a national system of education and was 'as opposed as any man to drunkenness, and would support any measure to prevent abuses in the liquor traffic, provided it did not interfere with the right of the working man to obtain refreshment.' It was a balanced, general statement from a brewer but was anathema to the local temperance vote, which switched to the two Liberals, William Briggs, a local cotton manufacturer and a popular candidate, and Richard Shackleton, a Quaker flour miller. On a cold, foggy February day, Blackburn went to the polls. Shortly before 10 o'clock that evening, the Mayor stood at the front door of the Town Hall to announce the result that Feilden (5,532 votes) and Briggs (5,338) had been elected, and Daniel had come third with 5,323 votes.

It was a disappointment, especially as the Conservatives returned to power with Disraeli as Prime Minister. 'We have been borne down in a torrent of gin and beer,' Gladstone famously observed, somewhat exaggerating the power of the drink interest, and minimising opposition to his Irish Land Act and Home Rule. Daniel did not have to wait long for another opportunity to seek election; Feilden died suddenly in the autumn of 1875 at Lytham. Before Daniel could make a declaration, two other candidates, both cotton men, announced their intentions to stand. Daniel assumed that, as a past candidate with the Hornby endorsement, he would be the automatic choice. At a turbulent meeting of some 3,000 local officials and party members the press had to be evicted and three rounds of votes taken before Daniel was adopted.

Of the other candidates, James Thompson, 'kingmaker' on local Tory committees, immediately publicly backed Daniel but William Coddington the Mayor was slower in offering his support. The Liberals tried to persuade him to stand as a 'Progressive Conservative' and split the vote. Once more, this led to Liberal stories circulating that Daniel had said he would stand regardless of what the party decided. Coddington had to issue a public denial of 'any coolness' between them or any sympathy for the Liberals.' The *Blackburn Times,* a Liberal paper, was convinced Daniel was swaying the voters with 'exhilarating drinks' and alleged 'if Mr Daniel Thwaites sold all the beer that was drunk on and off the premises this week in connection with the election, what a pretty penny he must have turned by the contest!'[55]

The by-election was fought on the slogans 'Thwaites for Queen and Constitution', and 'The Popular Candidate' for his opponent John Hibbert, former Liberal MP for Oldham. At the end of polling on 30 September, the unfamiliar sealed ballot boxes were brought to the Town Hall for counting. Coddington, as Returning Officer, announced the result: Thwaites 5,792, Hibbert 4,832. Visibly moved, Daniel declared to his cheering supporters, 'It is the proudest moment of my life, and I am sure it is a proud day to you. You have vindicated the principles of Toryism.' He was sure that Hibbert would think twice before venturing to Blackburn again. Hibbert was heard muttering that 'intelligence had been overcome by the beer barrel.' This election, unlike many of its predecessors, was remarkable for the absence of arrests for drunkenness or rioting. The last sounds to be heard, on that night of triumph for Daniel were the fizz and crack of sparkling fireworks outside the Central Conservative Club.[56]

He was fifty eight when he entered the House of Commons, and unlikely to change his character and habits. Described as a confident gentleman of 'correctness and respectability', he was, in public, forthright in opinion, reserved in manner and possessed a dry sense of humour; a combination that could make him appear brusque to strangers. His speeches in the House were notable for their

The Prince and Princess of Wales are welcomed to Blackburn in May 1888. 18 firemen manned this arch formed from two fire escapes. Such events constituted welcome opportunities for enjoyment at a time of economic uncertainty.

rarity and, as the editor of the *Blackburn Standard* noted, 'have not as a rule, carried us away with admiration' as to their power of oratory. In other words, he was no different from his fellow brewing MPs. In the 1870s there were over thirty brewers in the Commons, reflecting the increased prosperity and influence of the drink trade. Temperance advocates and critics exaggerated the brewers' ability to arouse fears of 'politics awash in booze, bribes and blackmail.' David Gutzke has found that while 'the rhetoric of the trade's power is impressive, the reality was quite different.' Brewers not only did not vote as a monolithic bloc, they mostly did not vote at all, preferring 'the asphalte of Paris and the bracing air of the moors to a Parliamentary conflict involving the vital interests of the trade,' grumbled the *Brewer and Publican*. Nor did Blackburn's other MPs display great volubility in the House. Harry Hornby successfully carried on the Blackburn tradition of silence by not speaking once at Westminster throughout a twenty-three-year parliamentary career.[57]

Daniel's Westminster career was much shorter. He sought re-election in 1880, standing with Coddington against the Liberals Briggs and Molesworth. A Liberal electoral pamphlet 'Cloggers Chips', depicting a conversation in a Clogger's shop in Blackburn, lays out the case against voting for Daniel. Strong, a tackler, states 'Ther's one thing certain – a w'se nod vooat for Daniel this time, an aw believe ther's mony a scoor o' my sooart i'th same mind.' When asked why, Strong replied, 'Wod hes he done for th' teawn after o his fine promises? Nowt.' 'Our Dan' had upset local opinion over his response to accidents on a railway crossing; when asked by a deputation of his constituents to help them 'protect lives', he had apparently replied that he was there to 'protect property'. This was held against him by the Liberals during the election campaign; as was his silence over cotton duties and his opposition to Sunday closing of public-houses. When the election results were declared at around 11 o'clock on 18 April he had been unseated by Briggs (6349) and Coddington (6267) and come third with 6008 votes in a general election that saw the return of a Liberal government under Gladstone.[58]

Thereafter, Daniel retired from politics. He was by now a substantial landowner. In 1878 he had bought the Gregory half share in Woodfold on the understanding that on the death of Miss Mary Gregory, then aged thirty-six, she would settle the money on his youngest grandchild. Daniel might have been criticised as aloof and uncaring as an MP in Blackburn but as a landowner he had an excellent rapport with his tenants in Mellor. Villagers reported how he had 'put his right shoulder to the wheel to roll away the vast incubus of damp, swamp, and dilapidations, the nurseries of ill-health, that encumbered miserably that manor, and so sorely impeded its occupiers.' Daniel was tireless in overseeing improvements to the eight hundred acre estate and never happier than seeing the land drained, draughty farmhouses and cottages repaired, walls rebuilt, hedges mended and plantations thinned. As Neil Summersgill, the Mellor historian, points out, this not only beautified the landscape but, practical as ever, Daniel provided employment during the winter months of an agricultural depression for labourers. In 1881 he donated land and £500 to build a village church school which he opened in 1883. The same care and improvement were given to his Leicestershire estate at Freeby in the heart of fine hunting country near Melton Mowbray, where he was a magistrate and a Deputy-Lieutenant of the county. In Scotland, he owned property in Perthshire and the Barwhillanty estate at Castle Douglas in Kirkudbrightshire. All these properties were immaculately maintained, for he was known as 'a good landlord' to his many tenants, to the undoubted benefit of future generations.[59]

He brought, what a friend William Tattersall, described as, an 'untiring diligence and the closest application' to everything he did. When he decided that Blackburn needed an up-to-date shopping precinct, he commissioned a splendid edifice of the best quality design and materials. Old buildings were demolished in Church Street and he had built the Thwaites Arcade to house twenty-six shops. The Arcade ran from Church Street to Lord Street and was closed at each end by beautiful wrought iron gates. Inside, each shop contained immense glass windows set in black and gold frames. Iron girders supported the arched plate-glass roof and the walls above the windows were covered in patterned blue tiles while the floor was bordered in mosaic. The effect was almost *fin-de-siecle* Parisian art-nouveau and altogether judged most attractive at the opening ceremony on 15 February 1883 conducted by the Mayor of Blackburn.

The prosperous trading years of the mid-1870 boom had been replaced by a general recession with a swift fall in beer consumption after 1880. 'Dullness seems to pervade every town in England,' noted Truman at Christmas 1884, 'even Messrs Bass & Co. at this the chief brewing season in the year are not in full work. This is owing to the great and universal Depression of English Trade in the country, and the extreme poverty of the working classes.' Competition in a declining beer market hardened as the Burton brewers increased their discounts, while other brewers had to resort to tying arrangements to keep their trade going. This unleashed a feeding frenzy to tie the free trade and, in order to buy property on an unprecedented scale, brewers raised the necessary capital by converting their partnerships into limited liability companies with public ownership of the shares.[60]

Guinness was the first to take the plunge in the London market aided by the celebrated company promoter Osborne O'Hagan. The issue was a gigantic success and whetted the public's appetite for brewing companies, just as prosperity returned in 1886. Over the following fifteen years, the large brewing partnerships took the path to limited liability company status so as to modernise their breweries and acquire public-houses. Daniel, too, was primed to take this route in 1886, judging from a letter which lies on file at the Brewery. Negotiations were in progress to form a limited company, Hargreaves Kay, a local solicitor, wrote. 'Mr Thwaites has expressed his willingness to dispose of the business upon terms to be agreed.' If the scheme was approved 'there seems little doubt that the applications for Shares will be much more numerous than can be met.'[61]

Daniel never went ahead with the scheme. He had several severe attacks of gout and was clearly in failing health. When he left Billinge Scarr for London in the spring of 1888, William Tattersall noticed a great change in his friend's appearance and 'a loss of mental activity.' Daniel had much to look forward to in London where his daughter Elma was to be married to Robert Yerburgh MP for Chester in the summer. The wedding had to be postponed for several weeks owing to Daniel's ill-health. It eventually took place on 8 August 1888, after which Daniel and Eliza travelled to Barwhillanty. The newly married couple were able to join them in September. Early on the Friday morning of 21 September, Daniel was seized by a stroke and died. Elma and Robert brought his body to St Mary's Church at Mellor where, on 25 September, he was buried next to his re-interred infant son in the Thwaites vault.

With 'well directed diligence' he had arranged his affairs. He left a probated estate of £464,516 [equivalent to about £28 million today] but this sum excluded the value of his extensive settled land estates in Lancashire, Leicestershire and Scotland. After many substantial bequests to his family and nephews and nieces, he left the Snig Brook Brewery to his nephew William Ward. He left the Eanam Brewery, hotels and public-houses to be sold at the discretion of his executors, William Ward and Joseph Aston, a barrister friend; and the proceeds, together with his personal estate, were left in trust with the entailed estates for his daughter Elma Yerburgh. Daniel directed that the two executors, while carrying on the Eanam Brewery until a sale, could employ William Ward as Manager at a salary of £800 a year. After Daniel's will was read, the future ownership of the Brewery looked to be anything but assured.[62]

The Thwaites arcade in Blackburn opened in 1883 and demolished in 1971. Amongst the businesses it also housed the Central Conservative Club.

The Public-House in 1857

*'The corner public[house] is radiant of gas, redolent of mahogany,
and glittering in mirrors! There are no settles, no stools, the old dun
coloured taps and parlours are all transformed into gorgeous saloons
or refulgent halls; or else the [upper]room is arranged as a theatre for
music, song and scenic performances ... At the bar the dropper in to
drink must stand their drink and move on when tired.'*
Building News, 15 May 1857[1]

A MAN, AND IT was still usually a man, dropping into his local in Blackburn in 1857 found the arrangements somewhat altered from earlier in the century. The scene of cosy domesticity furnished by the Regency alehouse, with its cottage-style kitchen and small parlour bar, had been exchanged for one of commercialised drinking provided by the urban Victorian public-house, with its horseshoe or 'O' shaped bar-counter and radiating partitions. The mid-19th-century public-house could not be mistaken for a private house. It was a place planned for the purpose of selling drink and, accordingly, its bar-counter dominated the room in which, for the first time, the customers' space and service area were designed as one unit.

No longer could a Victorian wander in, sit down and ensconce himself for an evening of chat with a few friends while the publican or landlady came out to take the orders for drinks and supplied some food. Instead, he straightaway went to stand by the bar where he ordered a drink, which was slapped down in front of him; he paid for it, drank it and then either ordered another or left. As a Parliamentary witness confirmed in 1877, men seldom used public-houses 'now as clubs for spending an evening in but rather went to them mainly for the simple purpose of drinking.' This enabled the publican to cope, first, with the new conditions of competition stemming from the 1830 Beer Act and, second, with both the larger numbers of customers and the changes in their requirements.[2]

This break with tradition owed much to the introduction of the gin palace in the 1830s. Its seedy precursor was the gin shop subsisting in the dank, dirty courts and alleys of the most miserable parts of London, Liverpool, Leeds, Manchester and the larger towns. After the Government reduced the duty on spirits in England in 1825, which had caused a jump in consumption, the widespread adoption of gas-lighting and plate-glass, which, like a contagious disease, had spread through drapers and haberdashers, chemists and hosiers, next 'burst forth with tenfold violence among the publicans and keepers of "wine vaults".' From that moment, in Dickens's description of the epidemic, 'onward it has rushed to every part of town, knocking down all the old public houses, and depositing splendid mansions, stone balustrades, rosewood fittings, immense lamps, and illuminated clocks at the corner of every street.'[3]

Looking back on this period, Henry Vizetelly wrote that Thompson & Fearon's of Holborn Hill, famous for the introduction of young barmaids, was the first London gin palace. He recalled its 'polished mahogany counters, the garish bar fittings, the smartly painted vats, inscribed "Old Tom" and "Cream of the Valley", the rows of showy bottles of noyeau [a liqueur of brandy flavoured with nut kernels] and other cordials, and above all the immense blaze of gas lights within and without these buildings as soon as dusk set in, were all so many novelties and came as a vision of splendour to the besotted denizens of the neighbouring slums.' And he also remembered that another 'of these so-called palaces had a second and lower counter for the accommodation of the children and juvenile thieves it counted among its patrons.[4]

At a time when gas-lighting in streets and public thoroughfares was in its infancy and rarely found in the poorer neighbourhoods, any gas-lit building was conspicuous, so that, at nightfall, the light blazing out of shop fronts and gin palaces acted as a siren to entice customers within. As Dickens noted, London drinking establishments were quick to adopt this novel form of advertisement; he saw at one place that '50 or 60 jets in one lantern were throwing out their capricious and fitful but brilliant gleams, as if from the branches of a shrub. And over the doors of a third house were no less than three enormous lamps with corresponding lights, illuminating the whole streets to a considerable distance. They were in full glare on this Sunday evening; and through the doors of these infernal dens of drunkenness and mischief, crowds of miserable wretches were pouring in that they might drink and die.'[5]

Although gin palaces appeared throughout London and other large urban centres, it was those in the slums that attracted the most notoriety, largely because the semi-starving become drunk very easily, and through both the caricatures of George Cruikshank (who later turned teetotal in 1848) and the journalism of Charles Dickens in *Household Words*, the better-off and educated classes were shocked to learn that the poverty-stricken drank themselves into oblivion in such luxurious surroundings. Furthermore, perpendicular drinking, reliant upon fast service and fast turnover, heralded what Girouard, the architectural historian of the Victorian public-house, terms one of the major 19th-century marketing discoveries: 'that if turnover is big enough there is money to be made out of the poor and

Tom and Jerry at a "Gin Shop" drinking Blue Ruin, by George Cruickshank.

they can be given something approaching the amenities of the rich' even though 'the rich found this very upsetting.'[6]

There was, moreover, much else that was novel, besides perpendicular drinking and gas-lights hung from curlicued wrought-iron brackets, to welcome the customer at a gin palace. From the spring doors – 'carefully hung so as to fly open with a touch and shut at an instant,' marvelled Edward Wakefield – to the gleaming long bar-counter – 'of French-polished mahogany, elegantly carved' which, Dickens reported, 'extends the whole width of the place'; and from the profusion of burnished brass rails to the intricately inscribed plate-glass doors and panels, publicans

and licensees vied with their rivals to provide the richest arrangements, and the experience of drinking amid such unimagined glamour and luxury offered people an ephemeral release from the meanness of their existence.[7]

While the dazzling splendours of the city gin palace barely penetrated the darkness of country towns such as Blackburn, publicans and brewers incorporated details of its style and marketing techniques into their mid-century public-houses. When, as part of a refurbishment programme, Daniel contracted to build the Grapes Inn in King William Street in 1849 and the Sir Charles Napier at Shear Brow in 1857, they were fitted with porticoes and ornamental parapets; their large plate-glass windows were unadorned with curtains so that, as Dickens wrote of a contemporary public-house, 'the transparent windows with the fire and light, looking so bright and warm from the cold darkness out of doors,' acted as an advertisement for the comforts to be sampled within. Gas lighting, which was widely used by the 1840s in Lancashire public buildings and the larger houses – Accrington was first lit by gas in December 1840 and Blackburn had formed its first gas company in 1837 – modernised the Thwaites properties; large gas lamps hung from wrought-iron or brass brackets outside all the public-houses. Inside, the carved polished mahogany bar-counters gleamed as did the bottles full of coloured liqueurs and cordials and the glasses arranged in the bar-back to be decorative as well as handy for dispensing orders to the perpendicular drinkers. The influence of the gin palace was also felt in the increased costs of the raw materials required to equip these public-houses to the higher fashionable standards of the day. Some idea of the costs incurred by the Thwaites partnership in 1857 can be realised from the opening of another Blackburn public-house at this date. The contract for the modest Hutchinson Arms states that it had to be built and equipped ready for inspection by the magistrates within three months at a cost of £668 [about £29,000 today].[8]

The impetus for brewers and publicans to build new public-houses and update old ones was, as ever, with a view to increasing trade; in the Victorian age that meant making them more conspicuous so as to differentiate them from the increasing number of competitors on every street. Whilst this had also been true of the gin palace, by the mid-century other influences were apparent in the development of the style associated today with the archetypical Victorian public-house. This style was characterised, first of all, by the prevalence of glass decoration used with evident abandon on door panels, partitions, bar-backs, bar screens and walls. The abolition of excise duty on plate-glass; the development in Bristol in 1850 of an apparatus for deep or brilliant-cutting of large panels of glass; and the inspiring effect of Paxton's design for the Crystal Palace, based on the great glass Conservatory at Chatsworth, and built to house

the successful Great Exhibition of 1851 in Hyde Park; all combined to inspire a fashion adopted by the retail and the brewing trade. As J. Callingham wrote about the art of glass embossing and lettering in 1871, 'Within the last few years it has been brought to a marvellous state of development; and its superiority over any other method of surface decoration has led to its very general adoption in the more tastily fitted-up public-house bars of the metropolis, and of the better class of public-houses in the leading provincial towns. It is now no uncommon thing for the inside walls of a richly decorated spirit bar to be entirely covered with glass, wither embossed or written on in burnished or matt gold.'

The apogee of this craftsmanship was achieved with the looking glass or mirror glass, which provides the second predominant element of the Victorian public-house style. It has been suggested that the published designs by Alfred Stevens in the 1850–1860s for the interiors of Robert Holford's palatial new mansion Dorchester House in Park Lane, London were the inspiration for the lush decoration so characteristic of later Victorian public-houses. In particular, the specially designed fittings for the saloon and dining room 'with their carved mahogany frames, cut and engraved mirrors,' introduced the large looking-glasses framed with or set into panels of carved, grained and marbled wood, a style popularised and adapted for the mass-market by the Exhibition of 1862, where embossed mirror-glass was fitted into furniture and hung in carved frames on the walls. Beautiful effects were achieved with scroll designs, gilding, back painting and led to the production of the brewers' advertising mirror: such a glass mirror advertising Daniel's best bitter still hangs in the Thwaites Brewery today.[10]

Any glimpses of bare wall interspersed between the profusion of glass and mirrors in the bar-rooms would clearly spoil the design effect. The brewing trade, unlike the rich landowners, could not afford the hand-blocked expensive

Decorative containers were deliberately introduced to make the environment more appealing.

wallpapers used to decorate mansions and London townhouses. It is highly likely, however, that when wallpapers first appeared in public-houses, they did so in Lancashire. For it was a local firm, Potters of Darwen, that in 1841 mastered the technique of roller printing paper on a calico printing machine and, thus, the production of wallpaper on a commercial scale. Later in the century, the familiar embossed wallpaper appeared on ceilings, walls and friezes when Lincrusta (1870s) and Anaglypta (patented in 1887) were developed and eagerly adopted by the trade as relatively inexpensive and durable; coverings, in the case of Anaglypta, still used in the present day public-house.[11]

The adoption of rich decorative and architectural effects in public-house design was made feasible by the growth of a national railway network, which transported these novel

building materials at a low cost. The resultant flamboyant styles did not satisfy everyone. When the brewing trade started to embrace medievalism in the style of High Victorian Gothic architecture, it infuriated John Ruskin. As the high priest of the Victorian Gothic revival movement and author of its seminal texts *The Seven Lamps of Architecture* (1849) and *The Stones of Venice* (1851), Ruskin famously deplored such commercialisation and corruption of his ideas, declaring in the *Pall Mall Gazette* in 1872: 'I have had indirect influence on nearly every cheap villa-builder between Denmark Hill and Bromley; and there is scarcely a public house near the Crystal Palace but sells its gin-and-bitters under pseudo-Venetian capitals copied from the church of the Madonna of Health or of Miracles.' Ruskin might have been expected to support the cultural aspirations of the licensed victualler; he was, after all, well-connected with the Trade through his prosperous father John James Ruskin, founder of the sherry business Ruskin, Telford & Domecq. Ruskin objected to the mass-production of materials but it is unlikely, however, that he ever patronised a public-house sufficiently to be able to form a measured opinion of the display of Gothic decorative effects.[12]

This is hardly surprising, for one of the changes registered by the 1857 public-house was in its customer base. The educated classes were abandoning it and, instead, preferred to drink elsewhere. The Regency young bloods, the professional men, the clergymen and the gentlemen no longer frequented the inn and alehouse as they had been pleased to do in 1807. It was a matter of reputation. As the Hon Algy Bourke, secretary of White's Club in London, loftily pronounced, 'The class I deal with and the class I associate with and the class I know do not go into public houses.' So they drank instead at home, in clubs or the smart new restaurants and cafes opening up in cities, and some of them even swallowed the Temperance propaganda. Public-houses became places lacking social cachet and, to some, respectability.[13]

Publicans, however, were far too busy to notice the finer points of social fashions. The years between the end of the Crimean War in 1855 and 1880 were notable for the

The busy scene inside a public-house in 1858 at 9 o'clock in the evening.

mounting prosperity of the nation. People had more money to spend and chose to spend more on drink. Consumption started to rise in the mid-1850s and public-house staff were rushed off their feet as, by 1876, the average Englishman drank more beer than he had ever drunk before, some 34.4 gallons in that year.

The man pushing his way in through the swing doors of a Victorian public-house in Blackburn was, therefore, most likely to be a working man. As the mid-century wore on, he might be accompanied by a working woman for Lancashire women were also wage-earners, often 'a t' mill', and independent working class women felt no shame about drinking in public-houses. If the man was a cotton, coal or factory worker, a labourer or a railway 'navvie', he came in his working clothes and stood in the public bar, resting a dusty boot on the brass rail below the bar-counter. The floor, as in 1807, was wooden and sprinkled with sawdust, interrupted by carefully placed spittoons. By the 1870s, most publicans had re-introduced some seating to the public bar area, usually a 'perforated wood back and seat' bench along one wall, though here the need for quick service and turnover remained paramount. Children were still legally allowed into public-houses to buy beer but it had been illegal for the under-16s to purchase spirits since 1839. The majority of children and women who came in did so to fetch drink for home consumption and went to the special jug-and-bottle area with its own serving hatch.

Drinking in the Victorian, as opposed to the Regency, public-house was a socially segregated occupation; and the social hierarchy was dictated solely by the requirements of the customer. Thus, if the man was a shopkeeper, a clerk, a craftsman and of the white collar brigade or anyone who did not wish to drink in the presence of what he doubtless termed the 'lower orders', the intricately embossed glass panelled entrance door that swung shut behind him bore the burnished lettering 'Saloon Bar'. Into this select room, the publican and brewing company had poured a great deal of money and the master craftsman had fashioned 'a scene of lavish opulence.'

Dominating the room and rising to the ceiling was a highly elaborate mahogany overmantel, containing a large

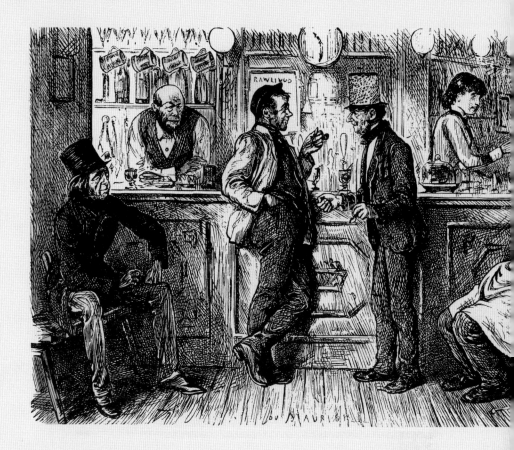

mahogany striking clock, all of which towered over the large open fireplace. Walls shone with patterned mirrored glass divided into panels framed in mahogany. The bar-counter carried an array of little screens known as 'snob screens' and composed of minature gilded or painted

Customers passing the time of day propping up the bar; many seats had been removed from inns during this period. Depicted by George du Maurier in 1879.

THE DRAM-DRINKER.—DRAWN BY KENNY MEADOWS.

CHARACTERS ABOUT TOWN.

The dram drinker and a child in her mother's shawl and bonnet likely to "slily lift the potion to their white withered lips"

brilliant-cut glass panels set in the typical mahogany frames, like half-opened windows, which pivoted on their vertical axes and screened the smarter saloon bar customer desiring privacy from both the common drinker in the public bar and the barmaid. The prolific use of glass and mirror was not purely for decorative effect; they enabled the publican and barmaid to keep an eye on customers in corners and alcoves or those with their backs turned to them, and were, accordingly, welcomed by licensing magistrates as suitable supervisory fittings.

The comforts of the saloon bar included flourishes of large green ferns in polished brass urns and smaller flowerpots dotted about the room. Beneath the wall mirrors and partition glass, horsehair padded leather seats and armchairs offered repose while, throughout the carpeted room, groups of customers perched on upholstered upright mahogany chairs clustered round heavy cast-iron circular tables with little brass rails encircling the marble tops to protect the glasses. In here, the more solid Blackburn citizen never needed to hurry over his drink and he could nurse all evening a pint of bitter or a glass of the by-now popular Scotch whisky for which pleasure he paid a higher price than in the public bar.

The Victorian public-house remained a focal point of local working-class life in Blackburn, as its leisure and culture still centred upon drinking. 'Strong drink is the secret of its own and Britain's greatness,' proclaimed the *Free Lance* in 1867, 'Be sober, and lead a decent and respectable life and your genuine Blackburner will wax red at the mention of your name, and dismiss you as a " – Dissenter"'. The publican offset any threat to his trade from proliferating beer houses by remaining at the forefront of sporting and social activities; the upper room continued to be used for meetings and large dinners, as it had been in 1807. When the Blackburn Cricket Club held an annual meeting in 1840, it chose the Bay Horse Inn 'and had an excellent dinner.' By 1852, with a larger membership of some 80 people, the annual dinner and ball was held at the Star and Garter, Stony-butts. Choral groups also frequented public-houses, with the Accrington Choral Society gathering at the Black Bull or the Red Lion Inn. The Blackburn Choral Society rehearsed at the Angel Inn, King Street before the annual concert held at the parish church. In 1850 Daniel was one of the patrons attending its performance of 'Handel's sacred oratorio' in aid of the new girls' charity school. John Dunlop was one temperance supporter who railed against the way publicans drummed up business in this way: 'Publicans use all manner of schemes to allure and attract by means of games, music, getting up country wakes, bull baiting, quoit playing, bowling, wrestling, running, boxing, horse racing, card playing, skittles, Dutch pins, bumble puppy, drafts, dominoes and other entertainments. And the intimate and inseparable connexion in this country between these amusements and drinking is most disastrous and an astonishment to other nations.'[14]

By the 1850s, however, customers, especially younger ones, were demanding entertainments over and above these pastimes, games and sporting activities organised or overseen by publicans. As reported in the *Northern Monthly* 'It is not in the concert halls, though professedly devoted to music for the millions, that one finds the real working classes, or learns what is the sort of musical entertainment that has the greatest attractions for the lower strata of the people. It is the singing saloon that is characteristically theirs.' The opportunity to provide variety shows and also serve drink, which was prohibited in theatres, as was smoking, was seized by publicans in Lancashire where ballad-singing in public-houses had long been customary. So popular did these new variety performances prove that the upper rooms of public-houses were soon far too small to hold the crowds seeking entry; publicans must needs commandeer any available space such as stable yards, billiard rooms and even their own sleeping quarters to create a long room to accommodate a wider public audience.

This room, the singing saloon or, in effect, the public-house music hall, contained seating in the form of benches and tables arranged in rows at right angles to the singers' table at the front, which served also as the stage. Amid the fug and noise of these saloons, people moved freely between tables, as did the perambulating barmen or waiters (who also doubled as singers) laden with liquid refreshments; publicans insisted upon frequent breaks within performances to order drinks and thereby increase the takings, which otherwise depended upon cheap entry tickets or 'nobbing' – passing the hat around. Singing saloons varied in sophistication and organisation. At the successful Star Concert Room opened in Bolton in 1840 and rebuilt in 1855, the landlord William Sharples offered as an evening's entertainment a string and brass band, madrigal singers, comedians, a Negro melodist and histrionic sketches, which attracted an audience of over one thousand people. Further down the performance scale was the saloon featuring 'a piano, a seedy gentleman with a violin, a remarkably easy and assured but debauched looking young man who sings comic songs, and one or more female singers, prodigal of their poor and faded charms.' And, finally, the small-scale public-house where 'you cannot hear a word; there is music, and there is a collier and his wife fighting, and a child crying, and that they call a concert room; it is all in front of the bar.'

One constant factor among the varied types of singing saloon was the youthfulness of the audience. According to a Manchester witness, of the attendance at a local singing saloon over seven Saturdays in 1852, 10 per cent were under 15 years of age, and 25 per cent between 15 and 20 years of

age, and the majority of them were unattached to any family party. The young loved singing saloons because they provided somewhere to go on Saturday nights where wage-earning adolescent men and women could drink, smoke, have fun and indulge in courtship out of sight of their parents. Concern over the corruption of these young people in such degenerate places spilled over in letters to the newspapers. In Bolton 'all the thieves, and bad characters of the town' were to be found on Saturdays in a 'notorious singing saloon' where 'no fewer than five hundred boys under or about the age of fifteen years congregated.' Middle class correspondents feared the degrading effects of the saloons as they were attended 'by our sabbath scholars, by the young lads of respectable families and by young women who are to be wives and mothers of a large and important class of our town population.' In Blackburn, Whittle noted that although the passage of the short time bill had given more leisure hours for factory workers, they were not spending their free time at concerts or at home but 'they run to foolish singing

The more acceptable face of the public-house with all ages enjoying conversation and fun epitomised by the bar billiards set up on the table. The picture itself is taken much later, showing the persistence of the games culture introduced in the 19th century.

The temperance movement draws attention to the Wheat and Barley destroyed to make gin and beer.

THESE are the *Drinks* that are sold night and day,
At the bar of the Gin-shop, so glittering and gay.

rooms in Shorrock fold and Darwen Street where depravity prevails and normality is at a low ebb.' Despite widespread criticism, the singing saloons of public-houses remained as popular as ever. It was not until the 1880s that the large formal music halls were opened as completely independent variety theatres and, gradually, they superseded the singing saloons in popularity.[15]

The Victorian public-house retained its traditional connection with musical entertainment, however, through the 'free-and-easies'. These were informal neighbourhood gatherings at the local where a miscellany of singing and recital was largely provided by volunteer talent from the audience. They were supervised by the publican with the assistance of a pianist and required neither extra premises, nor extra staff, nor any special licensing and would live on in Lancashire public-houses until well into the next century. In spite of any number of alternative attractions, such as social clubs, Mechanics Institutes, museums and public libraries, as the century progressed, nothing proved more comfortable and enjoyable for working people than their local Victorian public-house where 'they can combine the drinking of the Saturday night glass and the smoking of the Saturday night pipe with the seeing and hearing of a variety of entertainments.'[16]

A classic public-house interior showing the lack of seats, the partitions and the elaborate woodwork with the clock inset at its centre.

The Barmaid

THE MOST REMARKABLE aspect for Edward Wakefield about Thompson & Fearon, one of the earliest London gin palaces, was that 'Here gin is served by young women dressed up like the *belle limonadière* of a Paris coffee house.' In the 1830s 'four handsome, sprightly and neatly dressed young females, but of modest deportment were employed there and the opportunity of casting a scrutinising glance at the so-highly spoken of barmaids operated as a spell, and myriads … were drawn in thither.'[1]

Thomas Rowlandson's barmaid provides a singular example of freshness amongst her bibulous customers.

Barmaids started to appear everywhere. The first *Bradshaw* timetable in 1839 almost gasped that there was a refreshment bar at Wolverton railway station with 'a female in attendance'. When the male staff left a fashionable City public-house to fight in the Crimean War in 1854 and the landlord replaced them with barmaids, such was the sensation they caused that other public-houses rapidly followed suit. As did music halls; it was said of the first hall purpose-built in the West End in 1861 that 'the brightest, most glittering, and most attractive thing about the bars was the barmaids.' And luxury restaurants were not far behind; at the Criterion in Piccadilly, the barmaids operated in shifts: 'one corps would march out from behind the bars and others would relieve them like soldiers relieving the sentry.' In all of these places, the spectacle of barmaids serving drinks to customers was found to be exceedingly good for business.[2]

It was traditionally women rather than men who had brewed and served liquor in early England. They brewed the ale, first for their families and then for sale in alehouses, and were known as brewsters; men came into the trade later and displaced them as brewers. Women, however, continued to help their husbands and families in alehouses and later public-houses.

What was different about the modern 19th century barmaid was her position and status. She was a product of the new type of urban Victorian public-house, which was bigger, with higher ceilings, and designed to service a more rapid turnover of customers in the expanding cities and towns. The great innovation in the newly designed public-houses was the fixture known as the bar-counter which separated the barmaid from the customers, as a counter separated a shop assistant from the shoppers in a chemist's or grocer's shop. Drinks could be supplied more effectively and securely in a crowded public-house while the barmaid gained authority from her central position in charge behind a bar-counter, which also provided the necessary distance or buffer to protect her from unseemly attention.

The recognition of the barmaid's place in Victorian public life was confirmed by a contemporary cartoon showing Queen Victoria wearing her crown and jewels on duty as a barmaid behind John Bull's bar. The barmaid, in all but the roughest houses, adopted the universal rule that she 'must wear black dresses … and a large apron of the same material,' softened by white collars and cuffs; and under no circumstances enhance her appearance with false hair and busts. In this uniform the saloon barmaid considered herself superior to the domestic servants and shopclerks of Victorian and Edwardian England for 'behind the bar she is the mistress of the situation,' the journalist Barbara Drake observed, 'and an absolute despot.' She was no mere poor housemaid, who had graduated to service at the bar of a small public-house; she was a young lady from a higher social class, who preferred to be a modern barmaid working in a better establishment, be it public-house, music hall, theatre or restaurant bars which catered to the upper and middle ranks of society, and to earn a higher wage than a lowly clerk or governess. She earned a starting wage of 8–10s a week in Edwardian London and also received board and lodging; as an experienced saloon barmaid in a good public-house she could earn 15s and even more in the large music halls. Wages were lower in Lancashire but, even in Blackburn, where barmaids were introduced later, their wages were higher than other semi-skilled female occupations.[3]

Yet her work was also a great deal more arduous than that of, say, a clerk. Eliza Orme's report on the conditions of work of barmaids for the Royal Commission on Labour in 1893–4 stated that a standard working day of some 12 hours or so, making a 70–80 hour week, was usual in the trade. Barmaids started work at seven in the morning, had 4–5 hours for meals, dressing – they changed into more formal black clothes for the evening – and rest, and otherwise were habitually on their feet until they sank into bed at midnight. The journalist Maureen Cleave found that the barmaid of the late 1960s earned a weekly wage of up to £14 a week or £10 live and sleep-in. She started work at

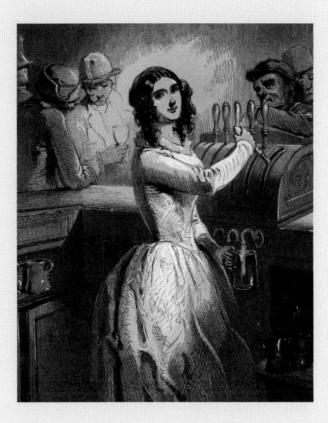

By 1849 the barmaid had become a stock (and welcome) figure in the nation's public-houses.

ten in the morning; washed floors, polished glasses and cleaned bottles, just as her Edwardian predecessors had; worked the lunchtime session from 11 to 3; took half an hour off for lunch; and worked from 5:30 till 11 in the evening, after which she cleared up.[4]

The long and tiring working conditions attracted the attention of evangelical and temperance reformers alike. In 1904, their lives suddenly became "the barmaid problem" and articles appeared in the national press about "the barmaid's lot." These campaigners prepared a memorial to the licensing justices against the employment of young women in public bars. They contended that much evil was occasioned by their occupation and sought 'to preserve the virtue, modesty, and physical strength of the future womanhood of the land.' Reformers cast the barmaid in the role of a moral victim, corrupted by drink and vulnerable to seduction; they were convinced of the publican's sexual and economic exploitation of these young women – why else

would they advertise in the trade for women under twenty years old and ask applicants for *carte de visites* (photographs)? And, they concluded, she was only 'employed by the publican as a decoy for men, and her very existence depends on her ability to attract.'[5]

The sirens of the bar fought back as best they could against the elimination of their jobs. They supported their employees' counter attack against the reformers, joined the Manchester Barmaids' Political Defence League, which was based in Manchester and organised by two suffragists to defend the women's right to work, and retained a self-reliant yet modest profile under the political scrutiny of opponents eager to catch the slightest hint in a deterioration of female delicacy and moral standards. The proposed licensing bill in 1908 included the phased but total extinction of bar-work for women, so there was much to fight for; fortunately for the barmaid, the measure failed, and she survives to this day as a central figure in the public-house. At Thwaites, the barmaid has more often become the women tenant, affectionately known as the landlady.

'Her graces are many, and her arts are countless,' an observer wrote and the barmaid undoubtedly succeeded in conveying to her customers a mixture of ministering angel and glamour. Described as 'a kind of moral salamander, living unharmed in the midst of the amorous furnace in which Destiny has placed her,' by a French visitor in the 1860s, she was 'protected from all human seductions behind the imposing serenity and the Olympian majesty of business.' A Lancashire man of the same period, cut through flowery foreign prose and put it, typically, more forthrightly when he wrote, in 1867, that 'Our Barmaid is good looking and she knows it ... We know it too. But she has to attend to business, as well as flirtation; and is unquestionably one of the industrial classes. From early morn to late at night she is ever on her feet. How many miles does she walk in the course of a day? ... How many orders does she take, and how does she remember them all? It's a mystery, how in spite of her slavery, she succeeds in looking so well, in being so brisk, and if it comes to that, in being so civil as she is.' For him and his fellow regulars, there was no mystery whatever about the universal appeal of the barmaid and the reason for her longevity as a great British institution. 'We like our barmaid, and would scarcely have her altered. With all her faults, if she has any, she is better than your man waiter,' he wrote rather endearingly. 'She is a civiliser as well as servitor. When she is present the conversation is decent, and any company with a spark of respectability about it is on its good behaviour. She works very hard, and is very badly paid. She conducts herself respectably and modestly. She is our Manchester barmaid.'[6]

Right Alma Bond in 1974 still pulling pints after 50 years at the Hand and Shuttle. *Below left* Thwaites Kaltenberg Hell lager and Lancaster Bomber are on offer at the Three Tuns. *Below right* Darwen "landladies", the term used for tenants.

Elma Yerburgh, Daniel's only daughter, who owned the brewery from 1888 to 1946. Painted at age 21 by Edward Fisher.

ELMA YERBURGH 1864–1946

CHAPTER FOUR

Elma Yerburgh 1864–1946

THERE CAN HAVE been few women in the late 19th century who became proprietors of a brewery whilst on their honeymoon tour, as Elma did. She was a married, financially independent woman of twenty-four and her education and upbringing had prepared her for a position in polite society, not for one in the rough male world of commerce. In contemporary eyes, there could be no doubt that her place was by her husband's side, demonstrating both her skills as a hostess and her devotion to the care of the children who would assuredly follow. Unlike so many genteel Victorian women, she did not need to endeavour to make a small income go as far as possible. On the contrary she was, like Thackeray's wealthy Miss Crawley in *Vanity Fair*, an object of great respect ' for she had a balance at her bankers which would have made her beloved everywhere.'[1]

Neither her father's advisers nor the Brewery managers would have been thought unduly precipitate if they held to the opinion that the Thwaites firm would shortly be for sale. It was, after all, a course of action sanctioned by her father's last will and he would have taken Henry Gornall and William Ward into his confidence. The staff at Eanam Brewery, however, would not have been previously enlightened as to their new proprietor's intentions; as in any work place throughout the ages, though, a change at the top generated uncertainty and must needs be of inexhaustible interest; and, when it concerned a woman in a man's world, could only inspire conjecture without end, such as, what would Mrs Yerburgh do? What would happen to Thwaites without "our Dan"?

Should Elma decide to continue the Brewery and become actively involved in the brewing business, however, she would risk transgressing the Victorian boundaries of female gentility. Married ladies of some means, whether aristocratic or middle class, did not then work; if they moved out of the domestic sphere into the male public sphere of trade and commerce, it was usually out of economic necessity and not from choice. Those ladies who did concern themselves with businesses were traditionally either widows or single women. This was largely because these women had had the same legal rights to property ownership as men. Upon marriage or remarriage, however, women had died 'a kind of civil death' for, in the words of the legal expert Sir William Blackstone, husband and wife were deemed to be one person and that person was the husband. Women thus had possessed no right to personal property except by means of a trust administered under the law of equity. This was the legal situation when Elma's parents married but, by the time she married in 1888, the Married Women's Property Act of 1882 had bestowed upon wives the same rights as single women to own all property and to have the right to dispose of it as they wished; all of which paved the way for a greater female participation in the economic and commercial life of the nation.

Gentlewomen, nevertheless, courted social opprobrium when they associated with such a male preserve. Lady Charlotte Guest, daughter of the Earl of Lindsay, was by birth an aristocrat but, after her father's death, her mother's second marriage to the family tutor was considered a *mésalliance* and Lady Charlotte could not therefore be presented to society. Her marriage to John Guest MP the

powerful iron industrialist, and a widower, pushed her further to the extremities, especially when she acted as his business helpmate and then successfully managed the huge ironworks after his early death in 1853. 'Though my husband is peculiarly formed to shine and rise, and is infinitely more eloquent than half the lordlings that I meet, and though I have my own rank which is high enough to assist me,' she wrote, she nevertheless had to struggle to achieve the social position to which she felt entitled by birth and wealth, but which her active role in industry had damaged. In examining the compromised femininity of her role, she observed that, 'the consciousness frequently obtrudes itself that in this aristocratic nation, the word Trade conveys a taint. I am determined to overcome the prejudice, I will force them, whether or no to disguise, if they do not forget its existence in my case.' And force them she eventually did. In recognition of her excellent day to day management of the Dowlais ironworks and the fortune and advantages she bequeathed to her family, her eldest son became the first Baron Wimborne.

Lady Charlotte Guest was an aberrant aristocrat in terms of her family situation and work; it was, however, still easier, for aristocratic women to manage estates, engage in public work and maintain investments without imperilling their femininity and their rank. Yet Lady Charlotte remained conscious of the disadvantage of her gender, reflecting that 'Sometimes I think I have succeeded pretty well – but every now and then I am painfully reminded that toil as I may, I can never succeed beyond a certain point and by a very large portion of the community my acquirements and judgements must always be looked upon as those of a mere woman.' It was even more difficult for women of middling rank who engaged in business; however genteel, they endangered their social position which, anyway, was less securely fixed than an aristocrat's, and they were generally considered and treated as the inferior sex. Elma was equally subject to the prescriptions of a woman's sphere and had to tread a careful path to protect her reputation against male doubts about the propriety of being engaged in business at all. Although she was by no means unique in her role as a brewery proprietor, her small

female peer group was, with one exception, widows.[2]

Sara Boorne (1859–1894) ran Wallington Brewery in Surrey for four years after the death of her husband. Elizabeth Gardner succeeded her husband in 1877, renamed the firm E. Gardner & Son of Coggeshall, Essex, and continued in partnership with her son until selling the Brewery to Greene, King and Sons in 1938. Another Essex Brewery at Foxearth was taken over and managed by widowed Charlotte Ward in 1878 until her son joined the partnership in 1887. Down in Dorset, Sarah Eldridge started

a brewery in Dorchester with her husband Charles in 1833. On his death in 1846 she ran it with a manager Alfred Mason whom she went into partnership with in 1850 and, in 1871, the Brewery became Eldridge Pope & Co.

When Elma became a proprietor in 1888 there were two other women in brewery partnerships in Lancashire. The widowed Mary Cardwell had become the sole owner of the Brewery in Preston in 1887. She would eventually sell out to Alfred Birtwhistle and Sons in 1895 and this business would eventually be acquired by a Thwaites

A characteristically male group on a day's outing from Bury to visit the Thwaites brewery in Blackburn in 1922.

competitor, Matthew Brown. The second Lancashire brewery, which became known as Hydes' Anvil Brewery, belonged to Annie Hyde, who was then in partnership with her brother William Hyde, in Manchester. Their father had died in 1880 leaving an insolvent business with debts of £4390 but the family came to an arrangement to pay their creditors 9p in the pound and succeeded in retaining the Brewery. Young and inexperienced, Annie and her brother thus had a difficult entry into proprietorship and had to work hard to establish a brewing firm that survives as an independent company today. Annie Hyde is remembered by her great nephew Neal Hyde as 'a tough and unyielding character who ran the financial side of the business to strict standards and with a rod of iron' yet 'could be extremely generous to people in trouble.' On one occasion, in the 1920s, her nephew was driving to Buxton when it started to snow. He realised that the car coming towards him was Annie's large chauffer driven Daimler; as it swept past him, he noticed that the rear hood was down and that her only concession to the inclement weather was to sit bolt upright with a raised umbrella to ward off the snow.[4]

Elma was more fortunate than Annie in that she had inherited not only a large fortune but also a solvent, prosperous business and had been placed under no obligation to continue it. Indeed, her father had directed his trustees to sell the Eanam Brewery at their discretion and place the proceeds in the same trusts as the entailed estate for the benefit of her and her children; the underlying assumption being that she would not want to be saddled with a brewery business in Lancashire when she could aspire to a great social position, and even become a leading political hostess, in London. This was certainly her mother's ambition for her and it was made all the more feasible by Elma's marriage.

Her husband Robert Yerburgh had been an M.P. for two years when she met him. He was experienced at the hustings, having unsuccessfully contested two elections before being elected as the Conservative Member for the formerly Liberal seat of Chester in August 1886. It was the first time that the Grosvenor interest was exercised on behalf of a Conservative as the Duke of Westminster had finally severed his political connection with Gladstone over the Home Rule Bill. Robert's win was part of a general swing to the Conservatives and enabled Lord Salisbury to form his second Cabinet. In March 1887, W.H. Smith moved from the War office to become leader in the Commons and Robert was singled out to become his private secretary. 'His appearance in Parliament will be welcome for he has an excellent knowledge of affairs,' enthused a London newspaper. 'He has great talents and will soon make a mark.'

He had long since made a mark in London Society. The Yerburgh family had been settled in Lincolnshire since the 11th century and from the earliest times had exhibited a partiality for the Church. Robert's grandfather, father and two of his brothers saw no need to deviate from this familial ecclesiastical preference and were followed into Holy Orders by numerous nephews. Although his grandfather and father were Cambridge men, in 1875 Robert went up to University College, Oxford after leaving Harrow. His choice was probably influenced by his mother's family from whom he inherited a small fortune and a connection with Lancashire. He was named after a godfather and great-uncle Robert Armstrong QC who died in 1869 and left him about £40,000 and several farms in the Lake District. The Armstrong and Higgin families were as partial to the Law as the Yerburghs were to the Church and, after a wonderful time at Oxford, Robert decided to become a barrister, probably through his uncle William Higgin, who was a member of Middle Temple, pleading on the Northern Circuit and chairman of Preston and Salford Quarter Sessions.

By this time, however, Robert, inclined to live in high style, had run through part of his Armstrong money after he and a cousin lost a considerable sum of money at the hands of 'a well-known man, of good family, but an unmitigated blackguard', who was afterwards imprisoned for fraud.

A beer container in the Thwaites museum.

Robert now had to find work as a barrister, which he managed to do through his uncle Higgin. Robert, however, found the Northern Circuit uncongenial and much preferred being in London where he enjoyed a reputation 'as a man about town'. He was considering whether or not to go out to South Africa at the invitation of his good friend Cecil Rhodes, when a fellow Oxonian, who was fervent about government policies, persuaded him to take up politics seriously. This Robert did, throwing himself heart and soul into it, and was rewarded with the customary political apprenticeship of contesting unwinnable seats. He graduated to the constituency of Chester and, after his election victory there in 1886, found himself at the centre of English public life.

Amongst his large circle of friends was Sir Harry Hornby, the Member for Blackburn, and it was while Robert was staying with him at Winfield House in 1888 that he met Elma. It was not at all surprising that Elma almost immediately agreed to marry him. Robert was the most extraordinarily attractive person. People spoke of how delightful he was and of his great charm and manner; they basked in his intelligent, persuasive company and enjoyed both his informed conversation and singular good looks. His closest brother wrote that 'Bob was, by nature, the kindest and most generous of men, and he was always ready to share with his brothers or his friends anything that he had.' He was popular, a fine horseman and a bold, skilled rider to hounds and he lived life to the full. In fact he was so busy enjoying himself that he had no time to exchange an innate modesty for arrogance and pomposity in the face of all this adulation.

Despite all his excellent personal qualities, he lacked certain attributes calculated to satisfy the father of an heiress, for he was a third son and had neither fortune nor estates. Daniel Thwaites, however, did not oppose the match. 'I believe he took a fancy to Bob from the very first,' Robert's younger brother Edmond Yerburgh explained, 'and Mrs Thwaites, who had great influence with her husband, was from the very first on Bob's side.' Robert and Elma had a very short engagement and, after their marriage, much to occupy them in settling her father's estate. Robert had

become through marriage a rich landed proprietor and concerned himself with both the management of Elma's estates and the agricultural issues of the day.[5]

The future of the Brewery, however, was quite another matter. Robert had no experience to bring to brewing management, and probably no inclination to involve himself in the business; he was, after all, already a busy man with many interests to engage him. Elma, of course, had no commercial experience either. What she did have to carry her through was a 'cool, cautious and deliberate temperament', her loyalty to her father and, finally, William Ward, the one member of the family *in situ* who could help her. William had been trained by her father, was his favourite nephew and retained his entire confidence and trust; furthermore, in his capacity as an executor and trustee of Daniel's will, he was also her trustee, and retained an interest in Thwaites through his position as General Manager and his inheritance of the Snig Brook Brewery.

Against all expectations, therefore, Elma decided not to sell Eanam Brewery. It was a courageous decision for a young Victorian woman to make, especially as she was going to start a family in the near future. She could only hope to continue the Thwaites firm with William Ward's co-operation and it says much for his character and the strength of their family affection that he remained at Thwaites and did not immediately leave to run his own brewery. He gave Elma unstinting support and the benefit of his experience and skills and, together with Henry Gornall, they set about maintaining the Thwaites reputation for good beer.

During the next seven years, Elma was chiefly occupied with family matters. Her two sons were born, Robert Daniel Thwaites Yerburgh in December 1889 and (Richard) Guy Cecil Yerburgh in November 1892. Her uncle John Thwaites died the year after her father, which entailed some financial restructuring of the public-houses in which he had retained an interest and which the Brewery continued to lease from his family. In accordance with her father's will, Elma had already transferred the sum of £200,000 settled on John's children. There was also a second Thwaites/Yerburgh marriage to celebrate, which delighted Robert. His brother, the Reverend Edmond Yerburgh married John's second daughter Constance Thwaites in 1890. Elma and Robert continued to spend the greater part of the year at 27 Princes Gate, which they kept on when they later took a house in Kensington Gore, interspersed with visits to Barwhillanty, to Woodfold, which they had finally moved into and refurbished, and to Caythorpe Court, a lovely house they had bought near Grantham and close to the Yerburgh stronghold at Sleaford in Lincolnshire.

By 1896, however, Elma was being drawn more closely into brewery affairs. Strategic decisions needed to be addressed about the status and management of the firm and about its growth in the face of fierce competition in the industry. Her father had clearly intended Thwaites to become a limited liability company and go public, but his ill health and death had prevented it. Elma's induction into the business had then precluded it, initially at least, at a time when the trading climate was against flotation. Beer consumption was stagnant, as the depression of 1876–85 returned, and the *Sharp* v *Wakefield* judgment in 1891, whereby magistrates could refuse the licences of those public-houses they believed were not required, reopened the prospect of losing licences on the whim of the magistracy without any compensation. William Ward was of the opinion that incorporation could be delayed no longer without damaging the firm's interests.

Thwaites was making good profits, the balance sheet for 1889–90 shows a net profit of £49,000. This amount equates to the profits of the Smiths at John Smiths of Tadcaster in West Yorkshire, a recent, modest brewery that, since 1847, had made a meteoric rise up the brewing ladder. When the brewery historian Barnard was entertained there 'in right royal style' in 1890, it elicited his comment, 'as well they might, on profits topping £50,000 in a good year', though more usually averaging £27,000. John Smith of Tadcaster, too, took the plunge in the second wave of flotations that seized brewing firms between Guiness going public in 1886 and the end of the speculative boom in 1899.[6]

In 1896, prosperity had returned as the economy improved, and in the fierce breakneck race to acquire tied house properties and restrict competition from rival businesses, brewing firms jumped into the surging flotation pool. Gourvish and Wilson described the years 1896–9 as 'the most extraordinary the industry had ever experienced. The number of incorporations more than doubled.' At Thwaites, Henry Gornall, who directed the property side with Henry Thompson, reported on the fierce competition in Blackburn. It was only to be expected that Duttons would waste no opportunity to buy up any public-house that came onto the market but, more worryingly, three other firms, Nuttalls, Shaws and Spring Vale in Darwen were aggressively entering the market. Thwaites could not allow itself to lose the competitive edge in its own sphere of influence. At a meeting held at Woodfold that year William Ward and Gornall urged Elma and Robert to take up the cudgels, as her father would have done, to maintain the Thwaites market share by raising the capital to fund a property spree.[7]

The Yerburghs were quickly persuaded that it was the right course of action to take, especially as Ward and Gornall were supported by the fifth member of the meeting, Benjamin Chaffers Roberts, whom Robert had brought into Thwaites. The only one present with extensive non-brewing business interests, Chaffers Roberts was a director of several Chester companies, the leader of the Conservative Party in Chester and the founder and Chairman of the Cheshire and North Wales Newspaper Co., a public company of which Robert and the Duke of Westminster were also directors. Elma had come to know and like him and had asked him to act with Robert and William Ward as co-trustees of the Daniel Thwaites Settlement Trusts.[8]

It was also as a result of this meeting that William Ward decided that the time had come for him to devote himself to the full ownership of the Snig Brook Brewery and follow the same route as he was advocating for the Eanam Brewery, namely to go public. Up to this point the properties of the two breweries had been managed together, and it made sense to separate the two businesses before the Thwaites flotation. It was also clear that, to retain profitability in such a competitive environment, Snig Brook would have to go public to increase its property portfolio of twenty-eight public-houses. Although he would have to

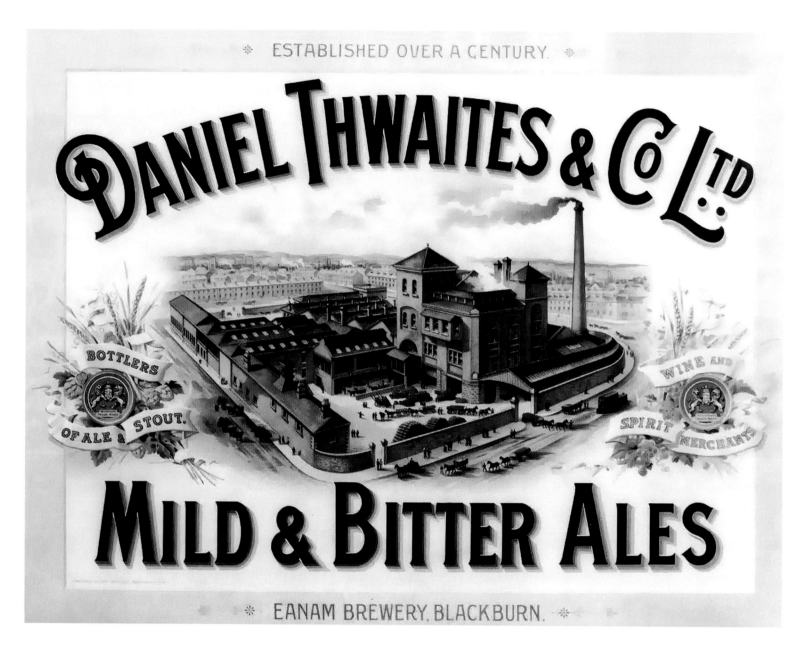

* ESTABLISHED OVER A CENTURY. *

DANIEL THWAITES & CO LTD

BOTTLERS OF ALE & STOUT.

WINE AND SPIRIT MERCHANTS

MILD & BITTER ALES

* EANAM BREWERY, BLACKBURN. *

The Brewery during Elma's chairmanship.

resign his position as General Manager of Thwaites, William Ward remained a trustee and even a neighbour, as he lived at Mellor near Woodfold Park.[9]

The race to float was thus set in train at Thwaites and, after lengthy consultations with a bevy of advisers, the company was incorporated as a limited liability company on 18 March 1897. The Thwaites approach was that most commonly taken for brewing flotations; the equity capital was entirely retained by the original partners who, as directors of the new company, proceeded to raise loan capital through the sale of preference shares and debentures. In the case of Thwaites, Elma transferred the business to a new company Daniel Thwaites and Co., for the sum of £850,000. The new Thwaites Company issued preference shares to the public in March and raised a nominal £134,000. In settlement of the £850,000 purchase money due to Elma, the Company issued to the Trustees (Robert, Ward and Chaffers Roberts) of the Daniel Thwaites Settlement Trust £250,000 in debenture stock and £64,925 in cash; and issued to Elma £400,000 in ordinary shares, £66,000 in preference shares and the £69,075 residue in cash. As Hargreaves Kay had prophesied back in 1886, the issue was fully subscribed. Thwaites was also at the forefront of a flurry of Blackburn brewery flotations. Shaws, with 114 public-houses, and Snig Brook, with 28, went public in April and were followed by Duttons and Nuttalls before the year was out.[10]

The first board meeting of the directors of Daniel Thwaites & Co. was held at 11 o'clock on 18 March 1897 at Woodfold Hall. Present were the chairman, Elma Yerburgh and two of the directors, Chaffers Roberts and Gornall, (Robert was unavoidably absent), the new secretary, Thomas Pickup and the company's solicitor John Mawdsley. The Eanam Brewery was fixed as the registered office of the company and Pickup's salary was agreed at £50 a year. This was most unsatisfactory to Pickup and, at the next Board meeting a week later, he made a case to the directors for a substantial increase and then withdrew while they discussed his salary. He was then called back into the room to be told that his salary was being raised to £400 per annum in addition to the £50 already set. He dutifully expressed his thanks to the directors and wrote up the rest of the minutes. He was not so fortunate at the May board meeting. Having taken the minutes for a discussion about staff wage increases and listed the exact amounts awarded to the nine senior staff in celebration of Queen Victoria's Diamond Jubilee, he submitted his own request for another addition to his salary. Elma was firm that his recent increase must suffice for the present and he was told on his return to the boardroom that his request had been declined. There was, though, an event

he could look forward to: the Jubilee Holiday granted to all the staff which took the form of a trip to Blackpool arranged and funded by Elma and the directors.[11]

After incorporation, the directors turned to the pressing task of buying tied property and building up an estate of good houses. At the same time a programme of modernisation and repairs to the existing properties was started. In all this, as the minute books testify, Elma took a leading part. At each meeting held throughout that Spring, Henry Thompson reported that 'On Mrs Yerburgh's instructions he had purchased this property' or that property; from King Wiliam Inn at Turton for £2500, to an Off-Licence at Fleetwood for £5910, or taken a lease on a hotel in Blackburn with a view to a future purchase of it. When repairs were sanctioned for the Black Bull at Ribchester it was Mrs Yerburgh, who pointed out that they must proceed in such a way as to interfere with business as little as possible.[12]

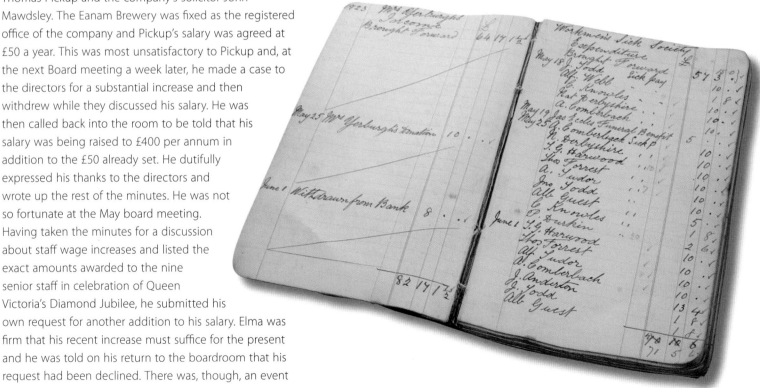

A page from Elma's meticulously kept charity books recording the welfare payments to sick members of staff.

In her careful attention to detail, conscientiousness in fulfilling her duties and decisiveness in business matters, she was her father's daughter. Constance Yerburgh thought Elma was 'so like her father,' and possessed his virtues and faults to a remarkable degree. Elma was an honourable, upright, just, unselfish woman and remained singularly modest and retiring all her life. As her father had sometimes appeared brusque and too forthright, so she sometimes appeared cold but, in both cases, a reticent nature and, in her case, shyness, lay at the root of their behaviour. Great wealth brought great responsibilities which Elma never shirked, but it did not automatically confer confidence and a wish to court publicity for the many kind and generous gifts and support she gave to others. She took a close interest in the welfare of her staff and many of the staff treats were provided at her instigation and often from her private purse. A sick workman or an ill member of his family would receive extra money and food. In December 1897, she introduced the tradition at Thwaites of a Christmas gift of 10 lbs of prime English beef to each workman and a goose or turkey for the office staff.[13]

She also proved to be, like her father, a good judge of character both in her appointments of senior staff at the Brewery and in the people from whom she sought advice. William Ward's resignation left a vacancy in the executive management of Thwaites. For this important position, and a Manager or General Manager then was the equivalent of a chief executive or managing director today, Elma took charge of the selection process. She engaged John Thorpe as manager of Eanam Brewery in April 1897. The son of a Lincolnshire vicar, Thorpe had gained a wide experience of the industry which included working at Mitchell and Butler in Birmingham. He was also well-connected in the trade as one brother held an important position with the large London brewers Mann, Crossman and Paulin and two others were at the Lion Brewery in Watford.[14]

Thorpe proved to be an excellent manager and, with the support of Chaffers Roberts in particular, set about introducing modern techniques and equipment to Thwaites. One of his first recommendations was for a wine and spirits division, an area of business that had somehow lapsed after the deaths in the 1870s of Daniel's cousins William and Daniel Thwaites of Beardwood Cliff. This Thwaites wine and spirit business was inherited by their brother-in-law Robert Coddington, who was a successful cotton broker in Liverpool and was delighted to put in a manager to run the business for him. After William Ward took over Snig Brook, he suggested a merger between the two firms and the new company Cunningham and T & W Thwaites floated in April 1897 with William Ward having a seat on the board and his brother-in-law Benjamin Ward Thompson acting as managing director. Thwaites, thus, needed to build up their own business in this area, and the decision was taken to start a wholesale wine and spirits division with Frank Rowe duly appointed Manager reporting to Thorpe.[15]

Next on Thorpe's agenda was equipment. New ice making machinery was to be built costing £1500; a new Hop store constructed; alterations had to be made to the Brewery tower to house new cold liquor tanks; three new boilers at £580 each were to be installed by Foster, Yates and Thom; when samples of water from the main well were found wanting, Thorpe persuaded the Board to invest in a new filter and connections for £210.

Thorpe certainly galvanised the operations of the Brewery. His chief innovation during the first year of tenure was to build and open a mineral and soft drinks department – called the Mineral Water Factory and Bottling Store – in Sparrow's Yard, Quarry Street, which was then connected by a bridge carrying the main steam pipe to the Brewery. He appointed Frank Hewitt as the manager in September 1898. This department proved profitable from the outset and a variety of mineral waters and soda siphons were bottled and supplied to the houses and clubs. Hewitt also established an essence store and the existence of numerous receipts, on cards and stuck into small books still at the Brewery, testifies to the variety and popularity of drinks bearing such names as "Rosebud", "Ginger Spice", and "Lemon Curl" as well as "Homemade Lemonade" and "Ginger Beer". These waters were bottled in thick but clear tapering glass bottles that contained glass 'marbles' inside the upper part which under pressure rose to the neck of the

bottle and became airtight. Bottled beer had little impact on the industry when it appeared in the 1870s – not one of the Burton Breweries bottled; it only began to become popular in the 1890s, even though the costs were high. Thwaites, like many brewers, had continued to produce a small amount of beer matured in bottles and closed by the cork or screwstopper. Thorpe and Chaffers Roberts, however, were keen to push the sale of bottled beer and use the bottles as a means of advertisement, especially

outside Blackburn where Thwaites was not so well known. It was decided to keep the matter 'carefully in view.' Advertising was approved, at Thorpe's suggestion, on show cards and in local newspapers at Christmas; Elma's only stipulation to this novel idea was that the words 'No connection with any other firm' be added.

All these innovations of 1897 were steadily increasing efficiency and bringing a greater professionalism to managing the company. Thorpe was able to report

increased beverage figures every month over the previous year and the Board was delighted when the sales figures for the first quarter of 1898 came in at 14,044 barrels as opposed to 10,617 for the first quarter of 1897.[16]

Modernisation, extension of the Brewery buildings, and the purchase of licensed property came at a price and, in December, the Board decided to increase the Company's capital and issued preference shares to the public, raising a further £100,000 to fund this expansionary programme.

At the same time, Chaffers Roberts had been astonished to discover that Board meetings were not held regularly: 'Mr Roberts is strongly of the opinion that the board should meet once a month', with the result that the second Monday of the month was fixed as Board day. In the same way, he stipulated that an Agenda paper be prepared for each meeting; that a statement of accounts for payment be submitted at each meeting and an arrangement be made for Thorpe and Pickup to be able to draw cheques for payment between meetings. None of this had been necessary in Daniel's day but it was now, due to the expansion of the business and the need for the company to meet the demands of a modern operation as the new century approached.[17]

The turn of the 20th century and its early years were unsettling for the brewing industry. The country was embroiled in the South African or Boer War during which four Thwaites men joined up and one man was killed. The new well bored near Quarry Street at a cost of £2165 was, in consequence, named Mafeking and the company contributed £100 to the South African War Fund. Henry Gornall's death in 1898 had ended an association with the Brewery lasting nearly forty years. Elma asked her cousin, John "Jack" Thwaites of the Troy branch to fill the vacancy

on the Board and Thorpe was promoted to become Managing Director and appointed to sit on several internal committees in place of Gornall. The death of Queen Victoria in January 1901 and the accession of Edward VII unsettled the nation; it was the greatest change to occur in the lives of three generations and few people could really remember the country under a king. H.G. Wells said that Queen Victoria was like a great paperweight that had sat upon people's minds, and when she was removed, their ideas began to flow haphazardly all over the place.

The brewers certainly felt that the licensing ideas of the magistracy, the Peel Commission (the Liquor Licensing Laws), the Liberal temperance lobby and, most of all the government, were blowing all over their industry with deadly results. The Edwardian period witnessed a decline in the standard of living of working people, which fell by some 14 percent in England. At the same time there was competition to expenditure on alcohol from mass markets in clothing and food stuffs, from music halls and football. Of great concern to brewers, however, was the decline in the popularity of the public-house. The directors at Greene King were warned in 1904 that 'there seemed a tendency among the public not to use the Public Houses as formerly.' If this continued it was bad news for Thwaites which had built up an impressive stock of houses. Returns for England and Wales in 1892, *before* the boom period of 1895–6, show that the largest owners were Greenall Whitley & Co. (681 houses); Steward & Patterson (473); Peter Walker & Sons (410); Bristol Brewery Georges Ltd (350); Colchester Brewery Co. (289); Truman (267); Bullard & Co. (260); Watney & Co. (289); Phipps & Co. (242); Thwaites & Co. (219); and Boddingtons' Breweries Ltd (212). It would be a bitter brewing pill to swallow if after, having expanded the ownership of tied houses, the public stopped going to drink in them.[18]

Thus, the campaign against drunkenness and the Licensing Bill furore could not have come at a worse time for brewers. Blackburn had long been stigmatised as 'the most beery town in the world', a reputation endorsed by the vicar of Holy Trinity Church, who spoke against the excessive number of licensed houses 'on behalf of the people and the poor, who have been treated,' he said in

Both the label for its bestselling 'East Lancs' beer, (above), and the one on its ginger beer bottle (opposite) carry the Thwaites trademark registered in 1898.

1890, 'as if they were born only to be ruined.' There was then one licensed house for every one hundred inhabitants in his parish; elsewhere, by 1892, the figure quoted was one licence for every thirty-four houses in the borough. It was said of the King Street and Northgate area that public-houses were as common 'as blackberries on a hedge.'[19]

The Licensing magistrates were concerned enough to order a survey in 1893 of the borough's 495 public-houses and off-licences (of which 219 belonged to Thwaites), with a view to reducing the numbers. From then on, the Brewster Sessions witnessed increasing pressure to combat drunkenness. In 1902, for instance, the justices reiterated that licences would be affected by supplying drink to drunken persons and permitting drunkenness on the premises, 'being offences which the Justices consider of a very severe character.' Most brewers condemned drunkenness and certainly Elma did not countenance either drunkenness or gambling in any of the Thwaites houses.[20]

After the passage of the 1902 Licensing Act, magistrates refused to renew 240 licences in England and Wales, a number well above the average of the previous five years. To the fury of the temperance lobby, Balfour's Conservative government enacted the Licensing Act of 1904 to regulate the removal of licences. Compensation for refusal to renew licences would be levied on each of their houses from a fund collected from the brewers. While the Liberals labelled the legislation 'the Brewers' Endowment Fund', the brewers called it 'the Mutual Burial Fund.'[21]

The effect of the Act in Blackburn was outright horse-trading, whereby, through the Blackburn Brewers' Association and the East and North-East Lancashire Brewers' Association, at both of which Thorpe was chairman, brewers negotiated amongst themselves which houses to surrender in order to keep others open. Thus, in Belthorn, the Blackburn Brewery Co. [BB] agreed to surrender a house in the district but 'the magistrates are particularly anxious for the "Victoria" a beer house belonging to Daniel Thwaites & Co. Ltd to be surrendered,' Thorpe reported in 1904,' and I have arranged with the Brewers' Association that we have the option either to sell the "Victoria" to the BB Co. Ltd to be surrendered, or if we agree to retain a licence in this

district, the BB Co. will allow us to take possession of their "British Queen" Beer house thereby meeting the wishes of the Magistrates.'

Then, another local brewer, Thomas Whewell & Co., undertook to surrender the beer house in the Duckworth Hall district because Thwaites had helped it in the Stanhill district. At the end of his lengthy report of these protracted negotiations covering just one Brewster Session, Thorpe wrote wearily to the Board, 'I venture to think that, after I have explained the trouble and anxiety we have been put to as an Association, on behalf of Daniel Thwaites & Co. Ltd I have made a very fair arrangement.' The Board entirely agreed and Thorpe received Elma's approbation for all his efforts on behalf of Thwaites.[22]

The anxiety he had been put to was as nothing compared to that caused by the 1908 Licensing Bill. The Liberals had returned to power, led first by Campbell-Bannerman in 1903 and then by Asquith from 1908; Robert had lost his Chester seat to a Radical Mr Alfred Mond and would not regain it until the 1910 election. When it came to the drink trade the Liberal bill was, in Churchill's words, 'a measure of plunder to satisfy spite.' Its main proposal was that at the end of fourteen years the ownership of all licences should revert to the State and the disposed owners should provide for their losses by means of a Sinking Fund, and any new licences issued would be paid for at a monopoly value. In addition to threatening local referenda on absolute prohibition, the bill proposed to prevent women from being employed on Licensed premises. Brewers reeled with shock while the Trade's associations organised petitions and demonstrations against the measure, which had easily passed its readings in the Commons. 'The Licensing Bill is an insult to the 100,000 barmaids who now earn an honest living in public-houses!' screamed one placard

Dray makers J. S. Leaver
of Eanam in 1919.

at the mammoth Hyde Park demonstration organised by the Trade against the Bill. As expected, the Bill was defeated by the Lords in November 1908.[23]

In the 1908 and the 1909 People's Budget, Lloyd George gave with one hand and took with the other. The introduction of the first old age pension of 5 shillings a week at the age of seventy to anyone earning an income of less than 10 shillings a week created enormous interest – with fatal results for some of the new pensioners. 'A woman dropped dead from excitement in Sandwich at eight o'clock as she was handed her 5 shillings,' a newspaper reported. To fund this social reform, Lloyd George increased the breweries' nominal licence of £1 to a rate of 12 shillings per fifty barrels beyond the first 100, and practically trebled the retail licences. The rejection of the Budget by the Lords caused a constitutional crisis and led to the 1910 election in which Robert was re-elected. The imposition of these taxes in the 1910 Budget added up to 60 per cent of brewers' earnings, according to Hoare & Co' *Brewing Trade Review*. As always, though, the volatile brewing trading climate suddenly improved and consumption increased in Britain between 1909 and 1913 by over 3 million barrels. This was the last statistic to cheer brewers for some years to come.[24]

The outbreak of the First World War affected all British industry as government controls were imposed on output and quality suffered. In brewing, the gravity of beer was reduced to 24°, output was reduced by 25 per cent of the 1914 barrelage and, as in all wars, the Chancellor increased the duties – in this case from 7s 9d to 23s per standard barrel (by 1919 it would have risen to £5). The severity of the duties reflected the gravity and length of this war as well, it was said, as the Chancellor's hostility to the brewing trade. 'Drink is doing us more harm in the war than all the German submarines put together,' Lloyd George declared, ever the temperance supporter. 'We are fighting Germany, Austria, and Drink, and as far as I can see the greatest of these three deadly foes is Drink.'[25]

The trouble was that, in consequence of his measures, which included drastically curtailing opening hours, retail prices rose, beer was scarce and output plummeted from 37 million bulk barrels in 1914 to 19 million in 1918. The meagre

supply had an unexpected result. The hard working munitions and heavy industry labourers finished their overtime shifts to find the public-houses dry when they came off duty. 'A curious lassitude seemed to pervade the workers' apparently, and, accordingly, production fell. Lloyd George had to introduce permits for brewers to produce what was termed Munition Beer in certain munition and heavy industry centres. The government's somewhat forced sponsorship of this increase in beer production for the war

A 1915 *Punch* cartoon showing David Lloyd George , then Chancellor of the Exchequer, fighting the demon drink which he ranked as serious an opponent as Germany and Austria.

David (to the Philistine) : "LOOK HERE, OLD MAN. I SHOULD HATE TO BE THE CAUSE OF ANY UNPLEASANTNESS. WHY NOT APPROACH ME AS A DEPUTATION AND TALK THINGS OVER?"

effort succeeded in silencing the organised temperance campaign, publicised nationally in posters declaring 'Beer versus Bread', which had advocated the suspension of all brewing.[26]

Thwaites not only saw staff called up but was also without its chairman at the outbreak of the war. Robert Yerburgh was suffering from heart trouble and, in June, Elma had accompanied him to the spa town of Bad Nauheim in Bavaria. As he later related, 'I was just going away into the mountains for the afternoon – you always take the "after-cure" following the baths – when the war between Germany and Russia was declared.' It was impossible for them to leave as every train was filled with troops and English visitors were promptly placed under curfew. After the declaration of war with Great Britain, the Yerburghs were amongst the English people detained as prisoners of war by the Military Governor of Frankfurt. Nine weeks later, all the English received an order enabling them to leave Germany on condition that each family left at different times, stayed in different hotels en route and travelled through Switzerland, where they had to give their word to remain for three weeks. 'The amusing part of the order,' Robert would later point out, 'was the reliance placed "on the word of an Englishman." I could have got over the border the very next day and come straight through to England. But we had given our word – so we remained.'[27]

In spite of his extended stay in the spa town, Robert's health had not improved; if anything, the anxiety attached to being a prisoner of war had been detrimental, although he passed the matter off lightly. His health rapidly deteriorated and, in December 1916, at the age of sixty-three, he died from heart disease. His sons were unable to be with him as they were fighting at the front, Bobby with the Royal Artillery and Guy with the Irish Guards. After his death, Elma followed his wishes and turned Caythorpe Court into a full time Convalescent Home where twenty officers were able to recuperate from shell shock and the misery of the trenches. She also lent their London house at Kensington Gore to the Red Cross Society and continued all his numerous hospital donations. Robert had been President of the Board of Management of the Blackburn Royal Infirmary and Elma

presented the hospital with a much-needed cheque for £3500. This was only one of the many donations that the Thwaites family had made over the years; after her father's death Elma had presented £10,000 to the Infirmary in his memory and, with some of her Thwaites cousins, had attended the opening of the hospital in 1892.[28]

By 1916, some 69% of the Brewery staff of military age was either serving or ready to serve in the War. Thorpe had to make numerous appointments to fill the vacancies, including that of a temporary head brewer, Swift, to replace Mr Griffin who was at the Front. While enlisted employees were away, Elma ensured not only that their wages were paid and their families were comfortable in their absence but that their jobs were kept open for them until the end of the War in 1918. There were many casualties from Blackburn among the war dead and three Thwaites men fighting with the East Lancashire Regiment died at the Somme, when the regiment was practically decimated, and four were killed in other battles. To the members of staff who returned from the War, Elma made a generous gift in addition to their backdated wages. A special holiday outing for all the ex-servicemen and their families was arranged to Blackpool where they received an envelope containing £25 for each year served in the Armed Forces. She would do the same in the Second World War, though the envelope contained a generous cheque rather than actual money. Another of her customs during and after the war was to confine tenancies on her estates to families who had members serving in the War.[29]

Post-war trading conditions improved slightly before the sales of beer declined to levels which would have been found impossibly low before the War. Thwaites fared no better than everyone else in the 1920s. Thorpe summed up the situation Thwaites and other brewers faced: 'The decreased consumption, combined with the forced brewing of a 4d and 5d beer, the restrictions on gravity, the question of altering prices to satisfy both Tenant and Brewer and the probability of facing an increase in duty, all tend to make trade from a Brewer's standpoint very difficult.' A price list of 1920 shows that a 36 gallon barrel of bitter cost £5 on which the profit was 31/6d; of mild ale cost £3–10–0 with a profit of 24/6d; and of stout cost £4–10–0 giving a profit of 26/6. It was in the early 1920s that Thwaites introduced the name East Lancashire for their popular bestselling Pale Ale and the name was quickly shortened to an 'East Lancs'. The head brewer also produced a new beer, a fine quality stout which he called East Lancashire Cream Stout, which sold in draught and bottle. Unfortunately, the line had to be discontinued later owing to trade restrictions on the use of the words 'cream' and 'milk'.[30]

In 1922 the directors decided to increase the capital of the Company to £1 million with a view to acquiring one of their brewing competitors, Henry Shaw & Co. Ltd's New Salford Brewery. The firm's public-houses were a particular attraction as they were in good condition and offered Thwaites a solid presence in Darwen, where it was under-represented. Henry Shaws had been established in Blackburn in 1834 by Henry Shaw and John Rutherford, whose son Colonel Sir John Rutherford Bart was the Chairman and driving force in 1922. Rutherford had been the Conservative member for Darwen since 1895 and it was said of him in 1900 that 'Every public-house – and Mr Rutherford himself owns a hundred – was a centre of influence in his favour' at election time. He was, however, undoubtedly popular with the electorate as a sportsman, who had played football with Blackburn Rovers and cricket with East Lancashire; and as a member of the Jockey Club. He was well known on the turf as the owner of the famous race horse Solario which would win not only the St Leger but also the Coronation Gold Cup and the Ascot Gold Cup in the 1925/6 season. He had a great respect for the Yerburghs whom he knew through political and philanthropic associations and when it came to negotiate the terms of the amalgamation Elma discussed them directly with him. In August 1923 Thwaites purchased Henry Shaw & Co. with eighty-seven licensed houses; Rutherford was appointed a director of Thwaites and, in the following year, Vice-chairman and he built up a large shareholding in Thwaites. On 29 August 1923, Thwaites closed the New Salford Brewery, which was eventually sold to Duttons and incorporated into its Salford Brewery building.[31]

and swallowed up the Thwaites wine and spirits department; it retained a separate banking account for which Jacob Walsh of Shaws and Rowe of Thwaites held signatory authority. The Board also decided that, although the Pickup books were now to be kept in the same manner as those of Thwaites, the accountancy firm appointed to look after Pickups was not Messrs Harwood Banner & Son, which had long looked after Thwaites, but Messrs J Adamson & Co. of Manchester, which had long looked after Shaws.

As with any acquisition, there were further changes to staff and working practices. Some duplication of staff was inevitable in certain departments and a small number of Thwaites and Shaws employees had to be let go. The custom of a daily allowance of beer to staff at Thwaites, for instance, was discontinued in November 1924 to bring it into line with Shaws, whereas the Christmas gift of a turkey to staff at Thwaites and Pickups was continued in the absence of such gifts to the Shaws staff. The question of the annual Thwaites brewery summer pic-nic vexed the Board in that Rutherford was opposed to its introduction for the new group. A compromise was reached whereby the Board granted one day's pay to every one employed by Thwaites, Shaws and Pickups in lieu of the pic-nic; the total cost in 1926 amounting to £141. The trouble, as Chesham pointed out, was that one day's pay meant that some staff received a tidy sum whilst some workers received only a few shillings each. He suggested that the whole of the fund should be pooled and a sum of 12/6d be paid to every employee irrespective of grade, which received Elma's agreement and was implemented in 1927; later, in 1930, Chesham would persuade the Board to increase the sum paid to married men to 17/6d.

A similar difference of opinion arose in 1926 over the Christmas gift when Rutherford stated that the Group Life Insurance Policy took the place of any such gifts and, on Chesham saying the policy was not entirely beneficial to employees, Rutherford opined that any additional premium could be considered in lieu of Christmas gifts. Elma held her counsel and calmly instructed Chesham to ascertain the cost of any additional benefits to the policy. Whatever

Thwaites sold Shaws Brewery building to Duttons which incorporated it into the Salford Brewery (above).

At the same time, Thwaites also acquired through Henry Shaw the plum that was James Pickup & Company. The wine and spirits business of 'Pickups', as it was called in the trade, was an efficient and profitable concern, bottling, since its establishment in 1790, its own special brands of Scotch and Irish whiskies and maintaining an excellent cellar. Elma decreed that it kept its own name as a separate entity

Chesham reported back to her, it was sufficient to enable her to insist upon the retention of Thwaites policy of a Christmas gift to everyone: the minutes of the Board meeting on 20 December reveal that a turkey would be given as usual to each of the Brewery officials and staff and the managers of the licensed houses; the only change being the replacement of a rib of beef for all other employees with £1 – the inauguration of the popular Christmas gift which was henceforth known as 'the Yerburgh pound'.

The dust had barely settled when the new Thwaites General Manager, Walter Chesham, who had joined after the retirement and death of John Thorpe, notified the Board about another acquisition. He was in negotiations to purchase Fountain Free Brewery & Co. Ltd of Rishton, which had been incorporated in 1898, at a price of £86,000. This Brewery's attraction lay in its eleven public-houses so that, once the purchase was finalised in May 1927, brewing at the Redcap Brewery was immediately discontinued, as it had been at Henry Shaws Brewery.[32]

Thwaites was hardly alone in its appetite for amalgamation. When the editor of the *Country Brewers' Gazette* observed that 'Still the tale of brewery amalgamation goes on. Scarcely a week passes without the paper announcing the amalgamation of two or more large breweries, or the absorption of one or more smaller ones. How long is this going on? How will it end?' his comments made in 1899, were just as pertinent to the activities of the local brewing industry in the 1920s. In 1926 Smith's Tadcaster Brewery Co. had taken over the Milnshaw Brewery of Accrington, originally founded by Elma's uncle Thomas Thwaites. In 1925 Thomas Whewell was acquired by Nuttall & Co. which in turn was taken over by Matthew Brown & Co., a Preston brewery company that now moved to Blackburn and became a main competitor to Thwaites. Lastly, in 1928, Duttons acquired the Blackburn Brewery Co. Ltd and one hundred public-houses. Thwaites had been minded to join in, partly to increase or maintain its sales of drink in an era of declining demand through having more public-houses, and partly to prevent its competitors from swallowing them up instead.[33]

Woodfold Park, the mansion outside Blackburn where Elma lived when supervising the Brewery.

Duke Street Mill, one of the many local businesses put out of business at the height of the depression, is demolished in 1930.

Elma remained an extremely busy woman, actively involved in brewery matters as well as all the business of managing three landed estates, which had devolved on her after Robert's death and in which she had the assistance of a good agent, John Howson. She was thus as occupied as ever during these years when she knew great sadness in her private life. Both her sons were settled in life and happily married with young families. Her second son Guy had married Hilda de Bunsen, daughter of Sir Maurice de Bunsen, former British Ambassador in Vienna, in 1921. They made a strikingly attractive couple and went to live at Bramshott Court near to where his regiment was stationed in Surrey. He had a distinguished war record with the Irish Guards, being made a CBE and awarded the Italian Croce de Guerra and the Belgian Croix de Guerre; a skilled golfer, he had captained the Cambridge University Team and played in amateur championships. In the winter of 1926 he was troubled by a mosquito bite which became infected, formed a blood clot and led to his death on 13 March 1926. He was only thirty-three and the shock from such an unexpected cause of death was immense. Hilda, then aged twenty-six, was left with two small boys, John and Oscar.

Then, in the following year, Elma's first daughter-in-law and Yerburgh niece Dorothea Gertrude died unexpectedly on 10 February 1927 leaving two daughters, Dorothy aged fourteen and Marjorie ten and a two-month-old baby boy, Guy, in their father Bobby's care. Two years later, on 10 July 1929 he was created a Baron in the Dissolution Honours List and took the title Lord Alvingham. Like his father, Bobby was an Oxford man and stood for Parliament, being elected as the Unionist Member for South Dorset in 1922. The conferment of this peerage was a posthumous honour intended for his father who had died after Royal approval of a peerage had been granted, but before the patent could be issued and gazetted. In celebration of this honour, Elma distributed £500 among the employees at Eanam Brewery.[34]

There was little else to celebrate at the Brewery and in Blackburn over the next decade. Mrs Lovell, a former Mayor, said of the 1930s in Blackburn: 'it was a dreadful

time.' Thousands were out of work throughout Lancashire as industry went onto short time, workers were let go and mills closed. One of the main differences between these years and those of the 19th-century depressions was the introduction of state aid in place of total reliance on soup kitchens and private charities. The poverty in Blackburn remained the same, however, at such times; it was made worse for the unemployed in the 1930s by the hated Means Test. 'I can remember men going to the Public Assistance offices,' Mrs Lovell continued, 'where they would give them vouchers to get tea, sugar, bread, and people lost their self-respect and dignity having to do such things but they had no choice. Then when the Means Test came, things went from bad to worse.' She saw families split up and boys and girls forced to leave home to comply with the terms of these tests, and a return to the bad days of the workhouse for older people. She reckoned that a quarter of the population left Blackburn for Southern England, where they had more hope of finding work.[35]

Staff and tenants at Thwaites suffered like so many others. Chesham reported in 1932 that 'our tenants are having a very difficult time, and in many cases we shall have to subsidise them.' Public-houses could not be let on any terms and, in the end, had to become managed houses. Managers and their wives were often so glad of a roof over their heads during the slump that they didn't mind the low wages; wives were paid 10/- a week for their work which included all the cleaning and laundry. Sales of beer at the Brewery had collapsed. Following two successive falls in 1932 and 1933, the figures for the year ending 31 May 1934 showed a further reduction of over 1000 barrels.[36]

To try to stimulate consumption of beer, the *Brewers' Journal* mounted the first national publicity campaign 'to tell the public the real facts about the national beverage.' The first collective advertisement appeared on the hoardings in 1933, proclaiming that 'BEER IS BEST.' This phrase quickly passed into the national consciousness and continues to be used in the present day. While the slogan was successful in promoting beer, it was unable to stem the decline in sales of beer. Nevertheless, trade did start to improve gradually and, after Chesham took up a new appointment in 1938 with Devenish Brewery in Weymouth, the new General Manager James Mather was instrumental in completing a renovation programme for the Company's public-houses. Extensive work was done to three important houses in Blackpool, namely the Gynn, the Fleece and the Duke of York which continued to enjoy a considerable trade regardless of the depression. And the popularity of Morecambe as a resort and an increasing business there made it essential to refurbish the Battery Hotel and the Cumberland View. Shortly after Mather's arrival in March 1938, the Board agreed to introduce the first Thwaites staff pension scheme, which Elma was keen to promote and it duly became fully subscribed.[37]

Elma in her later years.

There was a great exodus of staff from Eanam Brewery when Britain declared war against Germany on 3 September 1939. Many people had already joined the East Lancashire Territorial Army during a recruitment campaign the previous year and many more now left to serve with the regular forces. Those remaining in Blackburn were fully occupied with fire-watching, and Civil Defence duties and then with the Home Guard. Blackburn escaped enemy action unscathed except for two incendiary devices dropped outside the town which caused little damage. Manchester, however, was not so fortunate and was heavily blitzed in 1940. Boddington's Brewery was severely damaged and through Philip Boddington's friendship with Mather, Thwaites took over its brewing and managed to supply most of its public-houses. Demand for alcoholic beverages was stimulated by the presence of troops stationed around Blackburn, and the public-houses there and in the surrounding countryside enjoyed a good trade and were often overflowing with soldiers. The arrival of the American Forces added a certain glamour to the town's social life and introduced chewing gum, chocolate bars, cigarettes such as Lucky Strikes, nylon stockings and lipstick to the residents; while the public-houses introduced the best of British beer – the local brews – to the Americans.[38]

Elma lived chiefly at Barwhillanty for the duration of the war. She was in her eighties and less mobile than she used to be. 'John doesn't realise I can't get into a train & have to be well pushed in a car &c,' she wrote of her eldest grandson John to his mother Hilda in 1945, ' so I felt I must say no, also to his kind invitation to drive me in an open car.' Frail as she was, her spirit remained indomitable. When told that people could take advantage of her generosity, she replied briskly, 'As long as I don't miss helping someone in real need I can stand being bitten.' She was almost revered in Blackburn for the support she gave to so many local causes. She had become the first woman and only the sixth person to have the Freedom of the Borough of Blackburn conferred upon her. 'Today we meet to honour a lady who has rendered eminent services for, and done untold good in, her native town,' Alderman

Taylor said during the simple, dignified ceremony in the Council Chamber of the Town Hall on 5 September 1935. 'In honouring her, we honour Blackburn. The freedom of the borough is the highest dignity we can confer, and Mrs Yerburgh richly deserves it. She had ever shown practical sympathy with those less fortunate than herself.' And that was the essence of her approach; she liked to help where she could do the most practical good, such as providing fuel or a stove rather than writing out a cheque; her method of helping continues at Thwaites today in the form of the Charitable Trust.[39]

She continued to do her duty and to attend to all her affairs with the help of her loyal secretary but she was beginning to find it a strain. As with everything in her life, she had given a great deal of deliberation to the future of her estates and brewery business. It was traditional in English life for a title to be supported by a landed estate. Indeed such patronage had been withheld in the past to deserving candidates without sufficient wealth to uphold the position and responsibilities attached to a peerage. Elma therefore decided in principle to leave her landed estates to her eldest son Lord Alvingham and his son Guy and to leave her majority share of the Thwaites Company to her two grandsons John and Oscar, (the Rutherford family had retained Sir John's shareholding after his death in 1932). Several other landed brewers had taken this route in disposing of their property, such as Sir Andrew Walker. As John and Oscar were serving in the Army and Royal Air Force respectively, she could not teach them the brewery business but she did manage to introduce John to her legal adviser and a co-director, which as she told Hilda was 'a *load* off my mind after all these years & I cant quite coap with it now. He made a very favourable impression'.

She fell seriously ill at Barwhillanty in November 1946 and died there three weeks later on 6 December. Immediately, she was dubbed, on account of her generosity, 'Blackburn's Lady Bountiful'. She had always said that she preferred to give in her life than wait till after she died, and although she endowed and subscribed to numerous charities right up until her death, she nevertheless

remembered a large number in her will. Her most munificent gifts had been bestowed upon the Blackburn Royal Infirmary for which she was president for eleven years from 1932–1943. At the time she laid the foundation stone for the Memorial Wing in 1924, she completed arrangements for the Yerburgh Fund by providing an endowment of £5000. She also sent a cheque for £3000 as a testimony to her interest in the war memorial and Infirmary.

When she knew she was dying she wrote to her daughter-in-law Hilda, of whom she was very fond, 'To say good bye, & to *thank* you for the care you have taken of my son's boys.' She always called John and Oscar 'My boys', and thought that having a brewery would suit them for, as she put it when writing to Hilda of John's future ' after all he needs only to master the details, & its his income & Ockies, & decide later on if its Profit Sharing, Amalgamative, Selling out or forming a *Northern* Concern.' She had left the future of Daniel Thwaites & Co. almost entirely in their young and inexperienced hands.[40]

A stone set in the wall of Blackburn Royal Infirmary which had been the beneficiary of some of Elma's most generous munificence.

The Public-House in 1907

*' Railway Inn, Lower Darwen – Thorpe reported that he had met
the Magistrates regarding the Compensation for this Licence
and that he had made a claim for £1050.'*
Directors Minute Book No 3, 10 June 1907

*'We strongly oppose any conspiracy to exclude women from
the licensed house, for it is from the patronage of women …
that we shall hope to uplift the licensed house.'*
Brewers' Journal, 15 April 1918

Facing page
The Landlord painted
by Frederick Elwell.

THE OPTIMISM WITH which joyous crowds of Blackburn people greeted the new year in 1900, as church bells rang, mill whistles were blown, rockets fired and the Corporation Park gun boomed, had been displaced in 1904 by the despondency of an economic depression that threatened the whole decade, as looms were idle, mills fell silent and hundreds of distressed cotton workers and their families queued at soup kitchens. Moreover, the constant gloom of these years was by no means confined to the textile industry; the brewing trade, like other important industries, was also affected.

An Edwardian man aiming to have a drink in Blackburn was less likely in 1907 than at any time in the previous hundred years to find relief from 'the meanness of life' in his favourite public-house. Indeed, so unsettled was the liquor trade that he could not even be sure of obtaining a pint of bitter at his local: he might arrive there only to discover that it had been closed down. The licensing magistrates could easily have deemed it 'surplus to requirements', as of course they were empowered to do by several High Court judgements and the Balfour Licensing Act of 1904, which had established the principle of closure and the surrender of licences in areas where they considered public-houses to be too numerous. The licensing justices had therefore set about shutting down some 9617 licensed houses throughout the country, mostly between 1906–10,

so as to achieve a reduction of nearly 10 per cent.[1]

In Birmingham, a 'Surrender Scheme' organised from 1896 by brewers, such as Mitchell & Butlers, and the local Licensing Committee, had led to the closure of 182 licensed houses, at a cost of £173,738 by 1904. The Birmingham brewers had formed a company to negotiate with the licensing justices for the surrender of licences in congested areas in the centre in exchange for licences on new or renovated houses in the outskirts or suburbs of the city; the company contributed to a fund out of which it then compensated members who had lost their licences. This *quid pro quo* scheme was also used in towns such as Liverpool and Sheffield. The way it worked was later explained by the Clerk to the Birmingham Licensing Justices: 'The scale generally accepted for the removal of a publican's licence to a new site where there were no licensed premises before is 3 on-licences,' whilst for 'alterations involving considerable extensions as many as 2 on-licences have been surrendered.'[2]

In Blackburn, however, the long standing magisterial concern about the number of both licensed premises and offences arising out of drunkenness had produced the detailed report of 1893 on the condition of each house. Of the total number of 493 licensed houses, the magistrates had sought to reduce the number of houses in 'congested districts', earmarking principally those classified as 'poor'

(32 public-houses and 91 beer houses) and those sharing back yards with other buildings (59 public-houses and 109 beer houses), that prevented adequate police detection of the continuing and widespread habit of illicit Sunday drinking. The views and convenience of the customer and the publican were, not unnaturally, of little concern to the licensing magistrates. Those of the brewers were, naturally, of more import. As leading citizens the brewery proprietors were not only well acquainted with them but were also often themselves magistrates (Elma Yerburgh as a woman was unable to sit on the bench); indeed, John Rutherford of Henry Shaws had been one of the justices inspecting the licensed houses in No 5 District for the 1893 Report.[3]

Moreover, the proprietors were not entirely opposed to a limited reduction of licences as it maintained property prices, enabled them to dispose of their least profitable houses and, after the implementation of the Act of 1904's levy, compensated them properly for lost licences. In any case, in common with other Blackburn brewers, Thwaites had long worked closely with the bench. There had been no need to adopt the Birmingham model of 'Surrender Scheme' when John Thorpe, who organised all Thwaites licensing arrangements, regularly communicated with colleagues in other breweries, the clerk of the magistrates and the chief constable, to the extent that he was usually forewarned about the likely requirements of the local licensing justices and, accordingly, could forearm the Board.

The pages of the Thwaites minute books between 1899 and 1914 are filled with details about Thorpe's meetings and negotiations on this subject. Thus, in August 1899, he informed the Board that the police was likely to object to the renewal of the licence of White Hart Inn in the 'congested district' of Nab Lane and, as the magistrates were likely to support the police objection, his suggestion that the licence should be voluntarily surrendered by Thwaites was agreed. He was also able to alert the Board to the interest of the Darwen magistrates in reducing the number of the Company's licensed properties and their likely objection to five houses. By surrendering the White Hart Inn licence, Thwaites was granted permission to lay out a Bowling Green at the White Hart Inn, Subden; rebuild part

of the Black Bull Inn, Ribchester at a cost of £1068; and build another bar at the Walmsley Arms, Rishton – all three have continued to thrive as Thwaites 'pubs' to the present day. Customers and Thomas Kenlock the landlord of the Star Hotel, Darwen, were not so fortunate as this licence was refused on the grounds that 'there is no necessity for such a licence' and, after Thwaites lost its appeal at the next Preston Quarter Sessions, the house had to be closed down.[4]

As public-houses were increasingly kicked about like a political football in the Edwardian years by successive Liberal governments, suffused with temperance fervour and keen to demonstrate their skill on the pitch of anti-drink legislation, licensing justices imposed tougher rules. When Thwaites submitted plans to build the Mill Hill Hotel, a new public-house on a site in the Mill Hill district, a full licence was only granted in 1902 on the understanding that the licences of one other public-house, the Hornby

Arms, and seven beer houses were surrendered. On some occasions a licence would be renewed without difficulty one year but objected to another year, as happened with the Volunteer Arms, Southport; renewed in 1903, the magistrates nevertheless scheduled it for surrender in 1906. Thwaites decided to seek their permission to rebuild the house and to pave the way by giving a piece of land for widening the street to the Corporation but, should the magistrates still object, to appeal. In the event, the justices agreed, the licence was renewed in 1907, and the Volunteer Arms continues as a Thwaites public-house in Southport today.[5]

On other occasions, the back doors, having posed no problems for some years, suddenly presented an obstacle to renewal. In 1904, for instance, Thwaites received an order from the Burnley bench that 'the back door has to be closed within 28 days' or the Derby Hotel, Burnley would be closed down; the Darwen bench was also scarcely less forthcoming about the back doors of Thwaites houses within its jurisdiction. The issue was not as straightforward a one for the trade as the magistracy would have wished. Neighbouring customers liked the convenience of using back doors to enter and exit public-houses in their streets; publicans liked the trade conducted through them and

Fast Food c.1910. Hot
potatoes are sold
outside the Oak Tree Inn
in Accrington to its
customers. Such a
service continued in
places into the 1960s.

complained about losing it; and, as Thorpe reported to the
Board, 'some of the Brewers had defied the Magistrates by
keeping their back doors open, after having been requested
to close them.' Given the delicate and time-consuming
negotiations attached to the annual re-licensing sessions at
Blackburn, Blackpool, Darwen, Burnley, Bury and Southport,
Thwaites was not about to forfeit its good relations with all
the relevant licensing justices. As the Board minutes testify,
'the back doors of the property belonging to this Company
should be kept closed as arranged.' Besides which, the
Company always preferred to take the route of negotiation
rather than litigation in these matters and, instead of

entering an appeal at the Sessions at Preston, Thorpe
quietly paid yet another visit to Burnley and managed to
persuade a deputation of magistates and chief constable to
rescind the order to close the Derby Hotel's back door on
assurance of no illicit use on Sundays.[6]

The difficulty for Thwaites, and other brewing
companies caught in this magisterial web of licensing, lay
not so much with the surrender of licences but with the
attempt to improve their public-houses. Plans for alterations
and additions, however minor, were subjected to protracted
and expensive procedures at the end of which, as Basil
Oliver has pointed out, permission was 'all too frequently

refused' by the licensing justices owing to 'their misguided idea – and that of many of their contemporaries – that to improve buildings' was to increase the facilities for drinking and thereby encourage it. The bench hoped that by preventing alterations to a public-house, the premises would ultimately become unsafe and could be condemned and closed down. Brewers despaired of this policy; the North Cheshire Brewery in Macclesfield, over twelve years grown so weary of the annual protest against the justices' objections, was driven by 1917 to plead that it would raise no objection to the suppression of its houses 'providing they would leave just one alone.'[7]

For Thwaites, four of its most attractive and popular present day country public-houses were only saved from losing their Edwardian licences by the assiduous and costly endeavours of Thorpe, John Howson, the Woodfold agent and later director, and Henry Thompson, the estates manager, on behalf of the Board. The alterations to the Bay Horse, Osbaldeston, known then for the Shire stallion that used to stand outside it, and the Bonny Inn, Salmesbury were deemed unsatisfactory and had to be re-drawn and re-negotiated several times before the magistrates agreed to re-licence them. Improvements to the Buck Horse Inn, Clitheroe entailed the sacrifice of several other licensed properties before plans not just for the requested reconstruction but for a complete re-building were passed by the magistrates in 1905. After these experiences, when the firm decided that repairs were needed to the Britannia Inn, Oswaldtwistle, which would be managed by the Whewell family for many years, John Howson prepared plans but, instead of submission to the justices, the Board decided to start work 'as far as possible in the way of bringing the house up to date' and to apply later for any structural alterations to which the magistrates were bound to object. In this way Thwaites contained its costs to £750 - 10s and modernised the property without forfeiting the licences of a number of other properties – sometimes up to thirteen were necessary in any one Brewster Session – for an uncertain outcome to a profitable public-house.[8]

Thus, by 1907, it was evident that the onus of responsibility for the appearance and respectability of the public-house had shifted almost entirely to the brewing company. The publican-brewer of the previous century had virtually disappeared. Certainly, nearly all the licensed houses in Blackburn were tied houses; the figures for 1893, when the ratio of tied to free houses was 11:1 with only 43 free houses, had diminished considerably more by 1907. Thwaites had been an early proponent of a tied house portfolio and, with cautious, sound management, remained a competitive force in these testing trading years by continuing to acquire good properties, to extend its tied house portfolio and to pay a full dividend at a time when large concerns, such as Allsopps and other London and Burton brewers, were either unable or were struggling to pay any dividend. Thwaites, for example, advanced £500 to the tenant of the Old Red Lion Hotel, Burnley to release him from a competitor and tie him to sell the firm's beer, wines and spirits and mineral waters; over a century later, the Old Red Lion continues to provide Thwaites drinks and 'quality daytime food'. The Ship Inn, Caton which today offers customers 'a warm and welcoming atmosphere' was originally a free house doing a trade of 4 ½ barrels per week when purchased by William Farrer for £3000 in 1901. Thwaites lent him £2000 at 4% in return for a tie on cask beer, wines and spirits, which within a few years was extended to include mineral waters and bottled beer.[9]

The effect of all these developments was to leave the publican with less responsibility for, and the drinker with less choice of, public-house than had been the case fifty years' previously. Furthermore, both faced uncertainty not only about the fate of their favourite licensed houses but also about the quality and price of the beers served in them. It was a sorry turn of events when a drinking man could no longer enjoy a ha'pint of four [pence] ale without worrying that it might, literally, kill him. Yet, in 1901, over three thousand cases were reported of people falling ill from contaminated beer, of which seventy people died. Traces of arsenic were found in sugar used to manufacture beer in Manchester and Salford and all Lancashire was put on alert.

The Thwaites board immediately resolved to obtain a guarantee of purity for every consignment from its sugar

Judges sampling beers in a beer competition held in part to restore public confidence after major problems with adulteration.

suppliers and also agreed to contribute to the costs of an investigation into arsenical poisoning to be undertaken by the Manchester Brewers Association. Every possible precaution was taken at the Brewery to ensure the quality of the beers, including analysis by the head brewer of all malt and other materials used in a brew. The damage done to the trade was considerable and appeared likely to be prolonged with all the publicity generated by the appointment of a Royal Commission on Arsenical Poisoning in 1901 and the passage of the second reading through the Commons in May of the Pure Beer Bill, designed to protect the drinker from the use of deleterious substances in the manufacture of beer. Fortunately, the prompt action of brewers and the Country Brewers' Society to withdraw contaminated beer and be known to test all raw materials was able to contain the arsenic scare to the extent that the Commission reported favourably on the brewing industry and the Bill was withdrawn. Thwaites was only too happy to contribute £645 towards the costs incurred by the Manchester Brewers Association to restore public confidence in its beer.[10]

And public confidence was not something brewers could afford to shake at a time of rising costs and falling demand for their product. In spite of the closure of licensed houses, there were still less customers in the houses that remained open and they were drinking less. As wages stopped rising and spending power waned during the economic recession, beer consumption fell by 18.2 per cent between 1901 and 1908, even though the British population was increasing; in *per capita* terms, the decline was more pronounced, falling from 31.7 gallons in 1893–1900 to 27.3 gallons in 1911–1913. Whereas the price of most foodstuffs had fallen appreciably since 1880, the cost of beer remained relatively expensive and the working man was increasingly hard-pressed to afford his pint of bitter. Thwaites tenants' complaints, that the beers were too expensive and competition from other brewers was driving away customers, were taken seriously. The solution was to bring back the cheapest 'common' or mild beer which, according to Julius Baker in 1905, was 'still the beverage of the working classes.'[11]

Brewers, however, still blamed taxation for their woes, convinced as always and with some justice that they were taxed and controlled by government to a degree no other industry was. There was, they said, the duty of 1 shilling per barrel imposed to fund the Boer War but which was never removed after peace, so that duties of 6s 3d per standard barrel introduced by Gladstone as beer duty in 1880 had by now reached 7s 9d. Then, there was the compensation levy imposed on breweries in 1904, which meant an additional financial burden. Finally, came the nasty 1909 Budget: 'While the Licensing Bill chastised the Trade with whips,' intoned one Temperance M.P., 'the Chancellor of the Exchequer [Lloyd George] would chastise it with scorpions.' This he duly did, imposing a drastic increase in the rate of duty payable on retail licences, the licence to brew and spirit duties from 11s to 14s 9d.[12]

There was, however, a much more invidious threat to the survival of the Edwardian public-house than taxation and licensing schedules. Traditional patterns of drinking habits were changing so much that the public-house was no longer the most popular building in the community as a social and meeting place; it was not the focal point of working people's lives and had become only one of many centres of amusement for families. The first threat was close at (the brewer's) hand. An Edwardian working man could just as easily drink at his club as at his local public-house. Whereas his Regency and Victorian counterparts had attended gatherings and meetings of societies and clubs in the upper rooms of public-houses, the Edwardian did so at specially built or designated premises elsewhere. Furthermore, working men's clubs held numerous advantages over public-houses when it came to the sale of cheap beer. They had been excluded from retail excise licence duty and were usually non-profit making organisations so that they could sell their beer at lower prices than the ordinary publican could ever do.

From small beginnings, these clubs had grown to over 8700 by 1914 and offered brewers an opportunity for expansion of business in these lean years. Unlike the public-house, the club trade was unlicensed, outside magisterial control and had unregulated opening hours; yet, like the public-house, the clubs sold the same alcohol and mineral waters. As such they were powerful competitors to the licensed trade and Thwaites, in common with the Burton and Scottish brewers, went out of its way to capture this enlarged free trade. The Directors' Minute Books for these years list many local clubs: from Burnley Oddfellows' Working Men's Club, which obtained a £700 loan from the firm to build new premises and a bowling green in return for a five-year term of supply for beers, wine and spirits, to the Darwen Borough Brass Band Club which, already supplied by Thwaites, was given a £100 loan to make improvements to its club house. In 1907, for instance, Thwaites arranged a £600 loan to the Unity Club, Padiham and a £500 loan to the Working Men's Club, Rawtenstall; both in return for supplying their liquor trade.[13]

In the same way, Thwaites also supplied local sports clubs with both funds to improve their grounds and beer, wines and spirits to quench their players' thirst. In 1906, the Stanley Football Club, Accrington asked the Company for a donation; the club had long played on the ground adjacent to the Grey Horse, a Thwaites public-house, and with the support of the landlord, their application was successful. There was, of course, a long established connection between football and drinking in Lancashire. Public-houses provided at least a place for teams to meet and change before a game, if not a field for the match. In a famous Lancastrian example, the Newton Heath Club began life changing in the Three Crowns in Oldham Road before it became Manchester United and established headquarters elsewhere. Blackburn Rovers Football Club was founded in 1875 at the St Leger Hotel and was a founder member of the Football League in 1888, becoming League Champions in the 1911/12 and 1913/14 seasons. Although Thwaites did not provide or sponsor the club with its first premises, Sir

The Thwaites bowling team of which the Brewery Managing Director John Thorpe was for many years a pillar.

The Thwaites football team in 1911.

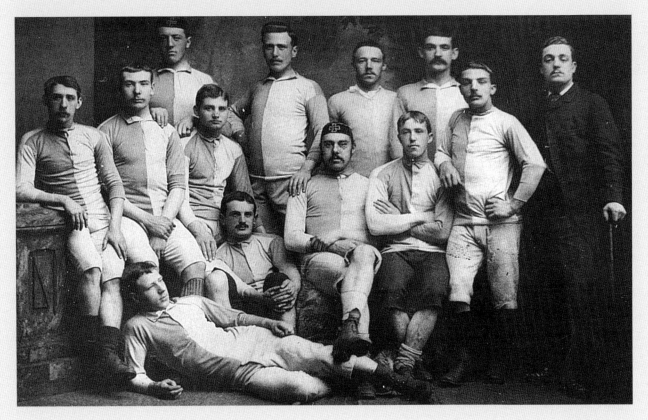

Blackburn Rovers football team in 1882 when they won promotion. Renowned for its forcefulness and closeness to the local community it was one of the first clubs to be founded.

Stills from a Mitchell & Kenyon film shows a beer seller outside a northern factory gate waiting for workers to quench their thirst. The seller can be seen pulling a pint.

John Rutherford, later Thwaites deputy-chairman, was closely associated with the club from the beginning, and Thwaites is proud to be actively involved with Blackburn Rovers today.[14]

The growing popularity of football as an Edwardian spectator sport increased drinking at public-houses in close proximity to football grounds to the detriment of public-houses elsewhere. When considering the overall decrease in trade in 1905, one brewery chairman, David Faber, suggested 'less beer and spirits were consumed, more money being spent on Games like football and similar attractions; all classes travelled more and in the towns very many cheap forms of amusement had been provided.' One of these cheaper forms of amusement that continued to enthral audiences and attract them away from the public-house was the music hall.[15]

The Edwardian music hall, however, was markedly different from its Victorian progenitor. It had become a much more professional undertaking, with the publican replaced by shareholders and managers; the emphasis on drinking first, and uneven, often amateur, entertainment second, had given way to twice nightly performances from professional artists with a national following; and the audiences no longer sat at tables or walked around for a set priced ticket but were seated according to varying admission prices in fixed places facing the stage in purpose-built halls, rather than an annexe or room in a public-house. In consequence, it was more difficult for the audience to buy drinks and, not surprisingly, the percentage of income derived from the sale of liquor declined sharply.[16]

There were three music halls in Blackburn, namely the Palace Theatre of Variety, the Princes and the Lyceum. Popular Edwardian artists who played them included Vesta Tilley in her legendary 'Burlington Bertie' routine, George Formby senior and Lottie Collins presenting her rumbustuous rendition of the song 'Ta-ra-ra-boom-dye-aye'. Even the famous Houdini graced the Palace Theatre with an appearance which caused a riot only quelled after the police evacuated the hall to prevent it being wrecked. Despite such hazards, Thwaites was keen to support the building of a music hall in Preston opposite its Cross Arms

Hotel and, in anticipation of an increase in trade after its opening, the firm applied to the Licensing Justices for alterations to improve this public-house.[17]

A new threat to the Edwardian public-house as the centre of amusement for all age groups appeared in Blackburn when a cinema opened near the Brewery, at Victoria Hall, Eanam Bridge, in 1907, to be followed by the Exchange Hall cinema in King William Street in 1908. Blackburn had been at the forefront of the development of moving pictures after two local film enthusiasts Sagar Mitchell and James Kenyon were inspired by the first commercial moving picture show by the Lumière brothers in 1895 in Paris, which came to the Lyceum Theatre, Market Street Lane, in 1896. Mitchell & Kenyon set up business in 1897 at 40 Northgate and began making feature as well as documentary films of Blackburn life under the slogan 'Local Films for Local People.' The mill workers captured on film in the day were able to see themselves on screen that evening under banners proclaiming 'See yourselves as others see you' at bioscope shows held in Corporation Park, at music halls and at local fairgrounds.

Thwaites, in common with other local brewers, had long supplied 'factory gate' beer which was sold from stalls set up outside the mills to provide mill hands of all ages with thirst quenchers of half pints and bottles of beer as they streamed out of the gates. Such scenes were filmed in the Edwardian years by Mitchell & Kenyon and, over a century later 800 reels of film were found, lying undisturbed in Mercers shop in Northgate, by workmen during demolition of the building. The reels were saved for restoration by a local historian Peter Worden and they provide a fascinating glimpse of Edwardian life in Blackburn.[18]

The craze for moving pictures continued unabated and led to the opening of two more cinemas in 1909. By 1911, a total of eight cinemas were surpassing the town's theatres, music halls and public-houses in attracting custom; it was the same story elsewhere. 'The times are different,' explained the chairman of brewers Strong of Romsey in 1912, 'your old toper who would sit in the public house until closing time is gradually dying out and is not being replaced. Popular amusements such as picture shows have multiplied.' There were, nonetheless, opportunities to be gained by enterprising brewers in the licensed trade. Thwaites was able to capitalise on the demand for cinemas by selling some of its sites for development. Land adjoining and forming part of the back yard of the Old Red Lion, Burnley, for example, rented for £180 a year was sold for £12,700 in 1919 to build a cinema. Thwaites, in turn, duly applied for permission to improve the Old Red Lion and to re-build the nearby Swan Hotel in anticipation of an increase in trade through offering refreshments to cinema-goers.[19]

There was one other significant development which inevitably altered the atmosphere of the Edwardian public-house and paved the way for a break with the past during the First World War. It concerned the growing presence of women customers in public-houses. A certain number of Blackburn women had always frequented their local, usually those working 'at mill' or living in the poorer 'congested districts'. Women had long provided the cotton trade with a cheap source of labour and, in specific occupations, such as weaving, they far outnumbered male workers; in 1905, for example, there were 8005 male as opposed to 16,604 female weavers in Blackburn. By 1910, Blackburn's population of nearly 133,000 boasted the highest percentage of working women in the country: 59% of all women over the age of ten, 78% of all unmarried and 44% of all married women worked, mostly in the cotton trade. Although their earnings were always lower than their male counterparts, these women were still relatively well paid when in work, and their financial independence lent them a reputation for being strong characters with 'a bit o'grit' in them. These women possessed the disposable income to be able to buy their own drinks and hold their own in an essentially male dominated environment.[20]

Women were also taking a greater part in national life through the suffragette campaign to achieve the vote for women. The movement had been publicised in Blackburn by the presence of Christobel Pankhurst, who visited the town in March 1906, shortly after the election of Philip Snowdon as Blackburn's first Labour M.P. The very fact of a woman speaking from a public platform was enough to shock the more conservative members of society although

her first speech pleading the cause of school meals was hardly contentious. Her second speech of the day was, however, more characteristic, a hectoring attack on the denial of women's 'right to vote'. As Asquith's Liberal government remained opposed to the female vote, the suffragette campaign adopted a more radical strategy and Blackburn women formed a support group. A local woman, Teresa Billington, was one of eleven women arrested and subsequently imprisoned for her participation in a demonstration outside the House of Commons that same year. Then, in 1907, another leading Blackburn suffragette, Louisa Entwistle, was imprisoned after another demonstration in London. Blackburn's suffragettes did not have the female political field to themselves for suffragists soon organised the Anti-Women's Suffrage League under the leadership of Fred Hargreaves, who claimed that, of the 363 women to whom he had spoken, only thirteen women were interested in gaining the vote.[21]

Whether suffragettes or suffragists, however, more women were interested in gaining a drink in a public-house. During the Victorian era women were rarely seen let alone heard in public-houses. Young unmarried women avoided them lest they be mistaken for prostitutes; respectable women would have lost any respectability by being seen entering them. In Blackburn, older working women and the poverty-stricken did drink in public-houses during the day but only with each other. Gradually, with the popularity of the 'free-and-easies', wives and families came to accompany the town's artisan and working men to the public-house on a Saturday night. Many women were also in the habit of calling at their neighbourhood house to fetch beer in jugs for the family lunch and dinner. A combination of the more prominent role of women in national life through political campaigns, the familiar sight of barmaids in public-houses, and middle class women undertaking public philanthropic work contributed to a change in women's drinking habits in the Edwardian decade.

Women were to be seen everywhere in public, on omnibuses and trams, shopping in the new department stores, at tea rooms, at Lyons tea shops, in rest rooms and restaurants, and even at ladies' clubs. By this time, women of

Scenes of northern life captured in a Mitchell & Kenyon film.

liked the Lounge, a new room introduced into the improved public-house and boasting upholstered seats, flowers, illustrated magazines, fashionable yet discreet interior design, carpeting, non-alcoholic advertisements, waiters and separate female 'powder rooms'. Nicely dressed woman could therefore drop into the lounge bar for a soft drink or cocktail as they could into a tea room for a cup of coffee. The men and families accompanying them were also expected to be tidy and behave as gentlemen. When Thwaites submitted planning details for improvements to its smarter licensed properties, increasingly they included provision for the Lounge. With a female chairman, Elma Yerburgh, at the helm, respectability continued to be the hall-mark of a Thwaites public-house. On the few occasions when lapses were reported, she always firmly reiterated that drunkenness, gambling and betting had no place in a Thwaites house.

Although the quantity of women customers remained small by comparison with male drinkers, female visitors were growing in the years immediately preceding the Great War. What historian David Gutzke has called 'a momentous social transformation' – the entry in unprecedented numbers of respectable women into public-houses – really occurred during the First World War. This represented 'the first major shift in popular drinking habits' in over a century. There was, however, opposition to such female defiance of convention, just as there was to the vote for women, usually from magistrates putting pressure on publicans to refrain from serving them. One Durham chairman of magistrates applauded placards being placed outside public-houses in Seaham Harbour; he recommended that instead of stating "Ladies are not served in this House", the word "Ladies" should be replaced by "women", for, he averred, 'a respectable women calling herself a lady would never be seen drinking in a public-house'. Women, especially the younger generation, nonetheless rose above policy, prejudice and pressure to attain equal access to the bar and their drinking rights. The entry of women into the Edwardian and, on a larger scale, into the First World War public-house laid the foundation for their greater freedom to drink publicly in the post-war era.[22]

A cotton worker dressed up for a visit by the Prince of Wales. It was her custom that brewers were keen to attract.

all classes had grown accustomed to seeking refreshment in public places and, as magistrates closed down many of the more disreputable licensed houses and brewers altered and improved the better and often more respectable of their properties, so women gradually felt more comfortable about using public-houses featuring snugs and special ladies' bars and, last of all, the Lounge. Respectable female customers

The off-licence became increasingly important to the brewers.

Blackpool

IN 1757 an insignificant "black pool" metamorphosed into an important Black Pool Town in Bowen's county map. Visitors expecting to find the society and amenities commensurate with an 18th-century town would have been disappointed, if not mortified, to discover a score or so of cottages and hovels, two small thatched inns, the Gynn and Bonney's, and only one sashed window. This town, in effect, remained a hamlet offering merely one narrow promenade over the green grassy cliffs of the Fylde coast, and vistas of windmills and the sea for amusement. Within forty years, however, a coach service ran between the town and Manchester via Preston, there were fifty houses, bathing machines, two small bowling greens and a theatre in a barn. Bed and board at the Gynn Inn, which had cost 8d a day

Mitchell & Kenyon show a typical beach scene in the North West in 1901.

in the 1750s, cost 3s 4d per day or 1s 6d without liquors in 1788. Perched at the northern extremity of the town, the Gynn's isolated position attracted a clientele of shipwrecked mariners and smugglers operating between the Fylde coast and the Isle of Man. By 1837, though, the waves of visitors had swept away the smugglers' dens, and prices at the Gynn had increased to 4s 6d a day and up to 6s for a private dining table. Blackpool was not only on the map as an increasing town but also as a favourite pleasure resort; one that in the Victorian and Edwardian eras would evolve into a famous working people's playground.

By the time that Elma Yerburgh introduced the annual summer 'pic-nic' for Thwaites staff, Blackpool had become a borough (1874); the Winter Gardens, where Caruso and Patti sang, had opened (1875); electric lighting on the promenade (1879) and electric trams (1885) inaugurated; the Opera House had staged its first show – Gilbert and Sullivan's *The Yeoman of the Guard* performed by D'Oyle Carte's company (1889); and the Promenade had developed into a grand broadwalk with two piers (1888, 1893). Moreover, at the height of patriotic pride in the British Empire, Blackpool built its own magnificent Empress Ballroom complete with an Indian Lounge (decorated at a cost of £129,000 in 1897). Blackpool's most famous landmark, the 519 foot Tower had been opened in 1894; the beacon fires lit as far away as the Lake District and the

Pennine Hills to celebrate Queen Victoria's Diamond Jubilee in 1897 could be clearly seen from the top of the Tower.[1]

There could be no finer and more fashionable destination for a staff outing than Blackpool; and no better way to celebrate the Queen's Jubilee than to give the Thwaites employees a day's wages and their first 'pic-nic' at the seaside. The trip was so successful that Mrs Yerburgh and the Thwaites directors thought to make it an annual event.

The 1902 pic-nic was typical of the Edwardian outings. Each employee was issued with a railway ticket, which also gave free access to the Central and North Piers, as well as special pre-paid tickets for entrance to the Tower and Winter Gardens and a tram ride to the Gynn Inn and back to the Central Pier. The famous Pleasure Beach, later owned by

the Thompson family and one of Thwaites oldest and most valued accounts, then consisted of a minstrel troupe on the sands, a photographic booth, phrenologists, an ice-cream stall, hobby horses and a skittle alley; in 1904 a switchback ride and a bicycle railway were inaugurated as the precursors of the incredible attractions of the present day. All the employees in 1902 were also given free tickets to the existing attractions for their wives, sweethearts or a friend – there were no female employees at the Brewery then.

At half past twelve everyone made their way to the Palatine Restaurant for a dinner consisting of soup, salmon hollandaise, turbot with lobster sauce, roast beef, mutton, lamb, vegetables and desserts. The General Manager and working Director John Thorpe presided over staff in the main room. His speech included a toast to the Royal Family and to the recovery of King Edward VII whose illness had postponed his coronation. 'Down to the humblest we had not only thought of our King and the pomp and ceremony but we had also thought of him as a man,' suggested Thorpe. 'Surely that was the one touch of nature that made the whole world kin. We have been drawn nearer to him in sickness and affliction and we had become closer in fellowship and brotherhood wherever our flag was flying.'

After another toast was drunk to the directors of Thwaites for their kindness and generosity, Thorpe read telegrams from them; from Mr and Mrs Yerburgh: 'Hope all our employees will enjoy their outing'; from Eliza Thwaites: 'Mrs Thwaites hopes you will all spend a very happy day, Addison Lodge'; from Benjamin Roberts: 'The weather seems promising. Hope everyone will enjoy their annual holiday'; and the final one from Jack Thwaites: 'Hope you will have a most enjoyable day.' Meanwhile, in another room, the secretary Mr Armistead presided over another

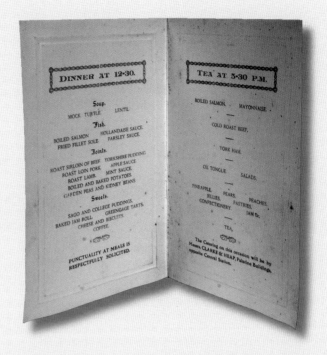

A brochure for the 20th annual excursion to Blackpool organised for the Eanam Brewery workers with its dinner and tea menus.

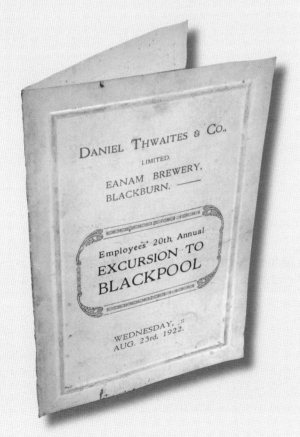

group of employees; similar speechifying and toasts were made. Mr Griffin, in answering the toast to Thwaites, said he was sure 'nothing would draw the firm and the men together more than these annual trips (hear, hear). No doubt they were all at times a bit pushed, but when they were they remembered these annual gatherings, put their shoulders to the wheel, and forced matters along (hear, hear).' Amidst such warm feelings of general bonhomie, encouraged by unlimited liquid refreshments, the staff was then free to take the sea air before assembling at the same place at six o'clock for a 'first-class' tea of cold salmon and cucumber, roast rib beef, York ham, boiled lunch tongue and sweets. They were then free to sample the delights of Blackpool at night before taking the ten o'clock train back to Blackburn.[2]

In the 1920s, however, both the Gynn and the staff picnic were relinquished. The Gynn Hotel, as it had become, was considered too small and old-fashioned for modern Blackpool. It was demolished in 1921, rebuilt as the Duke of Cambridge Hotel and in 1939 renamed the Gynn Hotel by Thwaites. As for the Brewery pic-nic, after Thwaites took

over Henry Shaw & Co. in 1923 Sir John Rutherford,
chairman of Shaws and the new deputy chairman of
Thwaites, voiced his opinion that such an event was
unnecessary when the staff already received one day's pay.
After consultation with Walter Chesham, then the General
Manager, Elma Yerburgh decided to grant every member of
staff the sum of 12s 6d irrespective of their occupation
rather than one day's wages, which had favoured the high
earners who 'got a very nice sum whilst some grades of
workers got a few shillings each only.'[3]

Although the annual staff summer outings to Blackpool
ceased in the 1920s, the Brewery's relationship with the town
did not. On the contrary, it went from strength to strength.
Thwaites continued to maintain both its property there in the
shape of, for example, the Fleece Hotel and the Gynn Hotel;
the Highlands Hotel, and the Princess Hotel were bought later
and enjoyed a large free trade presence. Every year, Thwaites
holds its prestigious annual Trade Show at Blackpool Pleasure
Beach.

In the 1930s the Brewery also forged a most enjoyable
and fruitful relationship with the Thompson family. This
continued throughout the difficult trading environment of
the Second World War; indeed, so appreciative were the
Thompsons of Daniel Thwaites & Company's successful
endeavours to keep the beer supply lines going during
war time that, despite fierce competition, they have kept
Thwaites beers on sale at the Pleasure Beach to this day.
Doris Thompson, the Chairman, and her son Geoffrey
Thompson, the Managing Director, struck up a great
friendship with David Kay, who recalls many an enjoyable
meeting with them at Blackpool to discuss developments
in the brewing industry. Furthermore, until his recent
death, Geoffrey Thompson was a non-executive director
of Daniel Thwaites & Co., where his knowledge and
experience of the leisure industry proved to be of great
benefit to Thwaites.

Thus, 'Funland by the Foam', the name given to the
Pleasure Beach when it was first formed as a company and
opened as an amusement park in 1910, also typifies
Thwaites's special bond, both for the staff and the Brewery,
with Blackpool.

Facing page John Yerburgh at the centre of a group celebrating the topping out of the new Brewery in 1965.
Left The Bridge Inn, a Thwaites pub in Accrington, showing a largely carless world at the time of John's inheritance in 1946.

CHAPTER FIVE

John Yerburgh 1923–

ON THE MORNING of 20 September 1946 the directors of Daniel Thwaites assembled in the Boardroom of the Eanam Brewery. On this occasion, however, the routine proceedings of the monthly Board meeting were punctuated by a *frisson* of nervous curiosity caused by the presence of a tall, red-haired, bespectacled, young man, who bore a familiar name, yet was a comparative stranger. Captain John Yerburgh, was not a director but he was attending his first proper Board meeting.

Despite his close family connection to the Brewery, he had only previously visited it once, about three weeks before the War ended, in the summer of 1945. He remembers entering the Brewery by a small door and going into a 'little, dark' boardroom where his grandmother

introduced him to three old gentlemen, Messrs Whittle, Ashworth and Kay. She then took him back to Woodfold, which he remembered as 'an empty, dreary, dark house', where he was staying with her and her secretary, Miss Petter, known to the family as P.D.S. (Poor Downtrodden Secretary).

'I had never seen it before; I had only once gone to Caythorpe and knew nothing about Freeby and other Yerburgh estates.' He also knew as little about the Brewery and its directors as they knew about him when he joined them there in September 1946. His grandmother could not be with them as Barwhillanty was still difficult to travel from; Ashworth was also absent as was her cousin, Jack Thwaites. The meeting was chaired by Jack's son, Gerald Thwaites, 'very good on brewing but weak on finance', according to Elma; and attended by Colonel Melville, who, as Elma told John, was 'chiefly used to sign certificates to get spirits out of bond'; Thomas Kay, the Company Secretary; James Mather, the General Manager and Alfred Whittle whom Elma chiefly relied upon for sound financial advice. The items on the agenda reflected the restrictions of war time trading more than post-war recovery: permission to use fuel oil from the Ministry of Fuel to offset irregular supplies of coal; report on the successful Victory Outing to Blackpool when grants made to the ex-service men were well received and 'created an excellent impression not only among the employees but with the public generally'; and permission to erect a new wagon garage behind Quarry Street, 'the existing garage being both unsuitable and impracticable for a valuable fleet of wagons such as we must have, and extremely dangerous in case of fire and road safety'. It must have been surreal for a twenty-three-year-old serving soldier, not yet demobbed; the fusty, old fashioned Brewery with its unfamiliar yet mundane concerns, far removed from the vivid, terrifying experience of war.[1]

Yet what seemed to a young man as a most Dickensian atmosphere, with clerks still perched on tall stools at high desks in the Estates Office, was not entirely unfamiliar. For, according to his brother Oscar, they grew up 'at the end of an almost Dickensian era.' John Maurice Armstrong Yerburgh was born on the 23rd of May 1923 at home in London with a midwife, a grand gynaecologist and a monthly nurse in attendance. His parents, Hilda and Guy Yerburgh, lived at 27 Princes Gate with a staff of a butler, a footman, an odd job man, a head housemaid, a second housemaid, a cook and a kitchen maid. The most important member of this retinue for John and his younger brother, Oscar, was their Nanny 'who was rather grander than the others and had her meals upstairs' and not in the servants hall in the basement. After the sudden death of their father, Guy, in 1926, they moved to 50 Ennismore Gardens, so as to be nearer their de Bunsen grandparents. There, what Oscar described as this 'set up "Upstairs, Downstairs"' continued. These were still the days of "Pea Souper" fogs when an unpleasant smell would descend as the streets disappeared in a dense yellow haze. John and

Oscar can recall that on one occasion, though, they were trying to get to the circus by car and, when the fog suddenly lifted for a moment, they discovered they were nowhere near but had arrived in the middle of Hyde Park.[2]

The boys were looked after by their "wonderful" nanny of whom it is said that, when asked once why she was so hot, replied, "Well I have got three vests on, one to keep the heat out, one to stop getting a chill, and one to soak up the perspiration". She was the anchor of their childhood and accompanied them on all their foreign travels and outings. Only once was her sang-froid disturbed. This oft-repeated family story concerned a shipwreck at Poole. Before their mother married Major Guy Salisbury-Jones in 1931, the boys and Nanny once accompanied them when they hired a speedboat to drive around the harbour. The young driver decided to demonstrate the power of his boat, 200m out into the open sea, whereupon the speedboat hit a submerged rock, broke the propeller shaft and water began seeping into the boat. "It was an unforgettable scene", recalled Oscar, as Salisbury-Jones cursed the trembling white-faced driver, who could not swim, and Nanny muttered to herself, "I must keep my mouth shut. I *must* remember to keep my mouth shut", interspersed with instructions to the boys to "keep their mouths shut", which would somehow prevent them from drowning! After a long, rather frightening time fearing the worst, their mother frantically trying to decide who should try to swim with whom on her back, the creamy vision of the Admiral's Barge of Poole Harbour rescued them. The incident was recorded in the *Daily Express* under the headline, "Guards Officer and Family Wrecked in Speed Boat".[3]

School, first to Glendower, then Wagners and finally to Eton College, must have seemed rather dull without Nanny's enlivening *bon mots*. By the time John was ready to leave Eton, however, dullness would have been preferable to the spirited action of warfare. He was nearly eighteen when the Second World War broke out but ineligible to join the army until he was eighteen and a half. Oscar was always struck by John's "immense curiosity as to how things work, and as to how they ought to work". In this respect and in his interest in science, he had much in common with his uncle, Robert Yerburgh, Lord Alvingham. John wanted to train as an engineer; being told by Magdalen College, Cambridge that a place would be kept for him after the war but that first, he should gain some practical experience, it was arranged through Sir Robert Micklem that he gain it at Vickers Armstrong. His experience at this vast, noisy engineering works near Newcastle might be described as "character building". The other fitter apprentices were Newcastle street boys who could not understand a word he uttered and decided he came from Devon. He was given overalls and a Union card and joined the thousands of workers streaming through the gates to clock in at 7:30 and out again at 5:00. No-one, however, told him where to sit or where to find the lavatories and lunch. He stood at a desk with a file to separate interlocking clamps for days on end but he knew that Vickers was building tanks with a new type of diesel engine with a super charger, and he was 'very interested in testing tanks'. Although his time at Vickers Armstrong was short, it gave him an insight into production methods, the operation of a large workforce, and the tanks he was about to drive for the Army.[4]

From Newcastle, he went first to Brigade Squad at Caterham as a guardsman, on to Pirbright for armoured training, and then to Sandhurst. In 1943 he was commissioned into the Irish Guards, took part in exercises and was sent abroad as Liaison Officer with Brigade H.Q. John's innate modesty would not easily reveal that far from failing Sandhurst, as he feared he would, he 'got a first *rate report*' there and, as Paddy Carew Pole told Bobby Alvingham, 'John has been given command of a troop (three tanks) on the exercise. Considering he joined yesterday this is a bit of a compliment!!'

The following year he participated in the British armoured advance towards Brussels where his scout car was one of the first to liberate the city: 'It was quite chaotic,' he recalls, 'as we had no proper maps of Brussels and I think we used school atlases!' Then came the less light-hearted battle for the Dutch bridges which he described as 'the most exciting time of my life'. Montgomery planned to seize the bridges over the tributaries and canals of the Rhine in a complicated,

combined armoured and parachute attack. He hoped this 'single knife-like drive' towards Berlin would end the war by Christmas 1944. John was with the tanks of the Irish Guards, chosen to lead the entire British Second Army into attack across a number of bridges over the Rhine. The Germans, naturally, did not just wave them through. 'I happened to be second in command of the leading squadron of the Irish Guards who led the Second Army from the bridge over the Escant canal,' John recalled to Peter Yerburgh. 'I think I was about sixth tank from the front. I was lucky as the nine tanks behind me were all "brewed up". Tanks were burning and slewing across the road.' In the event, the Irish Guards armour crossed the Niijmegan Bridge on 20 September 1944 but the advance was stopped two day later. The war in Europe would not be over by Christmas, after all. Having served with the Second Battalion in the Guards Armoured Division in France, Holland, Belgium and Germany, John retired in 1947 with the rank of captain.[5]

Although John was not in good health and had lost many friends in the war, he took up his place at Cambridge, where he switched from Engineering to read Economics. By this time he knew all about his inheritance and the Brewery business. He was in Hamburg on his way home to be demobbed when he happened to read in a newspaper: "Brewing Heiress dies". It was when he attended Elma's funeral at Barwhillanty that he learnt the exact nature of his and Oscar's inheritance and the choices they had to make about Barwhillanty and Caythorpe, and about the future of Thwaites. He was still only twenty-four and, as his grandmother realised, it would not be every young man's idea of fun to live at Barwhillanty in the south west of Scotland. The death of their father had inevitably propelled the boys more frequently into the orbit of the de Bunsen rather than the Yerburgh side of the family. They knew next to nothing about the Thwaites family, about the Yerburgh estates at Woodfold, Caythorpe and Barwhillanty and about the Brewery. Now the relatively inexperienced brothers were responsible for decisions that would determine the future employment of a large number of people.[6]

It was a relatively straightforward matter to settle the two estates. Their grandmother had willed them the option of buying them from their trustees at *The Times* price but had no wish to force them to do so or to live in them. Still, as she put it in her letter to Hilda, it would be nice for Oscar to settle at Caythorpe, 'the Ys being an old Lincs family … & he could do C(onservative) Council work!' Oscar, however, had no intention of doing any council work, nor much inclination to live at Caythorpe. Oscar was a pianist of considerable talent. While still at Eton, he was invited to study with Tobias Matthay and six months' later won the Senior Competition Medal of the Tobias Matthay Pianoforte School. He joined the RAF in 1944 and retired four years' later as a Flying Officer. On demobilisation he resumed his musical studies, travelling to study in Switzerland, Paris and Rome and toured South Africa by invitation. His intentions were, therefore, entirely bound up with his promising musical career and he wanted to live in Switzerland, not Lincolnshire. So he bought Caythorpe Court and then promptly sold it together with all the contents, and concentrated upon his music, with excellent results. His debut concert at the Wigmore Hall in October 1959 would receive brilliant reviews overflowing with unanimous acclaim from the critics, such as the *Daily Telegraph*'s judgement that he was 'an artist of unusual gifts and breadth of vision'. His mother, as it happened, found herself seated at dinner next to Edward Heath, who had no talent for small talk. "Oh Prime Minister", she finally ventured, "do tell me what you would do if you were not a prime minister?". "Oh", he replied, "if I could play the piano like a young pianist I have just been listening to at the Wigmore called Oscar Yerburgh". The conversation flowed thereafter.[7]

When it came to the Barwhillanty Estate, Elma had given John the wherewithal and the first opportunity to buy it from her trustees, in the same way her father, Daniel Thwaites, who had built the house, had done to her in his will. She had also told John what she had done, adding, 'You must please yourself about doing this'. She was concerned that if he settled at Bar, as she called it, he must be 'sure and remember that your wife will not find this as jolly as you do'. John had always loved Barwhillanty and as he could not yet conceive of being married, he felt no need to consider a wife's opinion. He felt more consideration for the fact that it had been his father's favourite place, and he decided to buy it and keep it on. The decision was braver than it immediately appeared to be. His brother recognised this, when he said many years afterwards: 'It must have taken a lot of courage for John, as a young bachelor after the war, to take on Barwhillanty and all that that implied'. Their uncle, Lord Alvingham, had inherited the Woodfold Estate and had been so defeated by the enormous unheated mansion when he already possessed a perfectly warm, sound house of his own, that he decided to maintain the estate but leave the house unoccupied and in disrepair. John, however, stuck to his decision, even when faced with a Victorian house that was far too big with dark brown wallpaper, boring prints on the walls, and whatever good pictures had once graced the walls were lying on the floor without their frames, which had rotted during the war.[8]

The question of the Brewery was more intractable. The first time John had ever heard about it was in the morning room at Barwhillanty when his grandmother had announced 'I'm leaving you some shares in a brewery, not all the shares, but some of the shares.' He was fifteen years old and a schoolboy. He thought no more of it, though at some point he gained a vague idea, no more, of a brewery in Blackburn. Elma Yerburgh never spoke to the family about the Brewery; it was trade and not something that a Victorian lady ever discussed in public or with friends and family. So careful was she to compartmentalise her private and business lives, that bottled beer served in her houses still bore no labels; Thwaites was, therefore, not a familiar name in her family. John's cousin Guy said his father Robert Alvingham, was thirty before he knew about a connection with Thwaites and the Brewery. John, in turn, had only learnt about it from his mother Hilda when he had returned home on leave in 1945.

Knowing about the Brewery, though, was quite different to taking an active role in its business. His grandmother understood this; that she was a wise woman and protective of her grandsons is clear from the letter she left behind for John. In it, she confirms first, that she has left some shares in Daniel Thwaites & Co. to him and Oscar and, second and importantly, that he does not have to make any decision

straightaway. He could wait until he was twenty-eight, (i.e. in 1951), before deciding what to do about the Brewery but then decide he must: 'if you carry on the business, or float it, or go in for profit sharing, or amalgamation with northern breweries or some similar concern.' Having said which, she also gives him her view 'I think you would be very wise to retain it, being a Director.' After all, she reasons, 'if I, as a woman, have attended monthly meetings from 1894 to 1940, you could do the same.'[9]

At the time of writing this letter, though unknown to John, she had made several new arrangements at Thwaites. Alfred Whittle had long been the partner at John Adamson & Co., accountants, who looked after the Thwaites accounts and attended Board meetings in that capacity. When he severed his connection with Adamsons in 1943, Elma had arranged for his appointment as a Consultant who would attend Board meetings. At the same time, she had confirmed to the Board her plans for the succession: that she remained Chairman during her lifetime but that C G Ashworth would become Chairman after her death; even though he was 'very good on finance, but on the cautious side for the liquor trade – "nothing venture nothing win"', as she told John. Jack Thwaites would remain Deputy-Chairman until his retirement, when Gerald Thwaites would take over until his retirement; and that James Hubberstey would go onto the Board upon his retirement as the Company Secretary.

When the War ended, though, Elma changed her mind about the Board positions. On 27 June 1946, she requested the directors to rescind her nomination of Ashworth to be her successor as Chairman, 'in view of the termination of the War and the return of Captain John Yerburgh to civilian life in the near future.' She was clear in her own mind that John should become Chairman but allowed that, although she had always been the Chairman, at first he might only wish to be Director. And she made sure that the best person was in place to guide him through the early years and teach him the business of proprietorship. While Hubberstey should be able to advise him about his yearly income, she wrote, Alfred Whittle would do so about his capital. Whittle was the ideal guardian, she explained to John. 'He has an interest in the concern, being the Trustee of Mr Rutherford

The White Bull Hotel in Blackburn, a Thwaites property where John Yerburgh stayed when in Blackburn.

(under the Public Trustee)' and Rutherford (Sir John Rutherfords's heir) was, next to her, 'the biggest recipient of the biggest dividends in D.T & Co.' She wrote more bluntly to Hilda about her plan for John: ' For another 10 years I am paying Whittle to guard him & teach him.'[10]

Thus, all was in order for John to take his place in the family business. At the first Board meeting after Elma's death, Alfred Whittle was elected Chairman and John was elected a director. On a freezing day in February 1947 John drove down from Barwhillanty to stay at the White Bull Hotel. It was bitter weather, quite the longest coldest winter people could remember, with snow and ice causing 'the Big Freeze' entered in record books. It was not the best time to be learning about a family business when fuel rationing, power cuts and black outs affected the smooth running of machinery and left people working in icy conditions with only candles for light. Many people, especially shopkeepers and licensees had deliveries and supplies cut off; bus and train services were severely disrupted so everything had to be done on foot, including collecting cash and orders from pubs and clubs. Under such conditions, the Brewery appeared more Dickensian than ever. It seemed 'full of old people' to John, and as he entered the yard, he had to walk past barrels and casks being washed outside in all weathers, even in the snow. The Brewery was an immensely old-fashioned place where virtually everything was still done by hand. He attended his first Board meeting as a director on 20 February and then stayed the night at the White Bull Hotel, which somewhat belied its reputation as the best hotel in Blackburn by then only being able to provide common bathrooms. He remembered the sound of clogs noisily

Working men in Blackburn with their beer served from a jug and clogs on their feet.

Satanic mills belching
smoke in the industrial
north. This is St Helens in
Lancashire but was not
untypical.

In 1949 Thwaites expanded its trading estate through the takeover of the Bury Brewing Company Ltd of George Street, Bury for £1 million. It was a small Brewery founded and registered as a company in 1868 but in its possession were 84 public-houses. These, together with its Free Trade outlets, provided Thwaites with penetration into new areas such as Rochdale, Middleton, Manchester and Bury itself. Many of the houses were in a poor, unmodernised condition with neglected pumps and beer engines but in good locations and, in spite of an initial reluctance from Bury's drinkers to accept Thwaites beers, the purchase was considered a very good acquisition. Although a few of the Bury staff were transferred to Blackburn, they soon found the travelling too difficult at a time when transport was affected by petrol rationing. There was, therefore little need for the staff integration procedures customarily associated with takeovers.[13]

It was around this period that James Mather, the General Manager, began to talk to Andrew Morton, the managing director and sole owner of Preston Brewery Ltd, about a possible acquisition. The two men knew each other well and Mather wanted to increase the Thwaites presence in Preston. As a prelude, Thwaites began to supply bottled beers to Preston Brewery houses, which were all managed houses with virtually a Free Trade, in that they stocked all the national brands because the Brewery no longer brewed its own beers. Mather also arranged friendly darts matches between Blackburn and Preston. Before a deal could be struck in 1952, however, James Mather collapsed in the office with a heart attack and died. The Preston Brewery business quite naturally went into abeyance as the Thwaites directors advertised for, and then interviewed, candidates to become their new General Manager.

Then Alfred Whittle took matters into his own hands and spoke to the Secretary Thomas Kay. "We have had many applications, but your's is not among them, how is that?" Thomas Kay replied that he was happy in his present position and would support whoever was appointed. To which Whittle's retort was "Put your application in immediately." Kay dutifully complied and was appointed

clanging down upon the cobblestone streets early every morning when the factories and mills started work as well as the grimy, soot-laden, dark buildings and tall chimney stacks belching forth smoke and grit. John would return to Barwhillanty the next day and largely kept to this routine for many years.[11]

In the first few months of his directorship, however, Jack Thwaites resigned as Deputy-Chairman and the Company celebrated the 50th anniversary of its incorporation by distributing a bonus of £2000 amongst the staff. In the summer it was decided to re-christen the Brewery with a more suitable name for marketing and advertising purposes. The name chosen was 'Star' and, on 22 January 1948, the Star Brewery became the registered office for Daniel Thwaites & Company, as it continues to be in the present day.[12]

General Manager forthwith. It was, therefore, Thomas Kay, who with Alfred Whittle, negotiated the purchase of Preston Brewery and its seventeen valuable licensed houses in 1956 for £278, 654. As a result of this acquisition, Thomas Kay's son, David Kay, was given the opportunity to look after the sixteen new managed houses and one tenanted house. Unlike the Bury properties, the Preston houses were in good condition and already familiar with Thwaites beers. David Kay transferred to Preston and combined support of the pubs with support of the Preston North End Football team. The trouble was that the Football Club had a midweek 'kick off' as they had no floodlights. Rather than ask for time off, David Kay, ever inventive, made sure that on match days he inspected the houses of three managers, who were keen football supporters. He did the first stock take at 6 a.m. and

the third at 10 a.m. and had finished by 1 p.m., just in time to see the Preston Football match 'kick off'.[14]

John Yerburgh was also visiting a great many houses as he followed a family tradition at the end of the 1950s. He had been selected as the prospective Conservative candidate for Blackburn in April 1959 and would oppose Barbara Castle, who held the seat as the Labour M.P. He was chosen from sixty candidates and pledged to fight the forthcoming General Election on the door knocker by visiting as many houses as possible. At the Annual Meeting of the Women's Association, held later that very evening, John admitted that, as a

bachelor, he was feeling a little frightened facing so many women. "But there is one lady I am not frightened of, and that is Mrs Castle," he said to resounding applause. "I am not frightened because I know that with your help we can throw her out." Unfortunately, he faced a difficult campaign in what had become a reasonably safe Labour seat. At the Election on 8 October he polled 24,490 against Mrs Castle's 27,356 votes, and, though he fought valiantly again in the 1964 Election, Mrs Castle won with an increased majority of 6893. Although 'it was a terrible wrench', he decided to stand down at the next General Election, saying that it was time 'for someone else to have a go.'[15]

He might not win an election, but he could further the cause of international understanding through education. In 1960, having returned from a visit to America, John inaugurated the Thwaites Travel Scholarship which was an award to be offered to young students from local schools to enable them to visit the United States. He invited the Mayors of Blackburn, Bury, Preston, Accrington, Clitheroe and Darwen together with their Directors of Education to discuss his plan. They enthusiastically accepted the responsibility of selecting suitable students while John got in touch with Mr Elphick, the national secretary of the organisation 'Experiment in International Living' which arranges accommodation with Host-families for up to four weeks for students travelling abroad.

There was great excitement the following summer as the first ever group of male Thwaites Scholars gathered for a tour of the Star Brewery followed by dinner at the White Bull Hotel. John made a brief speech in which he emphasised that the purpose of the Scholarships was to acquire knowledge of how other Nations lived and to present them with an image of what Britons were like. The Scholars, he said, are as important as British Ambassadors in promoting goodwill and better relations between peoples and countries and, therefore, 'it is very important to be a good ambassador.' Two days later, members of the group assembled at Blackburn Railway Station, posed for photographs and boarded the train for Preston and London en route to the United States. As Dick Cunliffe, who had succeeded Thomas Kay as Company Secretary, later recounted, 'It is needless for me to say that everybody comes back saying they have had the most wonderful time of their lives.' Since 1961, girls have joined the group to form mixed parties and, through Thwaites business links in Belfast, so, too, have students from Northern Ireland. Thwaites Scholarships' Students have travelled all over the world in the intervening years, from America to China and from Germany to Africa with great success to judge from the grateful letters John has subsequently received.[16]

Barbara Castle on a visit to the Brewery, and being shown the technological changes incorporated in the new building. Mrs Castle had won Blackburn against the Conservative candidate John Yerburgh who is standing behind her and to the right.

Above The Thwaites Travel Scholars from local schools embark on the first trip to the United States in 1961 Left The 2006 winners set out for Germany, seen off by the Mayor of Blackburn and Darwen, Dorothy Walsh, and Thwaites Travel Scholarship co-ordinator, Joan Halse.

The Public-House in 1957

'Our returning boys say "God Bless the British licensed
house." It saved our lives from loneliness; it is a
glorious institution and may it live and prosper for ever.'
The Agent-General for Ontario, c.1945

'Go round the country, go to the industrial towns, go to the
farms and you will see a state of prosperity such as we have
never had in my lifetime – nor indeed in the history of this
country. Indeed let us be frank about it – most of
our people have never had it so good.'
Harold Macmillan, Prime Minister 20 July 1957

THE SENIOR MEMBERS of the Brewery's staff who gathered at a licensed house on 14 May 1957 would certainly have seconded the Canadian sentiments and raised their glasses to the enduring prosperity of the public-house, should such a toast have been proposed that evening. The Chairman and directors had agreed that April to present every full-time employee with a pecuniary gift to mark the 150th Anniversary of the establishment of the firm and to hold a celebratory dinner. The size of the Company was then moderate. On 3 May each employee, from the newest office boy and the staff of the 37 managed houses to the oldest senior executive and pensioner, totalling only some 600 people, received from Alfred Whittle, chairman, and John Yerburgh, a director, the gift of a £5 note as 'an expression of appreciation of the part played by all personnel in maintaining the good quality and high reputation associated with the name of THWAITES which we are confident will continue in the years to come.'[1]

At the celebratory dinner, the number of executives and senior representatives of each department, who were accompanied by their wives, together with some pensioners and licensed house managers amounted, fittingly given the year, to a total of fifty-seven people. They assembled at the well-established Moorcock Inn at Waddington near Clitheroe, which offered superior, modernised accommodation in 'apartments' with baths, fires, morning tea, 'phone calls and cocktails. The Brewery dinner took place in the ballroom, where a good four-course dinner with coffee cost the Company a guinea a head. With the charges for drinks: a cocktail cost 2/6d [worth £2.18 today] a fine bottle of Sauterne 13/6d, a good red burgundy 19/0d [£16.53] , a liqueur 3/6d, and a mixture of drinks consumed afterwards at the bars £26–11–0, the bill for the evening came to £116–14–6 [£2033–35]. Under the guidance of the Master of Ceremonies, young David Kay, the two toasts 'The Company' and 'The Directors' were proposed by Philip Timson, the head brewer, and Richard Cunliffe, the company secretary, respectively, and replied to by Alfred Whittle and John Yerburgh respectively.[2]

It was announced that a new beer would be produced to commemorate the Brewery's birthday: 'We are confident it will satisfy the discerning palates of many old and new friends.' The directors' confidence in their head brewer and his team (which included a new assistant brewer, Philip Tann) was not misplaced. When the Board members sampled a glass of the new extra strong bottled beer in August, it more than merited their approval. All it needed was a suitable name. A competition was forthwith held within the public-houses and clubs, which provided the winning entry "Old Dan". Consideration was also given to the strength of the new beer. The lighter, weaker beers introduced during the First World War, and continued thereafter, had become so weak during the Second World War that in 1944 no less than *The Brewers' Journal* itself had urged the trade to promote beer as 'a temperance drink', in that it had become a 'relatively non-intoxicating product.' Lord Woolton, a former Minister of Food, even told the House of Lords that 'the greater barrelage of beer now being drunk consists largely of water – a beverage which is approved by the highest authorities.' The progressive decline in the gravity of beer during the war was called to a halt in peace-time by the public demand for stronger beers once restrictions and rationing were lifted – sugar rationing did not end until 1953 and rationing in general until 1954. Brewers, thereafter, gradually started to increase the gravity from the standard, ie. 1055º gravity, strength. Thwaites, therefore, decided to produce 'Old Dan' strong ale with a gravity of 1075º at a price of 1/6d per nip.[3]

The Traders Arms in Mellor.

Above The Load of Mischief with convenient if limited parking and *Below* Thomas Kay, the General Manager, overseeing the tipping of the pile of pennies collected for the Blackburn Ragged School at the Waterloo.

The directors had chosen the Moorcock for their function because it could provide not only a ballroom but also parking space and a garage. If public-houses wanted to compete in the more affluent market of the 1950s, they increasingly had to be able to cater for the motor car as well as the customer. This had not been the case for the Edwardian public-house, which had generally relied upon local trade or, at least, trade within the range of a horse or a bicycle. Early motoring was still then the preserve of the rich. As early as 1926, however, Elma Yerburgh was advising her directors that 'it would be advantageous to the Company if arrangements were made at some of our licensed houses for the parking of Motor Vehicles.' The first Thwaites parking ground was constructed that year at the Bay Horse, Osbaldeston and such was its success that parking grounds were also introduced at the Windmill Inn, Salmesbury and the Yew Tree Inn, Blackburn. This had presaged the inter-war fashion for 'a run in the country' by motor car and, especially in southern suburbs and along the coast, for the newly-built 'road house' type of public-house which offered ample accommodation for motorists and spacious dining rooms for coach parties. In the north, an increase in motor car ownership tended to accelerate the need to modernise the village public-house, rather than build 'road houses', so as to provide more modern amenities and drinking environment. By 1957, where feasible, any plans for improvements to Thwaites licensed houses, which possessed land, stables, outbuildings or were in rural areas, automatically incorporated parking facilities.[4]

All brewery directors in this post-war decade were concerned with the management of their tied house estate and, in particular, with the modernisation of their property and the replacement of tenants by managers. Usually, in these years, when a tenant retired from a successful house, a manager was appointed to replace him, as happened at the Fleece Hotel, Blackpool. While the process of keeping over 250 houses in good repair had always been a constant exercise at Thwaites, the implementation of a modernisation programme required the expansion of the estates department. In 1957 it employed an architect, a surveyor and some sixty builders, plumbers, carpenters, painters and decorators to renovate and refurbish these houses.

The sheer scale of the alterations and building programme, however, was daunting. No improvements had been carried out during war time but this had in no way affected the popularity of the public-house; it had been 'one of the few amusements almost universally still available.' Business had surged throughout the country as full employment, higher wages with a shortage of consumer goods, and the presence of foreign troops brought everyone into the local for a pint or three. The public-house heaved with customers, many away from home, such as the 'pint-pot girls', women who had discovered the delights of beer after a hard day's work. The difficulty for the trade lay not in selling but in producing enough beer to satisfy all the people in the bars; shortages of beer led to the familiar war time public-house notice 'No Beer.' In such times no one had minded about the appearance and old fashioned facilities of the typical licensed house.[5]

This was not to be the case, however, in peace-time and in the 1950s Thwaites, like the rest of the trade and the whole country, struggled to bring its housing stock up-to-date. Local authorities and licensing justices also pressed the Company to improve the level of sanitation and drainage in its licensed houses. Many properties lacked bathrooms, car parks, decent tenant accommodation and some even lavatories. In 1957 the Board's provision for this modernisation programme was £100,000. As part of a rolling programme lavatories and cloakrooms were added to or improved in all the firm's licensed houses such as the Hare & Hounds, Clayton-le-moors and the Traders Arms, Mellor, both still belonging to Thwaites, also received better car park facilities.[6]

One of its most popular residential hotels the White Bull, Blackburn was under scaffolding for many months that year as buildings were removed to create more room for manoeuvring cars in and out of the yard; new lounge and cocktail bars, a new luxury ballroom and bathrooms and lavatories were built; and the new Vaults (the northern name for a public bar customarily used by men only) were furnished in a way that would be conducive to turning into

Above The Boot & Shoe, Elswick and Saddle Inn Leatown, Preston.

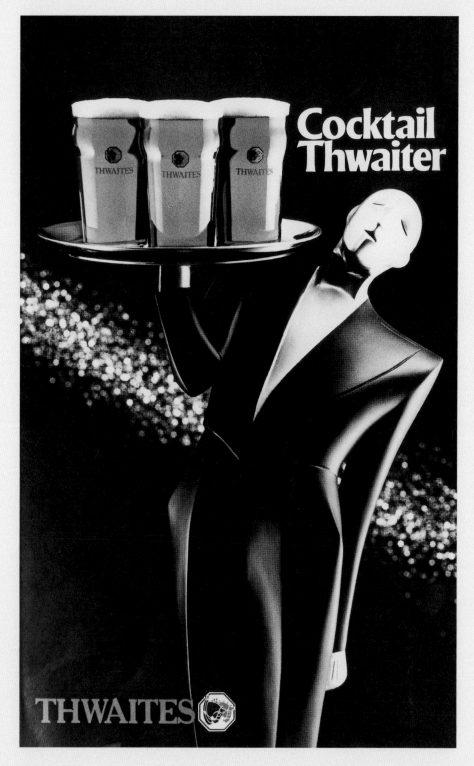

Cocktail Thwaiter

THWAITES

a modern 'Meeting Room'. When the new Cocktail Bar was opened just before Christmas, the General Manager Thomas Kay was able to report that 'It had been very well received by the public and the trade in the bar was very satisfactory.'[7]

Thwaites was not the only local organisation preoccupied with improvements. Blackburn's Borough Council had unveiled a town centre modernisation scheme in 1954, which led to the demolition of buildings including Duttons Golden Lion Hotel, a former ancient coaching inn on Church Street. Another familiar landmark there, the Old Bull Hotel had already been demolished. Meanwhile the Borough's Housing Committee had instigated a policy of clearance and redevelopment which swept away rows of cotton mill workers' old terraced houses on Audley Range, pulling down twenty-one of Thwaites licensed houses in the process. Other houses were forcibly destroyed through the redevelopment, those in Montague Street, in King Street and in the Griffin and Havelock areas. While some of these public-houses had carried on a small and diminishing trade, most of them produced a good barrelage, averaging at least ten barrels a week, and taken together presented a severe loss of trade for the Brewery. Elsewhere, Thwaites had long enjoyed a strong presence in Burnley, both tied and free trade, but a mixture of closure demands from licensing justices and redevelopment plans led to the loss of more profitable houses on good sites; in exchange, the Company built the 'Malt Shovel' on a new housing estate in Burnley. In addition, four houses were closed in Accrington and others at Darwen in the Brewster Sessions.[8]

To offset the effect upon production, Thomas Kay set out to acquire new houses and to extend the firm's trading area. In 1956 Thwaites purchased the Cottons Hotel in Knutsford, Cheshire (now a Shire hotel) though, unfortunately, a fire, which broke out on 4 December, resulted in protracted repairs. Other new acquisitions included the Grouse at Glossop and the Highwayman at Rainow, both still Thwaites houses. In 1957, Thwaites purchased the well-known Starkie Arms, Clitheroe from the owner-tenant and former mayor James Wilkinson for £21,000. The inn, originally the Rose and Crown, was developed in 1836 on the site of an older inn dating from Elizabethan days. Thwaites was able to install a Cocktail bar in time to catch the Christmas trade but other renovations had to wait until the new year. As Thomas Kay noted, though, the Cocktail bar was 'very well patronised' in Christmas week when takings amounted to £112.

The Company could also look to the public-houses added to its portfolio through the purchase of Bury Brewery Company in 1949 and of Preston Brewery Company in 1956, which went some way to compensate for the closure of the Blackburn properties. Of the original Bury licensed houses, the Swan & Cemetery remains a friendly family oriented Thwaites pub – the name by which the public-house was now popularly known. Just as the old Sun in Friargate, Preston retains its popularity as ' a town pub', and the Hole-in-One at coastal Lytham St Anne's continues to attract customers after a round of golf on the nearby links.[9]

Sporting links had always been a well-established feature of the Regency public-house when many landlords had been former prize fighters, dog coursers and even rat-catchers. This 19th-century tradition had continued and Thwaites had licensees who had been professional footballers, such as the well-known Harry Healless who had captained Blackburn Rovers when it beat Huddersfield Town 3–1 to win the FA Cup in 1928. Jim Smith was another famous Thwaites licensee; a Test cricketer who played for Middlesex County as a good all rounder, both a hard hitting batsman and medium paced bowler; according to a local cricketing fan, 'he drew crowds far bigger than any seen between the wars.' After retiring from Test play, 'Gentleman Jim' joined the East Lancashire Meadows Club where James Mather, a Club committee member, offered him the Millstone at Mellor.

Facing page Advertising began to reflect the social change as pubs went up-market.

Below Harry Healless who became a Thwaites licensee is here shown as Captain of the Blackburn Rovers FA Cup winning team of 1928.

Smith started there in 1946 and proved to be a popular licensee at what the Thwaites subsidiary Shire Hotels has since developed into an excellent country inn-hotel.[10]

'To be successful a pub needs to be warm and sociable,' averred a tenant in Hulme, Manchester, who reckoned a conscientious tenant in the 1950s needed to work sixty hours a week to run a pub well. The Second World War had resurrected the public-house as a place not just to have a drink but a place that was also at the heart of the local community. Indeed, the 'Morris' Committee Report of 1944, which resulted in the Licensing Planning Acts of 1945 and 1946 to redevelop war damaged houses, recognised the public-house as a national institution and 'an integral part' of British life. Thus, the 1950s public-house retained its popularity at the centre of post-war social life.

Crucial to its success were the landlord and the landlady and their ability to provide the right atmosphere and beer and to nurture their customers as well as their staff. 'A brewer can give a man good beer to sell in a well-designed house,' confirmed Alan Walker, former chairman of Bass, Mitchells & Butlers. 'He cannot give him the patience, tact and humanity which raise a good pub from being merely a place where drink is bought and sold to a house where there is warmth and understanding and an atmosphere of well-being.'[11]

An atmosphere of well-being was, nevertheless, furthered by the provision of good beer. Although there was an increase in the price of beer in 1951 of 1d a pint (the first for over a century not derived from beer duty), this did not unduly affect an overall downward slide in demand from its higher rate during war time. What did change more dramatically was the type of beer being drunk. The trend in the 1950s was away from traditional cask beers, which were often of variable and weak quality due to the rationing of raw materials and the neglect of cellar skills in unimproved

Bernard and Jean Houghton celebrate winning the prize for the best decorated Thwaites hotel. Three days had been spent trimming the tree and three weeks had been spent putting up the decorations.

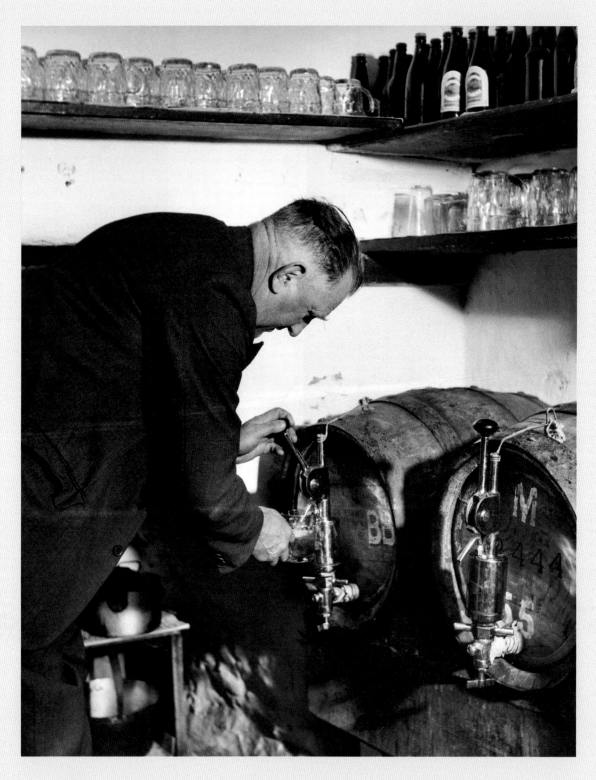

In 1955 glasses are filled straight from the barrel, a custom that was shortly to die out with the advent of technology.

pubs. Instead, wanting stronger beers, the public turned in ever larger numbers to bottled beer, which appeared 'clean, modern and high quality.' Returning troops, who had drunk mainly bottled beer during the war, continued to do so once back at home; women preferred its appearance; and the young employee, with a good disposable income in these more prosperous years, preferred and could afford a good reliable bottled beer.[12]

The rise in demand for bottled beer increased the sales of national brands such as Whitbread and Worthington pale ales and Guinness stout. Brewing figures for a typical firm showed that, by 1954, bottled beer represented 40 per cent of its bulk barrelage but 54 per cent of revenue, of which national brands contributed 21 per cent. Bottled beer also produced 'quite phenomenal' sales for smaller regional brewers. Such were the sales and higher profits on bottled beers at Thwaites that a new bottling stores plant was built and put into full operation by January 1957; the new plant was able to fill 900–dozen bottles per hour and the Bottling manager was more than satisfied with the machinery. Thwaites experienced an immediate success with its new bottled beer 'Old Dan'. Thomas Kay was delighted to inform the Board that 'sales of this beer had exceeded our expectations, and that it was going very well in the Company's houses.'[13]

Another change in the 1957 public-house which proved popular with customers was the installation of the television. The inaugural of a new television transmitter on the moors near Sheffield enabled television to be received in Blackburn for the first time in 1951. Sales in television sets soared in the town at the time of the coronation of Queen Elizabeth II in 1953. Many televisions were installed then in Thwaites licensed houses so that customers could watch her coronation and celebrate by drinking a glass of Thwaites special Coronation Ale.

With the mass popularity of television came televised beer advertisements. The Brewers' Society first used television in 1959 when participating pubs asked customers to vote for draught or bottled beers. The major national brewers started to place advertising campaigns for their premium priced national bottled beers onto television, which helped to make household names of the single

brand such as Guinness. The expense of such advertising, still in its infancy, was even then beyond the budget of most regional brewers. By the early 1960s, however, David Kay, the General Sales Manager, had moved the Thwaites advertising account to a new agency Bowden Dyble & Hayes of Manchester. One of the partners Ken Bowden suggested a regional campaign on Granada Television which would be localised and thus less expensive. The first such Thwaites advertisements consisted of one for Thwaites bitter beer filmed in the Elma Yerburgh, King Street (now closed down); one for Thwaites Cream Stout filmed in the Cock & Bottle, Tarleton; and the third for the best selling 'Old Dan'. The campaign was innovative and extremely successful and would lead to further national advertising featuring Thwaites Shire horses.[14]

The advent of television drew people, especially younger customers, who did not possess sets of their own at home, into the licensed house. In Blackburn, many of the cinemas, which had opened in the era of the Edwardian public-house, were now closing or being turned into Mecca dancing halls. When a craze for rock and roll took hold of the country and 'Teddy Boys' appeared on the streets of Blackburn, the elders of the town became so concerned about the threat to public disorder and decadent influence upon teenagers that they succeeded in banning the film 'Rock Around the Clock' from being shown in one of the few remaining cinemas. Five cinemas closed down in 1957 and the town's last theatre, the Grand, was demolished to make way for a new telephone exchange. By the end of the 1950s the appearance and amenities of Blackburn had begun to reflect the ongoing redevelopment programme. When the first set of floodlights were installed at the Blackburn Rovers' ground at Ewood Park and the Clean Air Act brought designated smokeless zones to parts of the grimy, smog-ridden Blackburn, it seemed to epitomise the approach of a bright new world to effect further modernisation in society and in the public-house of the future.[15]

CHAPTER SIX

John Yerburgh and the new Star Brewery

I N THE DECADE known as the 'swinging sixties', the emergence of a youth culture from the constraints of centuries of parental authority appeared to unleash the modernising tendencies of the once staid town planning authorities. Schemes for the redevelopment of town and city centres that had been refused or ignored in the past were suddenly regarded as being as up-to-date as the Beatles music and the mini-skirt. The Council in Blackburn climbed onto the contemporary bandwagon and resur-

rected the radical redevelopment plan for the town centre, which had lain dormant since the early 1950s. The plans for development of a 150-acre site that would involve the removal of the town's open air market and the demolition of rows of buildings, including the Thwaites Arcade, led to a public enquiry and a Royal Commission, which limited the site to a mere fourteen acres and approved the construction of the modern shopping block and covered market in the centre of Blackburn (still in existence today). In 1961

industry as companies bought into the 'bigger is better' philosophy. Within the brewing trade, for instance, wastage rates tended to be lower for the larger and more modern plant. The increased competition amongst brewing companies to maintain or grow market share led in the 1960s and 1970s to two strategic developments: concentration by acquisition, and diversification beyond the brewing industry. Large regional firms with well-established brands merged to form an even larger national group, as in the case of the merger of the Leeds firm Joshua Tetley & Son with the Warrington one of Peter Walker Ltd. to form Tetley Walker in 1960. This Company, in turn, merged with Ind Coope Ltd., and Ansells Brewery Ltd. in the following year and, in 1963, took the name Allied Breweries. It became one of the six major brewing companies, all formed in the 1960s; the other five being Bass Charrington, Scottish and Newcastle, Watney, Mann and Truman, Courage, and Whitbread.[1]

Of the three brewing companies then based in Blackburn, both Duttons and Matthew Brown were larger than Thwaites; where Thwaites had 350 houses, Duttons in comparison owned 500 houses and Matthew Brown 700 houses. The reason for the smaller Thwaites portfolio lay with Elma Yerburgh: she had resolutely held onto her shares and refused to issue more to finance expansion, as the other brewers had done. In 1964, however, one of the 'Big Six' brewers, Whitbreads, successfully bid £8m to take over Duttons. In fact, Duttons had earlier approached Thwaites about a merger with the proviso that John should become chairman of the new company. After conferring with Whittle, though, John had taken the view that, given the current high rate of taxation, it was not worth the risk; and, more importantly, he preferred to continue his grandmother's legacy and retain Thwaites as a family firm and remain independent. He later altered his opinion, though, saying 'I made a mistake over Duttons.'[2]

Where he certainly did not make a mistake was in his urge to diversify the business and, first of all, to rebuild and modernise the Brewery which had become quite out of date. 'We must have a modern Brewery,' he decided in 1964. Denis Robson, a Thwaites director but then still the partner

work started to culvert the River Blakewater at Salford, which destroyed the former Thwaites inn, the Bay Horse, and, in 1963, the centre of Blackburn degenerated into a noisy, dusty demolition site. The last vestiges of old Blackburn disappeared in 1964 when the outdoor market moved into the new indoor site of today and the ancient market hall and the fine clock tower were razed to the ground.

The urge to rebuild and modernise, which altered the British urban landscape in the 1960s, was not confined to shopping centres. There was a growing realisation within the business community of the economies of scale that could be achieved, especially in relation to the production and distribution functions of trade and industry. The trend for amalgamation and takeover adopted in the City in the 1960s, the' urge to merge', was also evident in the brewing at John Adamson & Co. who looked after the Brewery audit, believes it was key to the success of the Company. John, he maintained, 'did an extremely good job there and we have been complimented on our modern standards years hence.' It was a far sighted decision, enabling the company to achieve a better economy of scale and increase its standing amongst regional brewing firms at a time when so many of them were falling prey to larger predators. It was, however, not an undertaking for the fainthearted.[3]

The first stage was to build new offices to replace what Miss Birtwistle (always known as Miss B), executive secretary to Thomas Kay, described as 'the small, antiquated, dark old offices' which, apart from minor alterations, were essentially the same as in John's great-grandfather Daniel's day. The Company, therefore, purchased the site in Syke Street that had been occupied by Walsh & Co. Ltd., a pet food manufacturer, and erected an office block which, in 1964, was ultra-modern. It was spacious enough to house seventy members of staff and to provide a staff dining room and kitchen, 'which would make any housewife sigh enviously,' affirmed one newspaper report, complete with Catering Manager and kitchen staff. According to Miss B, on the Friday night, everyone packed up their belongings and papers and, on the Saturday, moved into the new building containing the spanking new Accounting Machinery, which replaced machines introduced in 1950 to supersede the traditional hand written ledgers, and a Computerised system.[4]

The old offices were then demolished to make way for the three storey cask handling unit with cellars, a new nine storey tower-brewhouse, and, eventually, a new bottling plant. On 22 September Oscar's wife Alicia laid the Foundation Stone for the new brewhouse. Underneath it lay a metal box containing two bottles of Thwaites beer, a typed history of the Brewery, a local newspaper and a record of the Four Pennies, (a local band) which had been prepared for the ceremony by Geff Palin and Miss B as a time capsule. Other aspects of the new beer house were not so easily managed. The most important, and most problematic, concerned the brewing process. Guinness in London had built a small experimental Brewery using a continuous brewery system. John went to see it and was most impressed. 'You put the malt and sugar in one end and like a sausage machine beer came out the other end,' was how he described it. Guinness, however, did not think it worked as well as expected and, as John and the Thwaites brewers discovered, there were, almost inevitably with experimental systems in a brand new Brewery, teething problems. Whereas the brewers knew the old Brewery 'like the back of their hands,' Philip Tann explained, in the new computerised one 'you couldn't see what was happening'. Not surprisingly, at first he found the sudden change nerve wracking.[5]

The other problem was how to retain uniformity in the taste and quality of the beer. In order to protect its product, the Company ended up running the old and the new brewhouses in tandem for twelve months, as the brewers were reluctant to use the new modernised one because the yeast had gone wrong and they were getting some bad brews; they preferred to continue using the old brewhouse. It could not produce enough beer, though, for either current business or the expansion that the directors were planning; it was three times smaller than the new Brewery, producing 300 barrels per week compared with about 1000 barrels in the new one. In the end, John insisted that a deadline was set for a transition to the new Brewery, which was beginning to dominate the skyline of Blackburn, as many of the old mill buildings were being closed down and demolished. The Brewery tower with its aluminium clad chimney faced the town's new market and shopping centre and an enormous neon sign proudly proclaimed THWAITES whilst on an adjoining building a clock face advertised 'Time for Thwaites'. It was, therefore, also time for the new Brewery to dominate production.

From the sales force's perspective, David Kay remembers that they had to be careful when opening the new Brewery and brewhouse in 1966 in case customers thought the beer had changed. In spite of some other hiccups, such as builders leaving a vent blocked, and the computer showing a flow of beer when none could be found, once everyone settled into the new brewhouse with its modern capsule control room, the beer was judged as good as ever and the

Right The old tun room showing brewing in open tanks.
Below The new conditioning tanks which replaced the tun room in the mid 1980s.

Barrels in the left picture have given way to the bottling plant below opened in 1972 with John Tate, the bottling manager, shown supervising the process.

to assume sole responsibility. He filled this role perfectly and assiduously: according to John, he was a good businessman who had always helped him enormously with Daniel Thwaites & Co., affairs. Whittle had a special gin bottle, which he kept half filled with distilled water, in the boardroom. At Board meetings he used to have two dry martinis and mark the bottle accordingly so that he always knew exactly how much he had consumed and, in old age, did not fall asleep at the meetings; in any case, over-indulgence or inattention were not habits Elma had ever condoned. Looking back at his early years at the Brewery, John believes neither he nor Whittle took enough risks with Thwaites, perhaps because neither of them then wanted the responsibility.[7]

John, however, was now well qualified to take on the role that his grandmother had planned for him and the decision that he and Oscar had taken in 1949 was the right one for the Brewery. At the time of the acquisition of Bury Brewery, Whittle had asked them to decide whether they would rather leave their fortune in the industry and expand in this way or 'get out while the going is good, say, by selling to the public DT&Co's ordinary shares' which would then have fetched nearly £3m and, at 3%, would earn them £90,000 a year. On the other hand, Whittle had pointed out, the Company had earned £400,000 in 1948 though for the purposes of their decision future profits should be taken as around £150,000, and the Bury Brewing profits of £80,000 in 1948 might drop to £50,000. Nevertheless, on the reduced estimated profits from the two concerns, the Yerburgh brothers could see profits of no less than £200,000 a year further reduced by interest of £40,000. 'I want you to try to weigh up the position carefully as it affects you & Oscar so much, one way or the other,' Alfred Whittle had written to John in 1949 before adding, 'We really should decide yes or no at the Directors meeting'. Against this, John had written '**Yes**'; the Yerburghs would keep their fortune in the Brewery and achieve concentration by acquisition.[8]

Thus, on 22 July 1966, he was duly appointed Chairman of Daniel Thwaites & Co., His fellow board members were Oscar, who in 1953 had become a director in place of C.G. Ashworth, and Arthur Birtwistle (known as Peter) of the

Above Alfred Whittle, who retired as Chairman of the company in 1972, on behalf of the directors presents a silver salver to Thomas Kay (on left) for twenty-five years service. *Facing page* the lager canning plant in full automated flow.

new Brewery, which had cost £5.5m, as a *tour de force*. When the new bottling complex, which cost £3m, was opened in 1972 it was considered to be 'the last word in bottling complexes in the country'. Vast numbers of people, and groups on arranged tours, came to see and marvel at this new brave new world of brewing at the new Star Brewery.[6]

This was also the year that Alfred Whittle retired from the Chairmanship, though he retained his seat on the Board and became the first President of the Company. 'He was such a powerful man' said Miss B, and John held him in great respect. A shy, quiet man, Whittle had been chairman of the large public concern Walpamur Ltd and Wallpaper Manufacturers, a well-known company with offices in Darwen. He was, therefore a part-time chairman of Thwaites, his main function having been to act as a safe pair of hands until the next generation of the family was ready

long established local cotton family, also since 1953. John and Oscar's brother-in-law Nathaniel Fiennes, a chartered land agent, had also joined the board. The senior members of staff who reported to the directors comprised Thomas Kay, General Manager; Alan Eatough, assistant General Manager; Philip Timson, Head Brewer since Frank Clubb's retirement in 1956; David Kay newly appointed General Sales Manager; and Dick Cunliffe, Company Secretary.

Having rebuilt and modernised the Brewery, John was now looking to increase the Company's sales of beer and, like the Big Six brewing companies, to diversify and grow the business beyond the brewing industry. First, he asked David Kay to investigate expansion into Northern Ireland. The result was the Company's purchase, in 1967, of Morton & Co. Ltd., a small family bottling concern, situated between the Shankhill and Falls Roads in Belfast, and the only firm to

have its own special label for Guinness: 'Red Heart'. John became Chairman, Morton McLure the Managing Director, and Kay father and son and Brian Morton directors of the Board in Belfast. David Kay every week thereafter used to cross over to Belfast on Mondays, spend Tuesday there, and return to Blackburn in the evening. Sales of Thwaites beers rose rapidly, and Mortons expanded into larger premises. Thwaites started to buy public-houses in Belfast and acquired twenty-seven of them. Soon, 300 kegs of beer per week were being transported from Blackburn to Belfast. Then 'the Troubles' started in Northern Ireland: the warehouse was bombed, pubs were blown up and the firm started to lose money. By the second year, John decided they had no option but to pull out and close down the once immensely profitable Northern Ireland operation.[9]

Another segment of the market in which initial success for Thwaites turned sour was the production of lager. Although the UK's beer consumption had been static in the 1950s it rose steadily throughout the 1960s and 1970s: from 24.6m barrels in 1958 to 42.1m in 1979, an increase of 71 per cent. This reflected a growth in population, greater prosperity, the emergence of supermarket off-licence trade, and a rise in the 'bulge' youth market of the consumption of lager. The increase in the popularity of lager started to make some inroads into the draught beer market, especially in the mid-1960s with the introduction of draught lagers, such as Harp. David Kay saw the need for a new competitive product to supply the demand in the free trade and pushed the Board to agree to produce its own lager. This, he thought, was the product to supply the extra business needed to keep the new Brewery at full capacity. Philip Tann remembers developing the Thwaites lager using a lager malt, Yugoslavian hops and English yeast. The name chosen to launch it was 'Stein' and David Kay arranged some television advertising.[10]

Stein lager was an excellent product and was extremely popular: 'We were selling 50,000/60,000 barrels of Stein a year, which was huge,' David Kay declared. Such success and the expansion of the lager market did not go unnoticed. It attracted the attention of the brands Carling and Carlsberg; the latter was spending £2m in one advertising campaign alone. 'Well, what chance had we got?' David Kay wryly admitted. This meant, as Denis Robson explained, 'that our customer, asked if he wanted a pint of lager, would ask for a Carlsberg or Carling. So, although we had a perfectly good product, we realised we could not sell enough of it.' Lager remained a problem for Thwaites throughout this period, when the sales of lager continued to rise but remained dominated by the brands. Moreover, overseas lagers were regarded as sophisticated and fashionable because holidays abroad provided an experience of drinking continental chilled beers, whereas home-produced lagers were condemned as second-best,

tarnished with an uninspiring image. 'It was a major decision for us to accept our Stein was not going to be successful,' admitted Denis Robson. Eventually, Thwaites arranged to stock Carlsberg in its pubs and to brew the sister lager Tubourg under licence in the Star Brewery, which was the first beer Thwaites ever produced under licence.[11]

There was, however, more than enough consolidation to be found in its other popular beers. The first time Thwaites ever entered for any award was, Philip Tann recalls, probably in 1955 when, at the behest of David Kay, it submitted an entry for Cream Stout and won a silver medal. From the 1970s onwards, Thwaites won a string of major awards for

Facing page In 1986 the Princess Royal paid a visit and was offered a drink by Philip Tann and John Yerburgh which she treated with some caution, only venturing a sniff.
Left Ray O'Brien, signwriter and George Leonard, maintenance painter working on a dray.

Right Philip Tann, head brewer, celebrates a CAMRA award in 1986.
Below The Thwaites team become the first north west England brewery to win the prestigious UK best cask-conditioned beer.
Bottom right Drayman Arthur Robinson and his driver-mate Michael Wright show off three gold medals won by the Brewery in the World section of the 1989 Championships.

the excellence of its beers, starting with the joint best beer of the year at the Campaign for Real Ale (C.A.M.R.A.) Great British Beer Festival where 'Thwaites Mild is Voted Tops' on 14 September 1978. It was the first time Thwaites entered its mild, brewed since 1958 for the competition. Ten days later, the *Sunday Mirror* announced that 'The North has once more proved it produced Britain's best beer'. Thwaites had won the coveted Supreme Champion Bitter Award and also claimed other medals for the best bitter in Britain. Alan Gregson, who had succeeded Timson as the head brewer and production director felt very proud: 'This has been a real team job all the way through,' he declared. The Company's beers continued to attract major awards under

Philip Tann's reign as Head Brewer in the 1980s. Starting with the CAMRA award for Best Mild in 1980, the ultimate accolade for any British Brewery came in 1983 with the brewing industry's own award for the Best Bitter in Britain. This was followed by the prestigious gold medal at the International Monde Selection in Geneva for canned Best Bitter two years' running in 1985 and 1986, and, again in 1986, Thwaites triumphed by winning the most significant award for CAMRA's 'Best in Britain' for its cask conditioned Best Mild. The critical acclaim from the industry for these awards enhanced the standing of the Brewery nationally throughout these years.[12]

There were further celebrations at the Brewery when the

John Yerburgh with his wife of a year and future company chairman Ann stand proudly beside the latest dray in 1974.

Chairman announced his engagement to Ann Maclaren in 1973. John, then aged forty-nine, appeared to be perfectly content to remain a bachelor, managing the Barwhillanty estate, entering into forestry matters with great determination and imagination, and attending to Brewery business. Then, commented Oscar, 'along came Annie (though she had always been just around the corner) a Cordon Bleu instructress no less, who seems to turn her immense vitality to almost anything,' and proceeded to turn John's heart and head into thoughts of marriage. His grandmother had advised him all those years ago: 'Don't marry a purely society girl; look and see if one wants the same person always to look at, say, at the breakfast table. I should say a Scots woman who would interest herself in the farm people'. Her words were most prescient for Ann Maclaren was all of this and more; full of life and laughter yet with a practical steadiness that would have delighted Elma as much as it did her grandson. John and Ann were

old family friends and neighbours, the Maclarens living at Brooklands, Crocketford, near to Castle Douglas and Barwhillanty. The couple were married on 3 March 1973 in Scotland. Everyone at Thwaites not only had cause for celebration but the means with which to do it. John had provided a £5 gift, so as 'to share in my happiness on this occasion,' to each of the Company's employees, pensioners and licensees. 'I have not been married before', he said, 'so I thought it would be quite a nice thing to do.'[13]

Throughout the seventies John and his fellow directors also thought it would be quite nice to get decent catering in their pubs. Food was becoming a more important part of the business in managed houses, which tended to be the biggest public-houses in the Thwaites portfolio. The rise in popularity of pub food is said to have been caused by the introduction of the breathalyser in 1967. At the time, dire predictions of the disastrous effect upon the public-house trade were voiced. In fact, the effect of the breathalyser had been to encourage breweries and publicans to produce more substantial food, not just bar snacks, for their customers; to the extent that catering courses offered by local technical colleges proved extremely popular with licensees and their wives. Yet the trend for better meals in pubs was not being followed in Thwaites houses, and the Board was aware that competitors were succeeding where its houses were struggling to get it right. 'We went through suffering and long board meetings talking about why we couldn't improve,' Denis Robson remembers. 'We also used several recommended food operators but no one seemed to make it work,'

At the same time John and Denis Robson, who had been a trustee of the Yerburgh family trusts since 1966, were also mulling over possible alternative revenue streams to offset, as Denis recalled, 'concerns about alcohol and legal restrictions because of the way smoking seemed to be going.' John was still keen to diversify out of brewing where possible, and into a related industry such as hotels. What he had in mind when he foresaw the idea of a hotel company was that certain of the bigger Thwaites houses could easily be expanded by adding a food operation and a bedroom block from which they could be made into hotels. He therefore wanted to find

Alan Eatough who had succeeded Thomas Kay as General Manager is handed a presentation silver tea service on his retirement in 1979. On the arm of his chair is his long serving secretary Miss Birtwhistle who also retired the same day

JOHN YERBURGH AND THE NEW STAR BREWERY

someone who knew about catering to run a new subsidiary company of the larger managed public-houses, which could more easily support a food operation. John's style of running Daniel Thwaites & Co. was to have other people to run the company for him; he allowed them great freedom of manoeuvre, never interfered with day to day aspects of the business, but there was never any doubt that they were answerable to him for results.[14] Alan Eatough, who had succeeded Thomas Kay as General Manager in 1970, had just retired after a successful nine-year term in 1979 and David Kay had been appointed Director and General Manager of Thwaites.

Shire Hotels

The new subsidiary company was named Shire Inns and consisted of five catering pubs and the small Millstone Inn at Mellor. John asked his equally new General Manager, 'Can we get someone to come and run the Company?' Through a mutual acquaintance, David Kay found Ian Harkness, a man with a good reputation, a specialist on the food and beverage side of Crest Hotels, a Bass Charrington company. In Ian Harkness's words, 'And that was it. What John Yerburgh had was a vision; that was as far as it then went, just a vision'.

After meeting John and the directors at Thwaites, Harkness was offered the post by letter from David Kay, 'We expect you to set up a hotel company, from finding and identifying the sites to opening and operating the hotels.' It was a marvellous opportunity to start a business from scratch but a high risk one. Although it was 1980, it was like stepping back fifty years; the Millstone was 'a mess with no baths or showers and charged £11 per night.' There were considerable problems with the other houses: one of them was managed by alcoholics; at another cases of a liqueur called Blue Bols had been purchased as part of some competition and never sold and the house was 'losing money hand over fist.'[15]

The first Shire Inns acquisition was a twenty-six bedroom hotel, The Crown at Wetheral, which, according to John, 'went quite well.' It made its return on investment and, after being remodelled, adding a gym and squash courts and

bathrooms, it became a good hotel situated in a lovely village. The next hotel, The Oaks at Burnley, was found by the Thwaites Property and Estates Manager and, according to Harkness, 'it was a disaster.' The old building offered a capacity for only thirty bedrooms as well as many other problems for a hotel developer. Harkness, still a one-man band reporting to David Kay and collaborating with Peter Eaton the company architect, remembers this as a low point for Shire. The subsidiary consisted of the Millstone, which was then not considered as a serious business 'although I always knew it would make money and now it does'; there was The Crown which was ticking over; and there was The Oaks, 'a potential nightmare.' Failure was staring Harkness in the face. Shire took it over, however, and at great expense converted it into a hotel, which later became the Group's offices. Then came The Cottons, at Knutsford, which was a large Thwaites pub originally bought by Thomas Kay in 1956. It was this time John, who spotted its potential as a hotel. 'He had this incredible vision of life,' confirmed Ian

An advertising card from 1946 for the Queen's Hotel, an early venture into the hotel business by Thwaites.

Harkness; he realised that the location of The Cottons near Manchester Airport would make it a good hotel. Harkness and his colleague Paul Le Roi started to develop it in 1983 and opened it in October 1984. Cottons was a storming success from the first day, with one of the best bedroom unit prices, and it set Shire Inns on course for profitability.

By then, Ian Harkness had already identified Shires fifth hotel or, at least, the greenfield site at Penrith upon which it

could stand. 'And I suppose that was the first real decision I made that was right, even though John Yerburgh was nervous about it'. Unlike the previous hotels, which had developed from existing buildings, this hotel would have to be built from scratch and would take a heap of money both out of the Company and out of the pot used by the brewery side for the acquisition of public-houses. It was, therefore, a major financial undertaking for the Yerburgh family. Although all the national companies had rejected the site, and Penrith had neither industry nor the amenities of a city to offer, Harkness believed that the leisure market was ripe for growth, especially in a tourist area such as the Lake District. He therefore set about trying to persuade John to build a hotel there. A hotel usually took about four to five years to build and open, and it was a much more capital intensive and longer-term project than the acquisition of a public-house which produces revenue straightaway. There were, however, tax advantages to consider which could offset the large costs over, say, twenty five years; even so, it remained a large investment. Yet John agreed to support the project and it turned out to be absolutely the right decision.

The addition in the building plan of a proper leisure club at Penrith was innovative and it would also provide weekend business. In those days, hotels did not contain health club facilities. Hotels might have small swimming pools but not large indoor ones complete with leisure and fitness centres and beauty spas. Ian Harkness, however, also had a vision and all the large Shire hotels would contain these attractions. This hotel, the North Lakes, with fifty-eight bedrooms, was opened in November 1985. In Denis Robson's words, 'it was done so well and admired by a lot of other hoteliers. That's when Ian's stock really started to

Opposite top left and right The exterior of the Millstone at Mellor and one of its bedrooms. *Opposite bottom* The North Lakes Hotel in Cumbria. *This page top and bottom* The Aztec Hotel outside Bristol.

rise after an early bumpy ride.' It was a very original and successful hotel, many people in the industry went to see it, and some even copied it.

It was after the opening of the North Lakes Hotel that the Thwaites Board agreed that the Shire hotel subsidiary needed to be developed further. It was clear that the central overheads necessary to run a hotel company with only three units could be reduced significantly when distributed over a larger number of units. In the 1990s, the Shire Inns concentrated upon opening hotels in business parks near motorways and ring roads. Between 1990 and 1993 the Aztec at Bristol, the Solent at Fareham and the Kettering Park hotels opened, costing Shire about £50m. Although designed with the requirements of the business traveller in mind and offering splendid conference facilities, each hotel also offers a haven of fitness, relaxation and beauty in its leisure centres

The ninth hotel could not have been more different. This was The Stafford, in St James's and as, Ian Harkness pointed out when describing its acquisition, 'this shows what a great company Thwaites can be when you need to do things speedily.' It took only three weeks from Ian Harkness first talking to Denis Robson and John and Ann Yerburgh inspecting it, to the due diligence and negotiation of the purchase. Trafalgar House, which owned the hotel, was undergoing cash problems and put it on the market; by January 1995 The Stafford was a Shire hotel. Trafalgar had not spent any money on it for a while so that Shire had to expend about £5m immediately on renovation and refurbishment. With this acquisition, Shire was entering a different section of the hotel industry, namely the luxury market, and appealing to a different customer base, namely

Top and bottom Kettering Park Hotel in Northamptonshire.

group is the modern gemstone of Thorpe Park, Leeds.[17]

In contrast with the speedy settlement of The Stafford purchase, it took five years to open Thorpe Park because the motorway had to be completed beforehand. It was, however, worth the wait as this was another 'storming success' when it opened in 2002; a stunning contemporary hotel with an internal courtyard which provides a natural centrepiece. 'It had the whole industry buzzing and we have already seen people try to copy it,' Harkness admitted. Under Gordon Jackson, the General Manager, the Leeds hotel aims to provide quality care in every area and a well-trained friendly staff who offer an informal yet professional approach to its guests. The Shire Hotels, as the group was renamed in 2001, are successful because they attract good teams of people to staff them and they train them to 'see' the customer. Tony Spencer, now Managing Director, emphasises the family mentality and atmosphere but also the challenge of anticipating what each guest is looking for from a particular stay and responding to the fact that next time that guest might be looking for quite

Ann, John and their son Oscar Yerburgh celebrate in a hot air balloon the opening of the Solent Hotel at Fareham with its own spa.

the American market, which stemmed from the Second World War when American forces were based in London and many of them have remained loyal to The Stafford Hotel ever since. There are thus special aspects to running this hotel that do not apply to the other members of the Shire group but the directors believe the Shire team led at present by Stuart Procter presents the right mix of a quietly lavish country house in central London that provides guests with the right balance between professionalism and friendliness during their stay. The Stafford has achieved AA Red Star Status and been voted number one in London by a travel guide. It is the traditional jewel in the Shire crown where the latest hotel to join the

The Stafford in St James's, London
which became the luxury flagship of the
hotel group in 1995.

Below left The Thorpe Park Hotel in Leeds with its internal conservatory courtyard; *Right* The café in the Conference centre; *Below right* Looking across the swimming pool to the Terrace Lounge.

In 2004 the hotel group celebrate winning the AA Hotel Group of the Year outside the Oaks Hotel which had been part of the group. The banner is held by Ian Harkness (left) and Tony Spencer.

different things for a different reason. 'You can never be 100 per cent better than your competitors but you can be 1 per cent better in 100 different ways,' is a favourite expression at Shire to sum up the approach to service. The former chief operating officer of an international chain was heard to say at Thorpe Park, for example, 'Why can't we get it right, the way these people get it right?' There is clearly a different style at Thwaites in terms of people.

And, every time Shire opened a hotel and John addressed the staff, he always reiterated that it does not matter 'how much is spent on the physical aspect of the hotel, how nice the rooms are, how good the restaurants are, it is all down to the staff. For it is the people who always make it work well.' The successful growth of the Shire Hotel group was recognised by the award of the AA Hotel Group of the Year for 2003–2004.[18]

In 1993, however, John decided it was time to relinquish the chairmanship of Thwaites but retain his seat on the Board – he would no longer have to control it and master the details but he would remain part of it and, he thought, enjoy the experience more. His philosophy throughout his years as Chairman had been to get the right people in to manage the business and then give them the freedom and respect to do so. Ian Harkness evaluated John's attributes: 'he is a fantastic guy, with a very clear vision of the business, he's highly intelligent, very articulate, and old school in that he has managers to manage everything for him'; while Denis Robson reflected that 'John has always believed that it is in the family interests to keep the business going and maintain independence; to that end he has built up a strong thriving company for his successors.'

The two men had always worked well together and shared similar viewpoints about the direction of Thwaites; it was not surprising, therefore, when John asked Denis Robson, still senior partner at John Adamson & Co., to succeed him. And so for three years, Robson combined the role of senior partner of Adamsons with the chairmanship of Thwaites. Denis jokingly said he was, like Whittle, 'an old codger who knew a bit about the background of the Company.' Yet he had a far more important part to play in that, like Alfred Whittle, he had come to know a great deal about the business and the Yerburgh Settlements, possessed the technical specialist knowledge to advise accurately about current concerns in a quiet, reflective way, and could protect the Yerburgh interests until the next member of the family was in place to become Chairman.[19]

There had by this time been changes both generally in the industry and specifically in Thwaites. Two changes had marked the brewing industry in the late 1970s and 1980s. The first was the heavy cost of promotion required to promote national brands; national advertising spending on beer grew from about £2.2m in 1955 to £33.4m in 1979 and television advertising, which had accounted for 5 per cent of the total spent in 1955, amounted to 75 per cent in 1975. Almost all of this was lavished on brands of keg beer. As sales of bottled beer began to languish in the 1960s, the technological development of keg beer (which was

pasteurised and filtered to make it less susceptible to poor cellar skills and more easily transportable as it remained within the keg) enabled the Big Six to create national draught beer brands such as Worthington E, Younger's Tartan, Red Barrel, Tankard and Double Diamond. It lent itself to centralised production and the achievement of economies of scale and all breweries, including Thwaites, were soon producing keg beer.[20]

The second major change in the brewing industry resulted from a reference by the Office of Fair Trading to the Monopolies and Mergers Commission in 1986, which produced an in-depth investigation into the brewing trade. No other industry has been 'so crawled over by officialdom' as brewing; it had been the subject of at least fifteen official reports in the previous thirty years, for, as a recent history of the industry noted, it manufactures a popular but potentially hazardous drink that has long

John Yerburgh handing over the reins of the company to Denis Robson in 1993.

been a major source of public revenue. These investigations whilst critical of the tied house system had not succeeded in any radical changes to the industry and the trade was minded to assume that such would be the case again. The Monopolies and Mergers Commission [MMC], however, was minded to prevent further concentration in the industry and ruled against the Scottish and Newcastle bid for Matthew Brown, and of Elders bid for Allied-Lyons in 1985, and eventually, in 1989, reported on *The Supply of Beer*. It concluded that 'a complex monopoly situation exists in favour of the brewers with tied estates and loan ties', and that this' restricts competition at all levels,' which 'operates against the public interest.' After the MMC's findings were subjected to a vociferous publicity campaign by the brewing industry, in which Lord Young, the Secretary of State for Trade and Industry, was accused of destroying more pubs than the Luftwaffe, the Government watered down the recommendations in the 1989 Beer Orders. These nonetheless, remained fairly radical, as the Orders required that, by 1992, brewers owning more than 2,000 on-licences had to dispose of their brewing business and become retailers or they had to free from the tie or sell half their pubs over the 2,000 limit. In consequence, the large players in the trade have either divested themselves of pubs or, in some cases, left brewing altogether while new specialist conglomerates have entered the retail end.[21]

Whilst Thwaites was not affected by the 2,000 limit, it had increased its ownership of pubs through the acquisition of Yates & Jackson of Lancaster in 1984. Yates & Jackson was not in financial difficulties when it decided to sell but, it admitted publicly that ' we can't go on trading like this over the next decade, so we decided to go now when we could choose a partner who was able to give beer of the same quality.' Thwaites added forty public-houses to its estate at a cost of £7m and was able to sell the Georgian brewery to Mitchell's of Lancaster. As a result of the Beer Orders, Thwaites also purchased some thirty public-houses from Bass, which extended its geographical reach into Yorkshire.

When Denis Robson became Chairman, David Kay was just reaching the end of his era as Managing Director but stayed on to see Robson settled in 'and did a very good job of it.' According to Denis Robson , David Kay 'made very good choices of people' and demonstrated it by his 'inspired' choice of a successor in Paul Baker, who became Managing Director in 1995 and proved to be a marvellous salesman with an ability as a negotiator second to none in technique. 'You have to wear lots of hats and drive everything,' he said of life in a regional brewery like Thwaites. He introduced new site agreements and modernised the management structure of the Brewery side by creating an operations board consisting of heads of departments. During his tenure, contract brewing also increased as the Brewery could brew the smaller lines which the larger groups wanted to outsource. Another change in internal procedures was the introduction of a five-year cash flow plan, common in the industry now but fairly novel in 1994 and an important planning tool. Denis Robson saw his role 'to be there and listen to the managing directors' so that they could bounce ideas off him. It was also important to balance the shopping lists of the two sides of the business, the brewing and the hotels under Paul Baker and Ian Harkness respectively. Denis Robson was also delighted to see a real improvement in the food in the managed houses under the tutelage of Paul Howarth, who was brought in by Paul Baker, and started a food revolution with the introduction of a couple of lady caterers.[22]

Denis Robson remained chairman until 2000 when Ann Yerburgh was ready to become the present Chairman of the family concern, Daniel Thwaites & Co. By then, the five Yerburgh children Henrietta, Arabella, Roseanna, Matilda and Oscar were old enough and she had the time to offer to such an appointment. Ann had also been on the Board for many years and gained sufficient business experience 'to have a go.' Denis Robson had no qualms about her qualifications for the post. She combines an ability of leadership with immense sociability: 'she gets on with anybody anywhere and is an absolute bundle of energy, amazing energy.' In terms of business experience, she had, as John before her, a good team upon which to rely. She particularly availed herself of the advice of Denis Robson; Winston Pickup, the Company Secretary for many years, who had started as a clerk in James Pickups in 1964 and was a fount of all Thwaites knowledge; her finance director David Lowe; the two managing directors and a strong Board of directors. That the family has continued in harmony throughout 200 years is notable and Ann upholds John's belief that the family will maintain the business and keep it independent for the Yerburgh generations to come.[23]

Thwaites celebrates its bicentenary with a specially built 200 Glorious Years dray.

The Public-House in 2007

*'The pub is the best run outlet for selling beer anywhere
in the world. It is a place to meet friends, to relax, to escape stress,
to have a laugh, a chat and even a grumble. In essence it is the
social ambience in pubs that accounts for its success.'*
Sir Charles Tidbury[1]

BY THE BEGINNING of the 21st century, the total number of alcohol retail outlets in Britain had grown by over fifty per cent since the mid-20th century. The public-house of 2007, however, faces competition from a greater variety and quantity of retail outlets than its Regency, Victorian, Edwardian and 1957 predecessors ever did. Beers, wines and spirits are sold today in pubs, restaurants, cafes, clubs, off-licences, supermarkets, corner shops, department stores and garages. The growth in sales has been accompanied by rising levels of *per capita* alcoholic consumption, especially of lager, spirits and wine, reminiscent of the boom years of beer consumption in the19th century. In 2007, however, a drinking culture has developed that is more fashion-driven, gastro-centric, bougeois and Europeanised. How has Thwaites adapted its public-houses, long used to a largely beer based drinking culture, to this new trading environment?

Thwaites started with some ten public-houses in 1807 and the Company now has a pub estate of over four hundred in 2007. Under the ownership of the Thwaites and Yerburgh families it has always paid meticulous attention to the refurbishment and maintenance of all its existing pubs. There is a rolling programme of redecoration so that interior design of a high and expensive standard, comfortable furniture and soft lighting are standard features. The Company has dovetailed its stock to meet specific customer markets. There are modern and traditional pubs; town and country pubs; and family pubs. And in all of them Thwaites aims for

excellence. Thus, one of its most modern and popular Blackpool houses, N.T.K. (Need to Know? In internet language), which opened in 2000, won the prestigious Gold Award in 2001 following a survey carried out by Blackpool's tourism department. 'The place has proved a massive hit and it is always particularly pleasing to win something selected by the customers themselves,' commented the delighted manager Mike Sugden.

The Company's guidance and provision of training for staff in both its managed and tenanted houses is thorough and supportive. Its high reputation as an employer and excellent care of its pubs won the Publican's Pub Company of the Year award in 2006. 'This is a fantastic achievement,' congratulated Brian Hickman, the current Managing Director of Thwaites, and shows 'that all the work we are doing as a business to focus the direction of our pub estate is giving customers the best possible service and surroundings.' In another example of the wide range of the Thwaites pub portfolio, the Grey Mare at Belthorn boasts breathtaking views as the highest pub in

Lancashire. A family-run country pub, it has recently extended the restaurant area and went on to win the Catering Pub of the Year 2006 award and also feature in the 2006 Good Beer Guide. As the Licensee Becky Price commented, 'The food side of the business is very important to us and we go to great lengths, to ensure these high standards are maintained.'

Thwaites has also met increasing competition and consolidated its strength as *the* Northern Brewer through geographical expansion: 'Our long-term strategy is to expand our pub estate with top-class community houses,' explained Paul Baker, group board director and former managing director. In 2000 Thwaites invested £7 million in buying nine flagship managed houses in the Midlands from Bass. Two years later it acquired twenty-eight houses from the Nice Pub Company, the tenanted arm of Tom Cobleigh Ltd, which provided a geographical reach stretching across Yorkshire and down into Derbyshire and Nottinghamshire. Then, in 2004, Thwaites expanded its trading estate further through the purchase of the Rosewood Pub Company and

fourteen pubs, which took the Company down into
Cheshire, Staffordshire, Shropshire and the West Midlands.
According to Paul Howarth, Retail director, 'These are
substantial and sustainable pubs run by excellent tenants,
and we view it as a great long-term investment.' The search
for quality well-run houses in prime locations is a
continuous exercise, as Malcolm Harrison, Property director,
pointed out: 'the buying has not stopped, far from it. We
remain in the market for attractive and desirable houses in
good locations.'

The firm has also expanded the range and quality of its
products to compete in the new trading environment. This
is especially the case with wines; there has been an
exponential growth in wine drinking in pubs and more

wine was consumed in the United Kingdom than ever
before in 2005/6. The demand for wines in pubs originated
with an increase in the number of people either taking their
holidays, or travelling more frequently for business, abroad
and becoming more familiar with the huge variety of wines
available. The leap in the sale of imported wines in England
since the 1960s has been spectacular and the expansion
continues unabated with a wide range of wines from Chile
and Argentina, for instance, joining brands from Australia,
New Zealand, America and Europe.

Thwaites is able to meet this demand through the
expertise of its own wine merchant James Pickup & Co.,
established in 1790 and a division of the Company since
1923. Cathy Swift, wine development manager, has seen

wine volume in Thwaites pubs grow by almost 20 per cent over the last two years. She helps the public-houses develop their own tailor-made wine portfolio from a choice not only of branded wine but also of wines that are a little bit different and less well-known, 'such as small *Domaine* wines direct from the vineyard, wines that can only be found in the on-trade, and [have] a wealth of different grape varieties to suit all palates.' The latest Thwaites wine catalogue incorporates a new section about wine and food, coupled with authentic recipes, so that the pubs can offer their customers a full 'wining and dining' experience every day of the week. However, as she points out, wine trends are now changing every year so it is necessary to keep abreast of changes in customer choices; in 2007, 'consumers are still finding that new world wines are much more approachable and fruity.'[4]

In spite of the growing popularity of wine, especially with the female drinker, it is still the quality of the beer upon which the overall reputation of the public-house rests in 2007, especially with the male drinker. 'The taste and appearance of the product is my concern,' reiterates Steve Fielding, the head brewer at Thwaites since 1999. As tastes have changed in the drinking population, so he has had to ensure that traditional methods are maintained while new

Thwaites Head Brewer Steve Fielding receives his award as Brewer of the Year 2006 from Michael Martin MP Speaker of the House of Commons.

products are developed. 'That's why we developed Thwaites Smooth Beer and it has proved to be a real success,' he pointed out in 2001. Since then, Thwaites has expanded its range of brands to offer more choice while retaining its global reputation for a quality pint; from Warsteiner premium lager and Kaltenberg Hell to Thwaites Original and the new Daniel's chilled blonde beer, all these beers have 'Drinkability'.[5]

In 2005, England Test cricketer and local Lancashire boy Andrew Flintoff became the face of Thwaites Lancaster Bomber and fronted the marketing promotion for this innovative beer, Brian Jenkins, Sales and Marketing director, was delighted with the success of this campaign, whilst Flintoff said, 'As a proud Lancastrian I am delighted to link up with Thwaites, one of the country's best known names and a brewery which continues to enjoy a great association with Old Trafford and Lancashire County Cricket Club. Add to that the fact that Lancaster Bomber is a superb beer and it sounds like the perfect partnership to me.' Steve Fielding and his team had produced yet another great beer with 'Drinkability' as Lancaster Bomber achieved excellent sales. In 2006 Steve Fielding was crowned for another beer, Kaltenberg Hell, when he was named Brewer of the Year and collected the prestigious title at the All Parliamentary Beer Group Awards. As the Parliamentary Beer Group Secretary said, 'To brew a credible lager in a traditional regional brewery is an achievement in its own right.' Now, in 2007, Thwaites has introduced the new 'Double Century' commemorative cask and bottled ale to mark its two hundred years as a brewery.[6]

In a similar fashion to the developments in wine, the 2007 public-house also offers a much wider and more interesting variety of food to its customers than ever before. The traditional bread and cheese found in the Regency public-house remains on the menus at the 2007 pub but its quality and presentation would not be recognisable to the 1807 customer. There is, nevertheless, a host of more exotic dishes representing both international and regional cuisine on offer in the present-day pub. At Thwaites, Judi Houghton, catering manager of the pub division and her team ensure that pubs are equipped to provide the gastronomic attraction of home cooked meals with fresh local ingredients to serve at lunch and dinner. In this bicentennial year, the success of Thwaites food operation has been recognised by several awards and notices. Judi Houghton is overall winner for the Training Concept of the Year 2007; she was a finalist in the catering development professional of the year and Thwaites was a finalist as food operator of the year. Most exciting of all, Thwaites was the overall winner of the Morning Advertiser Pub Food Excellence Awards for 2007.

The Brewery teams of Shire horses have been associated with the delivery of its beer to public-houses ever since the Eanam Brewery was first built and Daniel Thwaites joined the partnership in 1807. It is, therefore, most fitting that, in

Facing page Freddie Flintoff the Lancashire and England Cricketer was the face of Thwaites Lancashire Bomber in 2005.

The Brewery continues to sponsor a wide range of sports; here one sportsman celebrates with a pint of Thwaites Smooth.

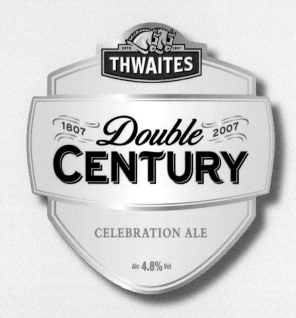

The new 'Double Century' beer commemorating Thwaites bicentenary.

the bicentennial year of 2007, the horses, who have won so many prizes and awards over the years and have provided a marvellous advertisement for Thwaites, have won yet more awards recently. 'A fantastic show for our horses!' was how David Kay described the latest Shire Horse Show to Ann Yerburgh on 19 March 2007. 'Hitched to the specially painted 200 Glorious Years dray, the four-horse team won Champion turnout!!!. They looked wonderful,' and were the object of widespread and expressed admiration, 'On the final lap of honour the public address commentator said,"How proud the Chairman of Daniel Thwaites Mrs Ann Yerburgh must be of this simply superb turnout."[7]

Throughout the years of her chairmanship, Ann Yerburgh has taken great pleasure in being able to praise the 'first-class performance of our Shire horses,' as they have won glowing praise and fresh awards and continue to be 'a marvellous advertisement for Thwaites.' Yet she is also keen to recognise, as both Elma and then John Yerburgh always were, that awards and good results are, in her own words of 2004, 'due largely to our excellent people who once again deserve praise for all their hard work and effort.' When announcing profits of £13.2m with record sales across the group in a good year, she took the opportunity to say "Well done to everyone and thank you." In the stringent trading environment of the present day, results cannot always be so uplifting and, as always throughout its history, the government of the day likes to add its own legislative contribution to the challenges facing the Star Brewery.[8]

In the 2005/6 year, the brewing industry had to cope with the complexities of the Licensing Act of 2005, whereby licensing responsibilities were transferred from Magistrates to Local Authorities; thus rendering all licences obsolete with one stroke of the pen. A torrent of applications for new licences occupied the brewing industry throughout the summer, whilst a tidal wave of articles on binge drinking occupied the newspapers and other media. The new licensing law introduced longer

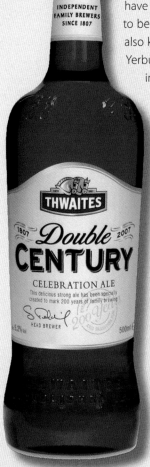

opening hours with fewer restrictions than previously for public-houses. Although most pubs only wished to vary their existing opening times by an extra hour or so at the weekend, the media concentrated upon twenty-four hour drinking to create a swell of moral anxiety and indignation. It was as if the nation was once again drowning in the 18th- and 19th-centuries' 'torrent of gin' with dramatic footage of images of town centres filled with groups of paralytic youths and scantily dressed inebriated young women staggering around in an apocalyptic vision of social chaos reminiscent of Hogarth's famous 18th-century illustration. Once again, the echo resounded down through the centuries of similar social behaviour: of street violence, the corruption of women and the threat to family life and English identity. In the event, however, as in 1807 and 1907, the threats proved short-lived and the damage slight. The new licensing laws came into effect without raising so much as a hair on a policeman's head.

The 2007 public-house met this legislative change, and will no doubt meet the impending smoking ban in the summer, as its Regency, Victorian, Edwardian and 1957 predecessors met their challenges, by continuing to serve customers in the best way possible, confident in the enduring tradition of the place of the public-house at the heart of the British community.

The changing face of
the Public-House in
2007 typified by the all
new NTK in Blackpool.

From left to right, Judi Houghton, Gordon Jackson, Tony Spencer, Ian Harkness, Mrs Ann Yerburgh, Mr John Yerburgh, Paul Baker, Brian Hickman and Mike Connell.

By 2004, Thwaites had consolidated its position as a leading northern brewery. In that year for example the group achieved widespread recognition for both its products and people when it received a host of awards. The Publican gave two awards to Thwaites for Pub Food Company of the Year and to Judi Houghton, catering development manager, Food Champion of the Year. The British Institute of Innkeeping National Institute Training Association awarded Professional Trainer of the Year to Mike Connell. Two of its beers were singled out for prestigious awards, withy Kaltenberg winning the Silver Medal and Lancashire Bomber winning the Gold at the Monde Selection. On the hotel side Shire was named RAC Hotel Group of the Year and *Catering and Hotelkeeper Magazine* named Thorpe Park Hotel and Spa, in Leeds its Group Hotel of the Year. Last but by no means least those perennial winners, Thwaites famous Shire horses were named Best in Britain at the Shire Horse Spring Show at Peterborough.

Ann Yerburgh takes Thwaites forward

This book has been a wonderful insight into the history and events of Daniel Thwaites PLC and the controlling family influence over the past 200 years. It is the family's commitment to the future and the long-term investment in the business that have always made the difference between Daniel Thwaites and many other independent companies, which have never achieved their bicentenary. The ownership and management structure have given clear vision and direction to the whole business, together with a set of values cascaded down to every employee. It is this controlling philosophy, together with the employees and the unique beer brands, that sets Daniel Thwaites apart from the rest, and continues to provide the foundation for the future. As Winston Churchill said on 10th November 1942; 'This is not the end. It is not even the beginning of the end. But it is, perhaps, the end of the beginning.'

The Group chairman and her managing directors: Ann Yerburgh with Brian Hickman (left) and Tony Spencer in 2007.

Acknowledgements

This book owes everything to John and Annie Yerburgh who asked me to write it and then had to wait much longer than anticipated to see it completed; their encouragement, wise comments, hospitality, friendship and numerous kindnesses have provided so much enjoyment and enhanced my writing life.

It would have been impossible to write a history of Thwaites without David Kay, whose knowledge of the Brewery and the people helped me enormously and made the research so enjoyable.

To my 'history committee', the Yerburghs, David Benson and David Kay, my heartfelt thanks for reading drafts of the book with unflagging interest and for offering pertinent suggestions.

I would also like to thank all the directors and staff of Daniel Thwaites Brewery and Shire Hotels who answered my questions and provided help and information. I am especially grateful to Denis Robson for deciphering old balance sheets; Brian Hickman for discussions about Thwaites; David Lowe for much-needed amendments to the text; Susan Woodward for enabling me to meet pensioners and for unfailing help with all my enquiries; Malcolm Harrison for help with the pubs portfolio; and Jane Waterworth for providing material about the hotels. Denis Robson, Paul Baker, Winston Pickup, Ian Harkness, Tony Spencer, Philip Tann, Miss Birtwistle, Eric Walmsley, Steve Fielding, Gordon Jackson, Kate Renicor, Ernest Halliwell, Frank Stones, George Stevens and Raymond O'Brien submitted graciously to being interviewed and gave me a wealth of material, as did so many other people. For assistance in a million other ways, I must single out Joan Halse, whose cheerful reliable efficiency worked wonders at crucial moments. Anson Bolton and the staff at the Millstone Hotel, Mellor, showed me the friendliness, quality care and delicious food to be enjoyed at Shire hotels. And Arthur Asteles made driving around Lancashire a pleasure.

As a non-Lancastrian I leant heavily upon the resources of Blackburn Library, where Diana Rushton and Alan Duckworth were generous with their time and extensive knowledge of Blackburn's history and people. Neil Summersgill lent me a suitcase of books on local history and kindly shared his encyclopaedic knowledge of Mellor and unpublished documents with me. My thanks also go to Derek Beattie and Gordon Hartley for providing information; to the Archivist and staff at Lancashire County Record Office; and, as ever, to the staff of the London Library and Kensington Reference Library.

Many others have helped and I am so grateful to Oscar and Alicia Yerburgh, Mr and Mrs Ken Bowden, Jean Magor, and Raymond Jepson with the excise serive. John Eatough of Roscoes kindly found old deeds and explained them to me. Howard Talbot was a wonder and produced marvellous photographs at short notice to bring the history visually alive. Roy Williams designed a great dust jacket. Jake Levy undertook research. Izzy Carnwath helped with the source notes. Katie Wake used her historical expertise to discover the excise career of Daniel Thwaites, investigate the Gregorys and so much else. Anna Goddard, Lucy Day and Adam Gregory at Carnegie were immensely supportive and unflappable when time was short. Fiona and Johnny Torrens-Spence were extraordinarily tolerant about my immersion in proofing a book long-distance.

Mia Stewart Wilson volunteered to help with the pictures and used far too much of her time and artistic skill in producing perfect images; her dedication, talent and friendship are treasured.

Writing and illness put pressure on the most understanding of families and William, Katie and David have been wonderful, as always, during the gestation of this book.

Picture credits

Accrington Library and Information Service 135 top and bottom, 146, 155, 163; Paul Agnew 206, 216; Blackburn with Darwen Library and Information Service 18, 22, 28, 56, 64, 75, 76, 82, 93, 96, 99, 103, 136, 138, 151 bottom, 171 top, 179; Blackburn Museum & Art Gallery 30, 38; John Bremridge 5, 6, 11; The Bridgeman Art Library/Ferens Art Gallery, Hull City Museums and Art Gallery/Frederick William Elwell (1870-1958) 143; British Film Institute Stills Library 152, 153, 156; Corbis/Hulton-Deutsch Collection 60, 148; Corbis/Hulton-Deutsch Collection/Raymond Kleboe 182; Corbis/Zefa/Martyn Rose 106; Daniel Thwaites Archive and Museum iv, 31, 85, 86, 95, 98, 117 bottom left, 121, 123, 126, 127, 128, 129, 130, 131, 132, 144, 145, 150, 151 top, 157, 158, 159, 165, 168 bottom, 171 bottom, 173 top, 176, 177, 178, 183, 194, 197, 205, 208, 209, 210, 211, 212, 213, 215; Paul Duxbury 217; Ivan Frontani 41 Guildhall Library, City of London 32, 35, 36, 42, 45, 55, 59, 61, 62, 66, 100, 110, 112; Harris Library, Lancashire County Library 97; Adrian Jenkinson 207; Malcolm Jennings 186; Lancashire Evening Telegraph, 65, 111, 119, 137 top, middle, bottom, 169, 173 bottom, 185, 189 bottom; Lancashire Lantern Archive 12, 14, 15, 19, 54, 83, 154; Lambeth Palace Library, Shelfmark TD20, 2; Allen Markey 212 right; Mary Evans Picture Library 10, 20, 25, 47, 50, 63, 78, 105, 108, 115, 116, 133, 161, 170; John Meek 44, 53, 58, 68, 114; Shires Hotels 198, 199, 200, 201, 202, 203, 204; Mia Stewart-Wilson, 57, 113, 141; Neil Summersgill 48, 175; Howard Talbot, vi, 24, 26, 27, 29, 70, 71, 73, 117 top right, bottom right, 162, 168 top, 172, 180, 181, 184, 188, 189 top, 190, 191, 192, 193, 194, 195, 196, 205; Bill Wilkinson, 23; Yerburgh Family 7, 74, 90, 94, 118, 122, 140; Westwoodcreative beer glasses on jacket.

Picture Research   Mia Stewart-Wilson

Source Notes

Chapter One

1. Articles of Partnership, 10 June 1807, Thwaites MSS.
2. B. Markland to Ld Hawkesbury, 25 Oct 1807, PRO/ HO50/172; Articles of Partnership.
3. *Blackburn Evening Mail*, n.d; T.S. Willan, *An Eighteenth Century Shopkeeper: Abraham Dent of Kirkby Stephen,* (Manchester 1970).
4. P. A. Whittle, *Blackburn As it Is*, (Preston 1852), 25, 221.
5. George C. Miller, *Blackburn: The Evolution of a Cotton Town,* (Blackburn 1951) 330–1; E. Duckworth, will, 1822, Lancashire Record Office, Preston; Brian Lewis, *Life in a Cotton Town,* (Preston 1985), 4–5.
6. Conveyence, Daniel Thwaites Co Ltd & William Parker, 1 July 1913, Thwaites MSS,
7. N. Redman, 'Dutton's Blackburn Brewery' *The Brewer*, Oct 1999, 515–6;
8. Dr. J. Aikin, *A Description of the County from 30–40 Miles around Manchester*, 1795; Whittle, *op cit*, 23; Ian Sutton, Blackburn's First Brewery, in *A Blackburn Miscellany*, ed. Bob Johnson (Blackpool 1993), 131; *Blackburn Evening Mail*, March 1794; TSS nd, Dutton MSS, DDX 2310/5/11, Lancashire Record Office, Preston; Miller, *Blackburn* .46; *Blackburn Evening Mail*, 6 May 1807, 3 June 1807, 29 April 1807.
9. Molly Lefebure, *Cumberland Heritage*, 1970, 35; W. G. Collingwood, *The Lake Counties,* 1949, 141.
10. *Cumberland Lay Subsidy: Being the Account of a Fifteenth and Tenth Collected by Edward III* ed. Col. J.P. Steel (Kendal 1912), 60; C. Roy Huddleston and A.S. Boumphrey, 'Cumberland Families and Heraldry' in *Cumberland and West Antiquarian and Archaeological Society Transactions*, 1978, 340; Edward Hughes, *North Country Life in the Eighteenth Century*, Vol. 2, (Oxford 1965), 1–2; Anon letter, TSS, nd in R. Jefferson, History of Thwaites, unpublished, Thwaites MSS.
11. Col. J. P. Steel, *Cumberland Lay Subsidy*, 55; Scott Michael Harrison, *The Pilgrimage of Grace in the Lake Countries* 1981, 21; M.Pearson, R. Warner and A. Warner, *Borrowdale*, (Cumbria 1995), 24.
12. Sheila Ricketts, *Lakeland Country Churches*, (Maryport 1994), 140.
13. *Thomas Grey's Journal*, ed. William Roberts, (Liverpool 2001), 45.
14. W.G. Collingwood, *Elizabethan Keswick*, (Kendal 1912), 1–2; William Rollinson, *A History of Man In the Lake District*,1967,103; Collingwood, *Lake Counties*, 145.
15. Collingwood, *Elizabethan Keswick*, 10.
16. Rollinson, *A History of Mant,* 107.
17. Collingwood, *Elizabethan Keswick*, 91, 135, 164, 193.
18. L.G.Wickham Legg ed., A relation of a Short Survey of the Western Counties made by Lt Hammond in 1635 in *Camden Miscellany*, 16, (London 1936), 42–43; *The Journals of Celia Fiennes*, ed. Christopher Morris 1947, 196–7; H. Moll, *A New Description of England*, 1724, cited by F.J. Monkhouse, Some Features of the Historical Geography of the German Mining Enterprise in Elizabethan Lakeland, in *Geography*, Vol.28, 1943.
19. D. Defoe, *A Tour Through the Whole of the Island of Great Britain,* 1971 edition, 549–50; Alms 106, fo.74, Armitt MSS, Armit Library, Ambleside; Daniel Thwaites will 1721, Daniel Thwaite will 1749, Carlisle Record Office.
20. Collingwood, *The Lake Counties,* 1949, 142; Molly Lefebure, *Cumberland Heritage,* 1970,100–1; John Thwaite, will 1748, Carlisle Record Office.
21. Lefebure, *Cumberland Heritage,* 114–15, 116.
22. Kenneth Smith, *Cumbrian Villages,* 1975,131; cited by Molly Lefebure, *Cumberland Heritage*, 45.
23. *The Cumberland Chronicle or Whitehaven Public Advertiser*, 7 June 1777.
24. Molly Lefebure, *Cumbrian Discovery*, 164, 21, 170; *The Cumbrian Chronicle*, 19 July 1777; Lefebure, *Cumbrian Discovery* 173–4; *The Cumberland Chronicle*, 24 May 1777; Lefebure, *Cumberland Heritage,* 131, 29.
25. Rollinson, *A History of Man In the Lake District,* 116; Collingwood, *Lake Counties,* 143.
26. Hughes, *North Country Life* vol.2, 26; *The Cumberland Pacquet*, 1777; Miss Noble, *History of Bampton*, cited in Collingwood, *The Lake Counties,* 142.
27. Anonymous, Jefferson file, n.d., Thwaites MSS.
28. *The Cumberland Chronicle*, 31 May 1777, 21 June 1777.
29. *The Carlisle Journal*, 28 November 1818; *The Carlisle Patriot*, 29 November 1817
30. Excise Records (TLB), 1355, f 229 & 1339, f.297, cited P. Mathias, *The Brewing Industry in England 1700–1830*, 1959, 344, 345; Edward Carson, *The Ancient and Rightful Customs,* 1972, 60.
31. Carson, *Ancient Customs* 41, 61.
32. T. Paine, *The Case of the Officers of Excise …,*1817, 14.
33. Catherine Hutton to Thomas Hutton, Lancaster, 12 July 1801, *Reminiscences of a Gentlewoman of the Last Century*, ed. C.H. Beale, (Birmingham 1891).
34. Arthur Young, *A Six Months' Tour through the North of England*, c.1770, cited by C. Hardwick, *History of Preston,* 1857, 383.
35. David Hunt, *A History of Preston*, (Preston 1992), 168; John Satchell & Olive Wilson, *Christopher Wilson of Kendal*, (Kendal 1988), 39.
36. Edward Baines, *Histor,y Directory & Gazetteer of the County Palatine of Lancaster*, (Liverpool 1824/5), vol. 2.
37. D. Defoe, *A Tour Through England and Wales* (1928 ed.), vol 2, 268; John Marchant cited by Hardwick, *Preston*, 248; Dr John Aikin, *A Description round Manchester*, 283, 286–7.
38. Rev. W. Ramsden to Elizabeth Shackleton, 31 May 1776, DDB72/192, and A. Parker to E. Shackleton, n.d. DDB.Ac 78861/24, Lancashire Record Office.

39. P.A. Whittle, *An Account of the Borough of Preston,* (Preston 1821), 30.

40. *Blackburn Mail*, 19 June 1793, 4, 19 March 1794, 3; Rev T. D. Whitaker, First Day Sermon in St. John's Church; *Blackburn Mail*, 4 June 1793, 1 March 1797, July 1793, 12 February 1794, 3.

41. Autobiography of the late M. Singleton Cooper, n.d. TSS, Bolton Archives & Local Studies Library, Bolton; Brian Lewis, *The Middlemost and the Milltowns,* (Stanford University Press, Stanford, California 2001) 22; *Blackburn Mail*, 16 July 1798, 3; PRO/CUST 47/419, Excise Minute Book, 37.

42. Ibid; PRO/ CUST 47/419, Excise Minute Book, 20 September 1798, 38.

43. B.T. Barton, *History of the Borough of Bury and Neighbourhood,* (Bury 1874), 80; W.A. Abram, *A History of Blackburn* (Blackburn 1877), 221; R.S. Crossley, *Accrington Captains of Industry,* (Accrington 1930) 62.

44. PRO/CUST 47/417, 4 September 1800, 37–8.

45. Roy Westall, *Stockport: A Pictorial History,* 1988, 151; H. Heginbotham, *Stockport: Ancient and Modern*, vol.2, 1882–1892, 323.

46. PRO/CUST/47/440, 1O September 1804, 26; E.J. Hobsbawm, *Industry and Empire,* 1969, 56; Roy Porter, *English Society in the Eighteenth Century,* 1991, 199, 186, 81.

47. W.D. Rubinstein, *Men of Property,* 1981, 182–3; Porter, *English Society*, 81, 78

48. T. Paine, *Officers of Excise*, 5.

49. Porter, *English Society*, 79; PRO/PRO/CUST 47/449, 13 November 1806, 128; Porter, 26.

Dray Horses and Drays

1. Ralph Turvey, 'Horse Tradition in Victorian London', in *Journal of Transport History*, vol. 26, issue 2, September 2005.

2. B. Pepper and R. Protz, *Beer Glorious Beer*, 2000, 149, 151; *Brewery History*, Number 78, Winter 1994, 33.

3. Pepper and Protz, 149; Barlow, *Recollections 1925–35*, part 5, Alex Johnson; Bob Potts, *Old Pubs of Tochdale Road and Neighbouring Manchester,* (Swinton 1985), 26–7.

4. Pepper and Protz, 150; David Kay, Testimonial Dinner; Forty Years' Service, 3 February 1993, David Kay MSS.

5. David Kay to author, interview 2006.

6. *Thwaites Times*, No.23, September 1979, 7; Benita Moore, *Lancashire Lives,* (Blackburn 1992), 58.

7. Daniel Thwaites Plc, Press Release, 24 October 1978; *Thwaites Times*, No.24, December 1979, 4.

Chapter Two: The Eanam Brewery

1. Peter Mathias, *The Brewing Industry in England 1700–1830*, (Cambridge 1959), xi; Brian Harrison, *Drink and the Victorians*, 1971, 41; Brian Spiller, *Victorian Public Houses*, 1972,.57; Frank A. King, *Beer Has a History*, 1947, 94; Harrison, *Drink*, 46; Porter, *English Society*, 217.

2. W.A. Abram, *A History of Blackburn,* 1877, 381; E.C. Midwinter, *Social Administration in Lancashire 1830–60,* (Manchester 1969), 73; S.C.H.L Intemperance, fourth report, Parliamentary Papers 1878 (338) XIV, Q.559 cited by Harrison, *Drink*, 37; Harrison, Drink,38, 39; William Cobbett, *Cottage Economy*, 1926 ed, 14–22.

3. Matthias, *Brewing Industry*, xxiv, *passim* 356–7.

4. *Blackburn Evening Mail*, April 1793, cited by Ian Sutton *Park Place Brewery* in A. Duckworth ed, *Aspects of Blackburn*, (Barnsley 1999).

5. Mathias, xxv, xxiv; *Hansard* 40, c.1030, 9 June 1819, cited Harrison, 62; R.G. Wilson & T.R. Gourvish, *The Dynamics of the International Brewing Industry since 1880*, 1998, 7; Harrison, 57 citing *A Practical Treatise on the Manufacture of cheap Non-alcoholic Beverages*, 1880, 21; Matthias, xxi.

6. Harrison, *Drink*, 59.

7. Peter Clarke, *The English Ale House*, 1983, 293, 267; Sutton, *Park Place Brewery*, 4; *Holden's Annual Directory*, 1811, LRO, Preston.

8. *Blackburn Evening Mail*, 10 December 1794; Sutton, 2–3; Peter Mathias, *The First Industrial Nation*, 1983, 138.

9. Matthias, *Brewing*, 3, 5, 6; Oliver MacDonagh, 'The Origins of Porter', *English Historical Review*, vol.16, (1963–4), 531–5; Matthias, 25.

10. Mike Dunn, *Local Brew*, 1986, 25; Matthias, 45–6 citing Malcolm, *Agriculture of Surrey*, vol. I, (1805), 291 & Parl. Papers 1806 II, Evidence to … Malt Report, 72; Greenall Records, Brewing books 1835 *et seq*.

11. S. Bamford, *Passages in the Life of a Radical*, 1842, *passim*; Indenture & Leaseholds Part III, f.49, Roscoe's; Abram, *Blackburn*, 298–9.

12. George Miller, *Blackburn: The Evolution of a Cotton Town*, 1957, 329; Brian Lewis, *Life in a Cotton Town*, 1985, 5.

13. Miller, 305–6.

14. *Blackburn Evening* Mail, 8 April 1807; Miller, 65, 67; *Blackburn Evening Mail*, 5 Oct 1825.

15. *Blackburn Evening Mail*, 13 May 1807; Abram, 193.

16. Abram, 1–3.

17. *Blackburn Evening Mail*, 6 May 1807; A Barnard, *Noted Breweries of Great Britain & Ireland*, vol.1, (1880) 67–70; T.R. Gourvish & R.G. Wilson, *The British Brewing Industry 1830–1980*, (Cambridge 1994), 49; *The Brewers Journal*, Centenary Number, 8 July 1965, 163; R. Jefferson TSS.

18. Dunn, 43–51; Sutton, 6.

19. William Black, *A Practical Treatise on Brewing*, 4th ed., 1866; Gourvish & Wilson, *British Brewing*, 55.

20. Raymond Jepson to author, interview, May 2005.

21. Mathias, 34.

22. Partnership Deed, 10 June 1807; T.S. Ashton, *The Industrial Revolution*, 1948, 97.

23. P. Wills, 'The Chale Brewery', *Brewing History*, No.61, 1990, 9; I. Donnachie, 'Sources of Capital and Capitalization in the Scottish Brewing Industry c.1750–1830', *Econ. Hist. Rev*, 2nd Series, Vol. XXX (1977), 281–3, *passim*; Mathias, 362.

24. Gourvish & Wilson, *British Brewing*, 202 f.52.

25. Mathias, 78–9; Letterhead drawings 1853/4, Thwaites MSS; R.W. Dickson, *View of*

the *Agriculture of Lancashire*, 1815, 585.

26. Richard Wilson, *Greene King: A Business and Family History*, 1983, 21; assorted deeds, Thwaites MSS.

27. Sidney Webb & Beatrice Potter, *The History of Liquor Licensing in England, principally from 1700–1830*, 1903, 51.

28. Ibid, 43, 44 n.1; *Leeds Intelligencer*, 25 April 1786.

29. Lancashire Quarter Sessions, Easter 1782; *Manchester Mercury*, 28 May 1782; Webbs, 58.

30. Clarke, 255, 257.

31. *Gentleman's Magazine*, LXXVII, (1807), 957.

32. Miller, 99; C. Aspin, *The First Industrial Society,* 2nd ed., (Lancaster 1991), 56

33. Dutton MSS, Whitbread Papers, LRO n.d.; *The Commercial Directory*, 1814–15; *Holden's Directory*, 1816.

34. Alan Duckworth, 'Blackburn and the Canal" in *A Blackburn Miscellany*, ed. Bob Dobson (Blackburn 1993), 138; Aspin, 6–7.

35. Lewis, *Middlemost*, 34.

36. Daniel Thwaite, will, I July 1816, Carlisle CRO; *Holden's Annual Directory,* 1811, 1816

37. *Blackburn Evening Mail*, 24 December 1822; Edward Duckworth Will, 1822.

38. John Wilkinson, Private Account Book, 1814, kindly lent by Neil Summersgill.

39. Aspin, 59.

40. Ibid, 62; Jehanne Wake, *Kleinwort Benson*, 1998, 46.

41. Sarah Whittaker to Rev William Whittaker, 12 Feb 1826, Whittaker Papers, G3 WHl, Blackburn Reference Library; Abram, 232; Wake, 46.

42. William Whittaker to Sarah Whittaker, 28 January 1826, G3 WHl, Blackburn Library; Abram, 232; Aspin, 70, 68.

43. Sarah Whittaker to William Whittaker, 26 April 1827, G3 Whl, Blackburn Library; *Blackburn Mail*, 26 April 1826; Abram, 233.

44. Miller, 395; William Durham, *Chronological Notes,* (Blackburn 1884).

45. Clarke, 334.

46. Gourvish & Wilson, *British Brewing*, 6–7 f. 11; Wilson, *Greene King*,.25; Angus McGill, *Pub, A Celebration*, 1969, 8.

47. Harrison, *Drink* citing 2 *Hansard 10*, c.951, (12 March 1824), 66; Jessica Warner, *Gin and Debauchery in the Age of Reason*, 2003, 195–6.

48. *Blackburn Mail*,2 July 1823; Miller,.27–8.

49. Harrison, *Drink*,.70, 41; Gourvish & Wilson, *British Brewing*, 9–10.

50. E. Bovill, *English Country Life*, 32; Clarke, 253.

51. Harrison, *Drink*, 74.

52. Ibid,.76; Gourvish & Wilson, *British Brewing*, 5; Clarke, 336; S. Smith to John Murray, 24 Oct 1830, Ly Holland, *Memoirs*, vol. 1, (1830), 310.

53. Clark, 336; Webbs, 125; Harrison, *Drink*, 81.

54. *Bristol* Journal, 1834; Gourvsh & Wilson, *British Brewing*, 17; Miller, 30; Rev. J. W. Whittaker, Report on Blackburn to Bishops of Chester, 1835, 28–9.

55. Harrison, *Drink*,.76; Gerald Curtis, *A Chronicle of Small Beer*, 1970, 180.

56. Wilson, *Greene King*, 29.

57. George Miller, *Blackburn's Old Inns*, 1993.

58. Gourvish & Wilson, *British Brewing*, 19.

59. Ibid., 20.

60. Whittle, *Blackburn*, 29.

The Public-House in 1807

1. George Miller, *Blackburn's Old* Inns, (Blackburn 1998), 13–15; Clarke, *English Ale House*, 11, 14, 5; *Holden's Annual Directory*, 1811, vol. 2.

2. Bovill, *English Country Life,* 133–4; J.G. Shaw & W. Hulme, *Bits of Old Blackburn* (Blackburn 1889, repr. Blackpool 1988), 10, *passim*.

3. Albert E. Richardson, *The English Inn Past and Present*, 1925, 40, 43; Bovill, 55.

4. Clarke, *English Ale House*, 5, 14; *Blackburn Evening Mail*, 4 November 1807; Clarke, 5.

5. Clarke, 278; William Howitt, *The Rural Life of England*, (1836, 1971 ed.), 484.

6. Clarke, 275–7.

7. S. Bamford, *Passages in the Life of a Radical,* 56–7.

8. Clarke, 287; Bamford, 57.

9. Rev. James Woodforde, *The Diary of A Country Parson,* (1924–31),.189–90; Clark, 307.

10. Valuation 1895, Thwaites MSS, 1895; *Edinburgh Review* XLIV, 1826, 446; C. Behagg, 'Secrecy, Ritual and Folk Violence', in. R.S. Storch, ed. *Popular Culture in Nineteenth Century England,* 1952, 156.

11. Miller, *Inns*, 66–7; Clarke, 317.

12. Miller, *Inns*, 54; Anne Secord, Science in the Pub', in *History of Science*, vol. 32, Part3, (Sept 1994), 297, 306 f.64, 279–80; Bamford, vol.1, 45.

13. Iain McCalman, *Radical Underworld*, (Oxford 1993), 114; Clarke, 325; Aspin, 106

14. Miller, *Inns*, 21.

15. Steve Earnshaw, *The Pub in Literature*, .95; *Blackburn Mail*, 2 July 1823;

16. Porter, 19; Samuel Pepys, *Diary*, 14 Nov 1660, 2 Dec 1660, and Roger Lowe, *Diary*, 4 Feb 1663, cited by Earnshaw, 95, 93; Porter, 19.

17. Earnshaw, 167; Porter, 20.

18. Ibid, Porter; Peter Haydon, *An Inebriated History of Britain*, (Stroud 2005), 157.

19. Clarke, 289; Rowland Watson, *A Scrapbook of Inns*, 1949, 114–5.

The Cooper

1. Robert W. Gilding, 'The Journeyman Coopers of East London', *History Workshop Pamphlets*, Number Four, 1971, 3.

2. A. Somerville, *Autobiography of a Working Man*, 1856, 28.

3. Gilding, 5, 10; John Dunlop, *The Philosophy of Artificial and Compulsory Drinking Usages in Great Britain and Ireland*, 1839, 11; Gilding, 55.

4. Gilding, 18.

5. *Morning Chronicle*, 12 September 1850; Tim Harris ed., *Popular Culture in England c.1500–1850*, 173.

6. *Inn Touch*, Summer 2005.

Chapter Three: Daniel Junior

1. Daniel Thwaites the elder, Will, 21 December 1843, WCW C1120, LRO, Preston.

2. Miller, *Blackburn*, 177, 181; Edward Baines, *Directory for 1824* (Liverpool 1824); Whittle, *Blackburn*, .271; Wilson, *Greene King*, 60.

3. 'A Historical Sketch of the Church of St. John' (pamphlet), 1908, & 'Parish Church of St. John the Evangelist 1789–1939' (pamphlet), 1939, Blackburn Reference Library; Geoffrey Trodd, 'Political Change and the Working Class in Blackburn and Burnley 1880–1914', (University of Lancaster PhD thesis, 1978), 72.

4. Aspin, *First Industrial Society,* 106.

5. J.T. Ward, *Chartism*, 66.

6. F.W. Hirst, *Early Life and Letters of John Morley,* 1927, vol.1,6; Lewis, *Middlemost and the Milltowns*, 257.

7. Whittle, *Blackburn As It Is*, 334.

8. Miller, *Blackburn*, 28–29; Lewis, *Middlemost and the Milltowns*, 74; Ward, 129.

9. Lewis, *Middlemost and the Milltowns*, 217–18; Lewis, *Cotton Town*, 37.

10. Miller, *Blackburn*, 138, 137.

11. Col. Wemyss to Phillipps, 5 June 1842, PRO/HO45/629, cited by Lewis, *Middlemost and Milltowns*, .84; Lewis, *Cotton Town*, 37.

12. Miller, *Blackburn*, 140.

13. Lewis, *Middlemost and Milltowns*, 87, 86.

14. Ibid, 89.

15. W.A.Abram, *Chronological Notes 1843–4*, (Blackburn 1884), 45; Catherine Jacson, *Desultory Retracings: A Personal Family Record,* 1895, 58; Mary Whittaker to Sarah Whittaker, 1 August 1825, G3WHI, Blackburn Ref. Library; Lewis, *Middlemost and Milltowns*, 312.

16. Hirst, vol. 1, 8.

17. Daniel Thwaites, Will, *op cit*; Wilson, *Greene King*, 69; K.H. Hawkins & C. L. Pass, *The Brewing Industry*, 1979, 16–17.

18. T.C. Barker and J.R.Harris, *A Merseyside Town in the Industrial Revolution*, (Liverpool University Press1954), 183; Robert Carlson, *The Liverpool and Manchester Railway Project,* (New York, 1969), 36.

19. Prospectus, 1843, Thwaites MSS; Lewis, *Cotton Town*,.11–12.

20. Alan Duckworth ed., *Aspects of Blackburn,* (Barnsley1999), 90; Miller, *Blackburn*, 315.

21. Abram, *Blackburn*,.244; J.A.R. Pimlott, *The Englishman's Holiday,* 1976, 87; *Preston Chronicle*, 20 July 1850.

22. Aspin, 41–2.

23. Charles Tiplady, Diary 7 June 1857, Tiplady MSS, Blackburn Ref. Library.

24. Jack Simmons, 'The Power of the Railway', in H. Dyos ed, *The Victorian City*, 1973, 277; Wilson, *Greene King*, 70.

25. Dorothy A. Canham, 'Extracts from A Blackburn Notebook', in B. Dobson ed., *A Blackburn Miscellany*, (Blackburn 1993),.42; Mike Rothwell, *Industrial Heritage*, vol I, 21.

26. Daniel Thwaites, Will, *op.cit.,*

27. G.C. Miller, *Bygone Blackburn*, cited in Duckworth ed., *Aspects of Blackburn*,.89; Whittle, *Blackburn* 275.

28. *London Gazette*, 10 Nov 1844; Whittle, 270, 268–9; Indenture, 2 Mar 1846, Thwaites MSS.

29. Deed of Partnership, 9 November 1844, Thwaites MSS.

30. Kenneth Neal ed., *Victorian Horsham,* (Chichester 1975), 12.

31. F. M. L. Thompson, *The Rise of Respectable Society,* 1988, p.260–1; *Fortunes Made in Business*, 1844, vol.2, 422–3.

32. Richard Wilson, 'The Introduction of Lager in Late Victorian Britain', in Thomas Riis ed., *A Special Brew*, (Odensee University Press) vol.65, 192.

33. Gourvish & Wilson *British Brewing*, 150, 156.

34. R. G. Wilson, 'Changing Tastes in Victorian Brewing,' in T.W. Gourvish & R.G.Wilson eds., *The Dynamics of the International Brewing Industry since 1800,* 1998; Riis, 193.

35. W. Abram, *Blackburn Characters,* (Blackburn 1894),.260–1, 265; *Blackburn Times*, 15 March 1924.

36. Durham, *Blackburn Chronology*, rev Abram, 1884, 51.

37. R. Jefferson, TSS, Thwaites MSS.

38. *The London Gazette*, 25 February 1859, 766.

39. Lewis, *Middlemost and Milltowns*, 338.

40. Geoffrey Carnall, 'Dickens Mrs Gaskell and the Preston Strike' in *Victorian Studies'*, Sept 1964; Charles Dickens, *Hard Times*, 1854, 1969 ed., 65–7.

41. *Preston Chronicle*, 3 Nov 1850;.

42. Duckworth ed., 164–5.

43. *Blackburn Standard*, 28 April 1852, 3 c.1, 26 May 1852, p.3 c.2; Lewis, *Middlemost and Milltowns*, 341; Charles Tiplady's diary, 19 &21 June, 1858; *Blackburn Weekly Times*, 26 June 1858.

44. Duchy of Lancaster Correspondence, cited by Anthony Howe, *The Cotton Masters 1830–60*, (Oxford 1984), 255–6; Acting Magistrate List 1841–51, Quarter Sessions records QSZ 1–17, LRO cited by Howe, 256.

45. J. Austen, *Pride and Prejudice,* 1901 ed,.1.

46. John F Hindle, Will, 1831; Woodford Estate MSS, DDX series, Blackburn Ref. Library.

47. George B. Gregory to H.B. Hollinshead, 30 Nov 1855, 7 Dec 1855, Woodfold MSS.

48. Elizabeth Hindle, Will, 20 April 1864.

49. H Gibbs, *Autobiography*, priv pr, 160–4, 169–171; Eccles Shorrock, TSS excerpt, 31, Thwaites MSS.

50. Charles Tiplady's diary, 1861–4; *Blackburn Standard*, 15 January 1862, 3

51. Accounts, 1878, Thwaites MSS.

52. A. Dingle, 'Drink and Working Class Living Standards in Britain 1870–1914', *Econ. His. Rev*, 2nd Series, vol.xxv, (1972), 615–6.

53. Harrison, 107, 115, 120; Haydon, 208.

54. Harrison, 247 et *passim*; *Preston Guardian*, 28 August, 1872, p.8.

55. R. Jefferson, TSS Bk 2, Thwaites MSS; Duckworth, 64–5; *Blackburn Times*, 2 Oct 1875, 6.

56. Jefferson, TSS Bk 2.

57. Ibid; David W. Gutzke, 'Rhetoric and Reality', *Parliamentary History,* vol 9, part 1, (1990), 79–83; Derek Beattie, *Blackburn: The Development of a Lancashire Cotton Town,* First edition (Lancaster 1992), 42–3.

58. Peter Piper, 'Clogger's Chips' (pamphlet), 1880, kindly lent by N. Summersgill.

59. Elma Yerburgh to Ld Alvingham, n.d note, Yerburgh MSS; N. Summersgill, *The History of Mellor in Lancashire,* (Mellor 1999), 62.

60. Gourvish & Wilson, *British Brewing,*.254–255.

61. H. Osbourne O'Hagan, *Leaves From My Life,* Vol 1,.1929; H. Kay to DT& Co, 1886, Thwaites MSS.

62. Daniel junior, Will, 1888, Thwaites MSS.

The Public-House in 1857

1. M. Girouard, *The Victorian Pub*, 1984, 33.

2. W.H. Palin, Evidence, *Select Committeet of the House of Lords on Intemperance,* P.P. 1877, 11, Q.1656.

3. Charles Dickens, *Sketches By Boz*, 1835 in *Dicken's Journalism*, ed. Michael Slater, 1996, 82.

4. H. Vitzetelly, *Glances Back Through Serenity Years,* vol 1, 1893.

5. Brian Harrison,'Pubs' in H.J. Dyos, *Victorian City* vol 2, 1973.

6. Girouard, 33–4, 30.

7. Spiller, 53.

8. Charles Dickens, *Bleak House,* Chapter LVll; Maurice Gorham, *Inside the Local,* (1949), 65; Paul Sykes ed., *The Book of Blackburn,* 1979, 11.

9. Gorham, 88; J. Callingham, *Sign Writing and Glass Embossing,* 1871, cited by Spiller, 69.

10. Spiller, 68, 66.

11. Gorham, 93.

12. J. Ruskin to the *Pall Mall Gazette*, 16 March 1812, cited by Girouard, 55.

13. Girouard, 5.

14. *Free Lance* (Manchester), 12 October 1867 cited by D. Beattie, *Blackburn: Development of A Lancashire Cotton Town,* First edition (Lancaster 1992), 117; M. B. Smith, Victorian Entertainment in Lancashire Cotton Towns', in S.P.Bell ed *Victorian Lancashire,* 1974, 173.

15. Smith, 'Victorian Entertainment', 174; Peter Bailey, 'Custom, Capital and Culture in the Victorian Music Hall', in R. Storch ed., *Popular Culture and Custom in Nineteenth Century England,* 1982,.181, 183–4; Smith, 174–5; Hugh Cunningham, *Leisure in the Industrial Revolution,* 1980, 168; Bailey, 183; Smith, 176; Whittle, 32.

16. Smith, 176.

The Barmaid

1. Brian Spiller, *Victorian Public Houses,* (Newton Abbot 1972), 8; Peter Bailey, 'Parasexuality and Glamour', in *Gender and History*, Vol 2, No.2, (Summer, 1980), 151.

2. A. McGill, *Pub: A Celebration,* .133; Bailey, 157, 152.

3. McGill,.133; Bailey, 162, 160; Barbara Drake, 'The Barmaid', *Women's Industrial News,* April 1914, 222–38.

4. Bailey, 159; McGill, 137.

5. *The Times*, 1904; Bailey, 162.

6. McGill, 133; Bailey, 162.

7. *Freelance* magazine, (Manchester), 1 June 1867, cited by Bob Potts, *Old Pubs of Hume,* Vol 1, (Manchester 1983).

Chapter Four: Elma Yerburgh

1. W. Thackeray, *Vanity Fair,* 1848, 87.

2. Revel Guest & Angela John, *Lady Charlotte: A biography of the Nineteenth Century,* 1989, 27–8.

3. L. Richmond & A. Turton eds., *The Brewing Industry: a guide to historical records* (Manchester 1990).

4. Neal Hyde, *Brewing Was a Way of Life,* (Cheshire 1999), 22–3, 62.

5. Yerburgh family records; The Rev. Edmond R. Yerburgh, Some Notes on Our Family History, 1913; Rev Edmond R. Yerburgh, Robert A. Yerburgh: A Memoir, priv. pr.,8, 6,11, 22.

6. D.T.& Co., Balance Sheet, 29 November 1890, Thwaites MSS. Gourvish & Wilson, *British Brewing,* 238.

7. Gourvish & Wilson, *British Brewing*, 266.

8. Directors' Book, Thwaites MSS.

9. Snig Brook Brewery prospectus, 1897, Thwaites MSS.

10. Daniel Thwaites & Company, prospectus 1897, Thwaites MSS.

11. Directors' Minute Book No.1, 18 March, 25 March 1897, Thwaites MSS.

12. Ibid, 23 April, 1897.

13. Edmond R.Yerburgh, Robert A Yerburgh, 16; Directors' Minute Book No 1, 20 Dec 1897.

14. Press cutting, Blackburn n,d., Thwaites MSS.

15. Snig Brook Brewery prospectus, 1897, Thwaites MSS.

16. Directors' Minute Books, 1897–1900 *passim* & 18 April 1898.

17. Ibid, 8 November 1897.

18. Gourvish & Wilson, *British Brewing*, 285, 279 f.33; Hawkins & Pass, *Brewing Industry*, 30.

19. Miller, *Blackburn's Inns*, 6, 68; Beattie, 118.

20. Blackburn Magistrates report on Public Houses, 1893, 1, *passim*; Directors' Minute Book, Sept 1900, Thwaites MSS.

21. Gourvish & Wilson, *British Brewing*, 289, 290.

22. Directors' Minute Book, No 2, 1904, Thwaites MSS.

23. Gourvish & Wilson, *British Brewing*, 292.

24. Ibid, 294.

25. Ibid, 318.

26. Hawkins & Pass, 43; *Brewers' Journal* (Centenary Number), 8 July 1965, 250.

27. Misc. press reports, *The Times, Blackburn Standard*, August – Oct 1914.

28. Jefferson, file 3, Thwaites MSS.

29. Ibid.

30. Director's Minute Book, 15 April 1918; Misc. papers, Thwaites MSS

31. Amalgamation papers, Henry Shaw & Co, Thwaites MSS; P.F. Clarke, *Lancashire and the New Liberalism,* (Cambridge 1977), 269; Directors' Minute Books, Thwaites MSS.

32. Directors' Minute Book, 22 May 1927, Thwaites MSS.

33. *Country Brewers' Gazette*, September 1899, cited by Norman Barber, '*Where Have All the Breweries Gone?*', Brewery History Society, (Swinton 1992).

34. John Yerburgh to author, 2004–6; Yerburgh family papers.

35. Jeremy Seabrook, *City Close-Up,* 1971, 225.

36. Directors' Minute Books & Balance Sheets, 1932, 1934, Thwaites MSS

37. *The Brewer's Journal* (Centenary Number),8 July 1965, 104–5; Directors' Minute Book, 8 March 1938, Thwaites MSS.

38. Jefferson, file 4, Thwaites MSS.

39. Elma Yerburgh, to Hilda Salisbury-Jones, c. 1945, Yerburgh MSS; Freedom of Blackburn scroll, 5 Sept 1935, Thwaites MSS; *Morning Advertiser*, 19 February 1954

40. Misc press clippings & obituaries, 7 Dec 1946, Thwaites MSS; Elma Yerburgh to Hilda Salisbury-Jones, n.d., Yerburgh MSS.

The Public-House in 1907

1. Hawkins & Pass, 38

2. Gourvish & Wilson, *British Brewing*, 288–9 f.62; Basil Oliver, *Renaissance of the English Public House*, 1947, 80–1.

3. General Report of the Justices of the County Borough of Blackburn, July 1893, M.851.BLA, Local History Collection, Blackburn Reference Library; Wilson, *Greene King*, 140.

4. Directors' Minute Books, 10 Aug & 14 Nov 1899, 4 Nov 1901, 11 Sept & 12 Dec 1899, Thwaites MSS.

5. Directors' Minute Book No 2, 9 July 1900, 9 Sept 1901 & Directors' Book No 3, 12 Feb 1906, Thwaites MSS.

6. Directors' Minute Book No 2, 14 March 1904 & Book No 3, 11 Apr 1904, Thwaites MSS.

7. Oliver, 19; Haydon, 252.

8. Directors' Minute Book No 2, 8 Feb 1902; David Kay to author, 2006; Directors' Book No 3, 14 Nov 1904, 9 Jan 1905; David Kay to author, 2006; Directors' Book, No 3, 13 March 1905, Thwaites MSS.

9. General Report of Justices; Directors' Minute Book No 1, 10 Nov 1898 & Book No 2, 11 Nov 1901, Thwaites MSS.

10. Directors' Book No 1, 10 Dec 1900, 11 Feb 1901, Thwaites MSS; Gourvish & Wilson, *British Brewing*, 296 f.90.

11. Hawkins & Pass, 37; Directors' Book No 2, 14 Mar 1904, Thwaites MSS; Wilson & Gourvish, *Dynamics*, 102.

12. *Brewing Trade Review*, 1 July 1909, 257.

13. Hawkins & Pass, 40.

14. J. A. Mangan ed., *Pleasure, Profit, Proselytism*, 1988, 76; Beattie, 119; Andrew Taylor, *20th Century* Blackburn, (Barnsley 2000), 27.

15. Gourvish & Wilson, *British Brewing*, 307.

16. J.M.Goldy & A.W.Purdue eds., *The Civilisation of the Crowd*, (Stroud 1984), 173.

17. Taylor, 17; Directors' Book No 3, 9 Sept 1907, Thwaites MSS.

18. Taylor, 24–5; Mitchell & Kenyon, internet at www.wikipedia.com.

19. Gourvish & Wilson, *British Brewing*, 307; Directors Book No 6, 1919–20 *passim*.

20. Beattie, 22.

21. Taylor, 21, 24.

22. David Gutzke, 'Gender, Class & Public Drinking during the First World War' in *Social History*, vol. xxvii, no 54, (Nov 1994), 368, 371, 369, 388.

Blackpool

1. Allen Clarke, *The Story of Blackpool*, 1923, 4–6; H.T. Perkin, 'Victorian and Edwardian Pleasure Resorts' in *Northern History*, vol. xi, (1976).

2. *Blackburn Standard and Express*, 5 July 1902.

3. Directors' Minute Book, 1923 *passim* & 12 July 1926.

Chapter Five: John Yerburgh

1. John Yerburgh to author, Oct 2005; Elma Yerburgh to John Yerburgh, November 1943, Yerburgh MSS; Minutes of Director's Meeting, 20 Sept 1946, Thwaites MSS

2. Oscar Yerburgh, speech on John Yerburgh's 75th birthday, 24 Oct 1998, Yerburgh Papers.

3. John Yerburgh, TSS notes for children; John Yerburgh to author; Oscar Yerburgh to author 2005

4. Oscar Yerburgh, speech 1998; John Yerburgh to author.

5. Ld Alvingham to Hilda S. Jones, n.d. postscript, Yerburgh MSS; John Yerburgh to Peter Yerburgh, 'War experiences, memo TSS p9, Yerburgh MSS.

6. John Yerburgh to author.

7. Ibid; Elma Yerburgh to Hilda Salisbury-Jones, n.d., Yerburgh MSS.

8. Ibid; Elma Yerburgh to John Yerburgh, Nov 1943, Yerburgh MSS; Oscar Yerburgh speech.

9. Elma Yerburgh to John Yerburgh, Nov 1943, Yerburgh MSS.

10. Minutes of Directors' Meetings, 18 August 1943, 19 May 1944, 27 July & 21 September 1945, Thwaites MSS; Elma Yerburgh to John Yerburgh, November 1943, Yerburgh MSS; Minutes of Directors' Meetings, 27 June 1946; Elma Yerburgh to Hilda Salisbury-Jones, n.d., Yerburgh MSS.

11. Minutes of Directors' Meetings, 21 January 1947, Thwaites MSS; Jefferson, TSS, Thwaites MSS; John Yerburgh to author.

12. Minutes of Directors' Meetings, 7 March 1947 & 22 Jan 1948, Thwaites MSS.
13. Jefferson TSS, Bury Brewery Share and Directors' ledgers, Thwaites MSS.
14. Jefferson TSS; David Kay to author; Preston Brewery Ltd ledgers, Thwaites MSS; David Kay to author.
15. Jefferson TSS; Press folder, Thwaites MSS.
16. Travelling Scholarship folders, Thwaites MSS.

The Public-House in 1957

1. Minutes of Directors' Meetings, 16 April 1957; Letter to all employees, Daniel Thwaites & Co., 3 May 1957, Thwaites MSS.
2. File on 150th Anniversary, Thwaites MSS.
3. Minutes of Directors' Meetings, 14 April & 13 June 1957, Thwaites MSS *The Brewers Journal*, January 1944; Minutes of Directors' Meetings, 6 July 1957, Thwaites MSS.
4. Minutes of Directors' Meetingst, 13 Sept 1926, Thwaites MSS.
5. Vaizey, 41.
6. Minutes of Directors' Meetings, 1957 *passim*; David Kay's Black Book, Kay MSS.
7. Minutes of Directors' Meetings, 16 April & 9 October 1957, 3 Jan 1958, Thwaites MSS.
8. Taylor, 85; Jefferson TSS.
9. Minutes of Directors' Meetings, 3 Jan 1957; *Preston Gazette*, 24 August 1957; Minutes of Directors' Meetings, 3 Jan 1958, Thwaites MSS.
10. Jefferson, TSS.
11. Bob Potts, *The Old Pubs of Hulme, Manchester,* (Manchester 1983), 14–15; Hickey, 101; *The Brewers' Journal*, Centenary Number, 10 July 1965, 115.
12. Hickey, 52; Millns, 143.
13. Vaizey, 68; Wilson, *Greene King*, 217; Minutes of Directors' Meetings, 3 January & 9 October 1957, Thwaites MSS.
14. Gourvish & Wilson, *British Brewing*, 559 f.80; David Kay & Ken Bowden, to the author, 2004.
15. Taylor, 84, 86.

Chapter Six: John Yerburgh and the new Star Brewery

1. T. Millns, 143–44.
2. John Yerburgh to author.
3. Denis Robson to author, May 2006.
4. Miss Birtwhistle to author, June 2004; *Lancashire Evening News*, 14 March 1964.
5. Miss Birtwhistle to author; John Yerburgh to author; Philip Tann to author.
6. David Kay to author; Jefferson TSS.
7. Miss Birtwhistle to author; John Yerburgh to author.
8. Alfred Whittle to John Yerburgh, 1949, Yerburgh MSS.
9. David Kay, and John Yerburgh to author.
10. Wilson & Gourvish, *The Dynamics of the International Brewing Industry*, .451–2, 455; David Kay to author; Philip Tann to author.
11. David Kay and Denis Robson to author.

12. Philip Tann to author; the *Sunday Mirror*, 24 September 1978.
13. Oscar Yerburgh, speech, 24 October 1998; Elma Yerburgh to John Yerburgh, n.d., Yerburgh MSS; Jefferson TSS.
14. Denis Robson to author.
15. Ian Harkness to author, June 2006; David Kay to Ian Harkness, 1980.
16. John Yerburgh and Ian Harkness to author.
17. Ian Harkness, John Yerburgh and Denis Robson to author.
18. Ibid, and Tony Spencer to author.
19. Ian Harkness and Denis Robson to author.
20. Millns, 151–55.
21. Gerald Crompton, 'Well Intentioned Meddling' in Wilson & Gourvish eds., *Dynamics of the International Brewing Industry*, 1998, 160–1, 166, 172, 175.
22. Yates & Jackson papers, Thwaites MSS; Denis Robson and Paul Baker to author.
23. Denis Robson and Winston Pickup to author.

The Public-House in 2007

1. Lord Asa. Briggs, 'Beer and Society', in *The Brewer*, vol. 69, August 1983, No. 826, 318.
2. *Inn Touch*, Issue 4, Summer 2001.
3. *Inn Touch*, Issue 11, Summer 2004.
4. *The Northern Brewer*, Autumn 2006, 4.
5. Steve Fielding to author, summer 2006.
6. *Inn Touch*, Issue 14, Summer 2005, 1; *The Northern Brewer*, Autumn 2006. 11.
7. David Kay to Ann Yerburgh, email, 19 March 2007.
8. Anne Yerburgh to author; *Inn Touch*, Issue 11, Summer 2004, 5.

Index